Poetics of the Flesh

MAYRA RIVERA

POETICS OF THE
FLESH

Duke University Press   Durham and London   2015

© 2015 Duke University Press
All rights reserved

Designed by Heather Hensley
Typeset in Whitman by Westchester Publishing Services

Library of Congress Cataloging-in-Publication Data
Rivera, Mayra, author.
Poetics of the flesh / Mayra Rivera.
pages cm
Includes bibliographical references and index.
ISBN 978-0-8223-5987-6 (hardcover : alk. paper)
ISBN 978-0-8223-6013-1 (pbk. : alk. paper)
ISBN 978-0-8223-7493-0 (e-book)
1. Flesh (Theology) 2. Human body—Religious aspects—
Christianity. 3. Human body (Philosophy) 4. Christian philosophy.
I. Title.
BT741.3.R58 2015
33ʹ.5—dc23 2015015083

Cover art: Wangechi Mutu, *Non je ne regrette rien*, 2007.
Ink, paint, mixed media, plant material, and plastic
pearls on Mylar, 54 × 87 inches. Courtesy of the artist
and Victoria Miro Gallery.

CONTENTS

vii Acknowledgments

1 INTRODUCTION Both Flesh and Not

PART I: **Regarding Christian Bodies** 15

19 CHAPTER 1
Becoming Flesh: The Gospel of John

29 CHAPTER 2
Abandoning Flesh: The Letters of Paul

43 CHAPTER 3
Embracing Flesh: Tertullian

PART II: **The Philosophers' (Christian) Flesh** 55

59 CHAPTER 4
Incarnate Philosophy

87 CHAPTER 5
The Ends of Flesh

PART III: **A Labyrinth of Incarnations** 111

117 CHAPTER 6
Inescapable Bodies

133 CHAPTER 7
Carnal Relations

153 CONCLUSION

159 Notes   193 Bibliography   203 Index

ACKNOWLEDGMENTS

This book has emerged slowly, shaped by conversations with students, colleagues, and friends. I cannot name every person who shaped the project, but naming those who commented on it most directly I acknowledge my debt to many others.

Among the students who affected this project most directly are Nicholas Dials and Eleanor Craig, who assisted me diligently in the research, and Cassie Houtz, who also read the manuscript and offered helpful comments. Without the competent research assistance and relentless challenges of Andrea Quiñones-Rivera, I would not have dared to devote so many hours to reading through and discussing scientific literature. I am grateful for all I learned and aware that the subtlety of her analyses often escaped me. Mónica Quiñones-Rivera helped me think about the significance of metamorphoses, offering insights into classical texts and helping with Latin and Greek translations.

The research for this project was supported in part by a Lilly Faculty Fellowship during the academic year 2011–2012. I am also grateful to Harvard Divinity School and its faculty for their support. My colleagues Mark Jordan, Jonathan L. Walton, and Laura Nasrallah read parts of the manuscript and offered invaluable comments. Laurel Schneider, Dennis Buell, Ellen Armour, Michael Nausner, Shelly Rambo, Catherine Keller, Inese Radzins,

Marion Grau, Krista E. Hughes, and Andrea Bieler offered comments and challenges, as well as timely encouragement.

I am thankful for Ulrike Guthrie's editorial advice. Julie Meadows's perceptive reading and brilliant suggestions were an unexpected gift in the last stages of this work. My deep gratitude for the wise contributions and generous spirit of the team at Duke University Press, especially Jade Brooks, Danielle Szulczewski, and Heather Hensley.

INTRODUCTION
Both Flesh and Not

Flesh carries memories of theological passions. In Christianity, flesh evokes a creative touch, divine love, and suffering. More prominently, it alludes to sin, lust, and death. To be described as living "according to the flesh"—as Jews, women, and sexual minorities have been—is to be considered trapped in sinfulness.[1] Outside Christian circles, in everyday uses of the term "flesh," those memories might be barely recognizable; but they are not inconsequential. Desire and instincts are said to inhabit flesh, or even to be indistinguishable from carnality. These associations have earned flesh a bad reputation—but also the admiration of many followers of Eros.

Ironically, it is the religious aura of flesh that most troubles postmodern philosophers, not its bad reputation. For them, flesh functions as an essence, the self-identity of the body. As a subjective interiority, it fosters the illusion of unmediated sensibility and thus of absolute truth. They also consider flesh to be irremediably Christian, always haunted by the incarnation. Those associations lead some thinkers to denounce flesh and proclaim the end of the passions that "flesh" once named. These philosophers' gestures may be hasty, betraying irritability toward the persistence of Christian ideas in Western thought, but their critiques cannot be taken lightly. Flesh is a concept prone to metaphysical excess, used not only to demonize corporeality but also to spiritualize it—in both cases losing touch with ordinary bodies.

Flesh is an ambivalent term that names a rather slippery materiality. Its propensity to change distinguishes "flesh" from "body." Body commonly denotes an entity complete in itself and visible to those around it. In contrast, flesh is conceived as formless and impermanent, crossing the boundaries between the individual body and the world.

Flesh is always becoming. Air, water, food, sunlight, and even societies of microorganisms enter our bodies to weave the delicate tissue of our flesh. Imperceptibly to the naked eye, cell by cell, day after day, the world constitutes your body and mine. And our bodies enter into the constitution of the world. They are intimately our own, singular and irreplaceable, and yet formed by and given to the world. "I am spacious, singing flesh, on which is grafted no one knows which I, more or less human, but alive because of transformation," writes Hélène Cixous.[2]

Words also become flesh. Words mark, wound, elevate, or shatter bodies. Social discourses divide the world and mark bodies differently. Some bodies are made to bear the weight of race. Gender norms "surface as . . . styles of flesh."[3] Laws prohibit or authorize practices that infect bodies and produce illness and death. Literally. Social hierarchies become flesh. We speak casually about a touching account, biting comments, or deadly policies. The term "sarcasm" comes from the Greek *sarkasmos*, "to tear flesh." These intuitions concern the corporeal effects of common words, yet they resonate with what preachers and poets have for centuries recited: "And the word became flesh." Enigmatically, enticingly, this statement has traveled widely, crossing the boundaries of the properly Christian, being adapted and transformed by those who repeat it.

Poetic Affinities

Thought . . . spaces itself out in the world.
It informs the imaginaries of peoples, their varied poetics,
which it then transforms, meaning,
in them its risks become realized.
—Édouard Glissant, "Imaginary," *Poetics of Relation*

Poetics of the Flesh is inspired by the practice of Édouard Glissant's *Poetics of Relation*, and more indirectly by its contents.[4] For Glissant, poetics refers not only to styles of writing, but also to modes of knowing, being, and acting in the world. The poetic approach is indispensable for addressing histories marked by disruption, displacement, and irrecoverable loss—such as those of Caribbean peoples, whose very existence emerged from the obliteration of African and indigenous cultures, religions, and languages. An intellectual practice attentive to such events shuns totalizing forms of thought and writing. It questions the search for legitimacy in genealogies and the drive to produce ontological systems, theories of the nature of being itself. Instead of privileging the genres of stable, ordered unity, Glissant is inspired by Caribbean poetics, which Derek Walcott describes as a "gathering of broken pieces." "Break a vase, and the love that reassembles the fragments is stronger than the love that took its symmetry for granted when it was whole," Walcott writes. "This gathering of broken pieces is the care and pain of the Antilles." The pieces might be disparate and ill-fitting; they contain more pain than the icons and sacred vessels from which they originated. "Antillean art is this restoration of our shattered histories, our shards of vocabulary."[5] For Glissant, poetics is an approach to knowledge that values processes of creation from "shattered histories" and "shards of vocabularies" and acknowledges their discontinuities.

Poetics aims at expressing in style this stance toward knowledge by being attentive to loss and opacity, interruption and silence. While poetry is the literary genre defined by this sensibility, some of these traits may also influence other forms of writing. Prose can be poetic—learning from poetry, adopting its attentiveness to the creative potential of words, and adapting some of its strategies.

In addition to relating poetics to modes of knowing and ways of writing, Glissant links it more broadly to being in the world. "The world's poetic force," he writes, "kept alive within us, fastens itself by feeling, delicate shivers, onto the rambling presence of poetry in the depths of our being."[6] A poetic force emerges from the world itself and links human expression to it. "The expression of this force and its way of being is what we call Relation: what the world makes and expresses of itself."[7] The world's poetic force creates and expresses itself as Relation.

"Relation" is the most encompassing category in Glissant's work, but it is decidedly not (simply) one. It is manifold and dynamic, elusive and opaque. These traits are at the heart of the imaginative elements of poetics, which is contiguous with *poiesis*—"creative making." He explains that because Relation is indeterminate, it cannot be fully known. Not knowing Relation is thus not a weakness, Glissant assures us. But "not wanting to know it certainly is."

For our inability to grasp Relation is no excuse for indifference. To the contrary, one shall seek to sense the "entanglements" of worldwide relations. We cannot fully know Relation, but "we imagine it through a poetics."[8] Poetics is a practice of engaging the world, in which one risks being transformed.[9]

I use poetics in this book in all the senses that Glissant gives to the term: a stance toward knowledge, a style of writing, and the creative dimensions of thought. I share Glissant's interest in poetics as sensing, joining, and contributing to broader worldly relations. Writing and reading about flesh this way help me convey the complex qualities of sensation: the silences, disruptions, and opacity that characterize the body's relation to the world. They help me be attentive to how flesh shifts between empirical description and imaginative affirmation, which envision alternative modes of being and seek to foster their materialization. A poetic orientation guides my readings, as I attend not only to the conceptual logic of the texts I analyze, but also to their literary dimensions and affective charge. I observe the peculiar tonalities of their words and the distinctive contours of their images; I trace the movements, transformations, intertwinings of the images they use. This is particularly fruitful for registering the marks of Christian imaginaries in widely different contexts. For as Virginia Burrus explains, "drawn and lured by scripture, Christian writing emerges in late antiquity as a crazy quilt of biblical fragments, each piece placed in a new relation to the others, yet still haunted with the ever-multiplying memories of prior contexts of meaning."[10] In engaging ancient theological texts I do not seek to uncover their meaning in a unifying origin. This is not a genealogy of Christian flesh. Instead, I explore evolving relations between different interpretations.

Attention to the poetic dimensions of theological notions sheds light on elements of body-words that tend to be occluded by other modes of philosophical inquiry. The Christian texts that I engage describe experiences in which the most mundane touches upon the inexpressible. They tell stories of divinity becoming flesh and flesh striving to become divine, of flesh that sings and shines, as much as it rots and dies. Instead of assuming a simple opposition between theology and literature or between metaphysics and critical thought, I follow the poetic longings and creativity in all these modes of thought. I approach them as part of ongoing, sometimes painful processes of remaking visions of corporeality—out of pieces of shattered histories and shards of vocabulary.

Poetics of the Flesh explores the intersections between bodies, material elements, and discourses through the concepts of "body" and "flesh." The definitions for each term and the relationship between them unfold throughout the chapters of the book, connecting Christian theology, continental philosophy, and political theories of corporeality, particularly those theories concerned with the corporeal dimensions of gender and race. Much needs to be said to justify bringing together, for instance, the ancient poetics of the Gospel of John, the philosophies of Maurice Merleau-Ponty, and the analytics of the social of Frantz Fanon. I will explain. But before sketching the structure of the book in the last section of this introduction, I present theological and theoretical discussions that precede and inform my work. A quick glance at Christian theologies of the body of the past three decades shows where they may—and I think should—meet theoretical debates about the social-material dimensions of corporeality.

Christian Bodies

The body appeared in religious studies in the second half of the twentieth century. Defiantly. At least that is how we, scholars of religion, like to tell the story of the turn to the body. We know it is hardly the first time that Christian thinkers have been puzzled and challenged by corporeal phenomena. Miraculous feedings and healings, the power of relics, the transformations produced by ascetic practices, and many other such phenomena have been the subject of formative debates throughout the history of Christian thought. But the conversations to which I am referring here are about the body in "our" times. In this context, we associate the body with eroticism and sexuality. The large and growing corpus of literature on Christianity and the body includes a substantial number of works on the role of Christianity in occluding, forbidding, and/or inciting such desires.[11]

Still, there are other stories that have also shaped postmodern visions of the body—accounts of multitudes bearing wounds inflicted in the name of the people, the nation, the economy. In our times, images of human bodies all but destroyed by concentration camps, the atomic bomb, or hunger represent the shattering of myths of human progress. If these bodies reveal anything, it is the likelihood of corporeal destruction.

Recognition of human vulnerability led early liberation thinkers to the Christian body as they sought to bring attention to its material needs—basic necessities such as food, health, and protection against violence. For Latin American liberation philosopher Enrique Dussel, this orientation required an ethics grounded in corporeality.[12] Thus Dussel turned to Hebrew Scriptures, Greek literature, and the New Testament in search of models for a corporeal anthropology that avoided the separation between body and soul.[13] As long as the essence of human life was assumed to reside in an eternal substance such as the soul, he argued, material necessities would be deemed to be secondary or derivative, merely supporting something more lasting and true.

It was clear that theologies concerned with poverty and violence could not ignore the body; neither could those confronting sexism. But these problems required different strategies. The bodies of the poor were mostly absent from modern theological discussions of salvation, liberationists argued. Thus they sought to bring attention to the cry of pain of those suffering from hunger. In contrast, the bodies of women were written into the texts that subordinated them. Discourses about gender and sexuality—like those about race—deployed the body as a foundation of knowledge and a source of unquestionable truth. In order to unsettle that logic, feminists tried to liberate themselves from the body-as-foundation—from biology as destiny. If genders are culturally constructed, then we can transform them. But would that mean abandoning the body to its destiny?

Clearly not. Part of the theoretical task of these theologies has been questioning the idea of "nature" and "body" as passive or immutable and the dualisms on which the opposition between materiality and transcendence rests. The body/spirit dualism was one of the main targets of these projects, which would reach the heart of Christian doctrine. For, as Grace Jantzen argued, the immateriality of God was the linchpin of the Western masculinist symbolic.[14] Feminist theologians have tracked biological essentialisms and spirit/matter dualisms, in all their versions, to deconstruct them. They have also sought to provide alternative visions of the relationship between divinity and materiality, such as the influential metaphor of the universe as the body of God, as well as other models that assert the "relational" (instead of dualistic) structure of the cosmos.[15] Reclaiming the value of bodies further entailed attending to elements of human experience that had been dismissed as irrelevant for theological reflections because they were deemed carnal rather than spiritual. Sexuality has been the preferred site for such reappraisals of corporeal experiences; and there are similar aims and sensibilities in recent theologies of food, dance, and the like.[16] These theologies reenvision the body affirmatively. Drawing inspiration from Christian poetics, they represent the body as created and embraced by the divine, its pains and desires inseparable from its spiritual longings.

So why turn to the body again? Because countering the opposition between spirit and the body has revealed additional challenges pertaining to the relationship between the body and the socio-material world. "The body" remains a highly contested category. "The body" names the physicality of human existence. It is invoked as a solution to the devaluation of flesh and materiality and yet "the body" is also described as an *effect* of arrangements of power, an artifact produced for social control. It is described as "natural" yet shaped by social practices and representations—biological and ideological. Both flesh and not.

Theologian Sharon Betcher analyzes the limitations of the theological turn to the body for questioning the social objectification and standardization of bodies. She observes that feminist accounts of the body at times reflect dominant cultural values and have not always disrupted "disability abjection."[17] "The body" itself might be part of the problem, she argues. As a theoretical category "the body" fosters an illusion of completeness and wholeness easily naturalized, normalized, and deployed as part of cultural systems of representation. Indeed, the body tends to function just as nature does, as "a transcendental term in a material mask." Even "loosed from any conscious religious scaling," the body "might likewise hide its transcendental demeanor in a corporeal overcoat." It represents the unattainable stability that social norms demand but that corporeality cannot mirror. "Whereas 'body' can invite the hallucinatory delusion of wholeness, and thus the temptation to believe in agential mastery and control, flesh . . . admits our exposure, our vulnerability one to another, if also to bios."[18] Betcher counsels us to "learn to think flesh without 'the body.'"[19] For the flourishing of diverse forms and capacities of human embodiment requires communities that recognize their interdependence, shared vulnerability, and the social obligation to provide the conditions to sustain carnal vitality.[20]

This book seeks to unsettle the reifying tendencies of "the body" by evoking carnal interdependence, vulnerability, and exposure. And yet I do not replace the body with flesh but focus on how they constitute each other. Carnal flourishing requires interactions where social standards are always already at play. I do not encounter flesh without a body. Racialized people, like those living with disabilities, are seldom allowed to forget the critical effects of their visible identities in social interactions. I examine social hierarchies that depend on reifications of the body; I describe social identities, particularly race and gender, as markers that influence how social norms affect particular bodies. I explore how those hierarchies affect even the most intimate elements of life and shape the materiality of flesh.[21] Part of the critical task of this book is thus to unsettle the assumed separation between social ideals and materiality, between social constructs and carnal vitality. The distinctions between cultural and material dimensions of corporeality are established discursively and they have material consequences. Between body and flesh there are always words.

The Matter of Flesh

Recent developments in science and technology are troubling and transforming received assumptions about the relationship between the sociocultural and material dimensions of corporeal life. Even though biological essentialisms have hardly disappeared, we are believers in the transformability of the body—in the power of fitness regimes or meditation practices, drug enhancement or genetic modification. We are more intentionally involved in reshaping our bodies—for good or ill.[22] We are also more capable of affecting the bodies of others and the material conditions of the earth. And thus we face new ethical and religious challenges that require more robust understandings of the material effects of social relations. As Judith Butler argues, "if we are to make broader social and political claims about rights of protection and entitlements to persistence and flourishing, we will first have to be supported by a *new bodily ontology*."[23] This "implies the rethinking of precariousness, vulnerability, injurability, interdependency, exposure, bodily persistence and desire, work and the claims of language and social belonging."[24]

Broadly speaking, the demands for more materialist approaches in a variety of fields across the humanities reflect a sense of dissatisfaction with predominant methodologies of the past few decades. Scholars advocating a return to materiality often describe their task as overcoming the problems caused by the focus on language and the prominence of constructive models.[25] The study of corporeality has focused mainly on how discursive practices define and position people in society. Important as this project has been for understanding mechanisms of power, its emphasis on discourse has come at the expense of engagements with other dimensions of corporeality. The efforts to denaturalize gender have at times led to an "allergy of 'the real,'" or even an incipient "somatophobia," Vicki Kirby contends.[26] Too often allusions to materiality are dismissed as foundationalism—as betraying a desire for an unquestionable source of truth. Whether the aim is to relate the body to the broader worldly processes in which it participates or to reach out for a lost aspect of "the real," new materialisms consider postmodern approaches limiting.[27] Addressing ethical challenges of the twenty-first century, such as climate change, biotechnology, and genetics, among others, requires theories that go beyond the critique of discourses toward better understandings of the material conditions and effects of human practices.

Materialist approaches seek deeper understanding of the relationship between bodies and social and scientific practices. Therefore, they build on the insights of postmodern theories about the relationship between bodies and language. They presuppose the analyses of how representations are used to naturalize and thus justify hierarchies of power, linking social categories such as taxonomies of gender and race to visible bodily traits. Words do not simply mirror what is, or express the thoughts and desires of a person, but rather shape reality and subjectivity. Discursive practices incite passions, create and negate identities, enticing even our interest in theorizing the body. The efficacy of words is intricately connected to the experiences of bodies. As Butler has argued, even the claims that bodies exceed language must be understood as assertions—and thus as discursive.[28] To assume otherwise would imply claiming an extra-cultural, universal, absolute foundation for a particular view of reality—a type of argument that scholars have challenged in their efforts to denaturalize gender and race assumptions. However, human practices, including discursive ones, are also shaped by material creativity.

This interest in materiality as a dynamic element in our environment and in our bodies is much more than the result of our having exhausted the prevalent methodologies. Rather, that interest responds to broader cultural changes prompted by developments in science and technology. As models based on postmodern physics replace Newtonian mechanics in science, theoretical discussions in the humanities and other fields are also transformed. Instead of passive matter characterized by inertia, materiality is described in terms of forces and energies in complex networks of relations. We are interested in *processes* of materialization—not just in *matter*.

Not only do we understand materiality differently, we are experiencing new material phenomena as technological advances become part of our everyday engagements with the world. Organ transplants and stem cell experiments have captured the imagination of writers, producers, and philosophers who wrestle with the significance of such exchanges of bodily matter, where part of one body becomes part of another. But new technologies force us to think beyond the exchange between humans to include the participation of the nonhuman—animals, bacteria, and inorganic matter—in the production and reproduction of corporeal matter. The boundaries between human and nonhuman flesh are porous and provisional. So are the divisions between socioeconomic and biological processes. The use of new reproductive technologies, the proliferation of genetic testing and treatments, the debates about cloning, and the like are foregrounding not only the productivity and malleability of materiality, but also how the potentialities opened by these technologies are enmeshed in social and economic relations. Social factors influence what technologies are developed and who has access to them; technological practices and discourses reshape understandings of subjectivity and communal relations.[29] The processes of material transformation and becoming are deeply, if ambiguously, relational. The emerging vision is one where bodies are not simply *located* in society—as suggested by the commonly used phrase "social location"—but *constituted* in relation to the world.

Flow of the Argument

Poetics of the Flesh elaborates a view of corporeality woven by its carnal relations to the world—spiritual, organic, social—describing the folds of body and flesh, flesh and world, body and word.

The book is organized in three parts, which engage in turn theological, philosophical, and sociopolitical texts, while pointing to the relations between them. It follows "flesh" as it unfolds from a Christian poetics of incarnation. It also traces its significance in Maurice Merleau-Ponty's philosophy, as well as its constructive potential in dialogue with Judith Butler, Frantz Fanon, Michel Foucault, Luce Irigaray, and Jean-Luc Nancy—all of whom have critically engaged Merleau-Ponty.

The work begins by laying out the Christian categories around which it coheres—body (*soma, corpus*) and flesh (*sarx, caro*). The difference between body and flesh reveals their distinct semantic histories and affective charges. Of the two terms, it is "flesh" that carries the most ambiguous connotations: of lust, instinct, sinfulness, and death. Tellingly, flesh is also feminized. These associations derive from Christian views of "flesh," but

Christian traditions are more ambivalent about carnality than the well-known attributes suggest.

The first part examines ancient texts—the Gospel of John, the letters of Paul, and works by Tertullian—that have had formative roles in Christianity and are also invoked in relevant philosophical allusions to "the Christian body," especially by the thinkers that I engage in this book. The choice of texts and the orientation of the readings respond to contemporary provocations. *Poetics of Flesh* engages scholarly discussions about the meaning of those ancient texts, but its approach is literary. Its readings foreground the semantic associations of these notions and illuminate the poetic resonances that have led so many scholars, poets, and preachers to turn to these particular texts. I trace two distinct Christian visions of the flesh. Simply stated, the Pauline narrative contrasts "spiritual bodies" with "carnal bodies," treating flesh as a negative metaphysical principle, whereas the Gospel of John envisions salvation through the "flesh," rather than "body." "Carnal" views—exemplified here by the Gospel of John and Tertullian—tend to emphasize metaphors of flesh, carnal exchanges, and transformation. "Somatic" views, inspired by Paul, tend to imagine bodies as less firmly attached to their flesh.

Foregrounding the differences between these views allows me to move beyond generalizing critiques of Christian flesh and identify elements in those traditions that can nourish contemporary ideas about corporeality. In their most poetic, imaginative versions, Christian allusions to flesh unsettle stasis and elude claims to absolute corporeal knowledge. Rather than trying to conceive corporeality without recourse to the notion of flesh or seeking to free flesh from its implication in Christian discourses, I engage the concept critically. I suggest, moreover, that conceptualizing bodies entails risking ontological gestures and that a simple rejection of flesh may lose sight of a crucial aspect of corporeality—its material vitality.

In the second part of the book we witness the reappearance of flesh in the twentieth century in the works of Maurice Merleau-Ponty. He acknowledges the Christian provenance of his metaphors, which I read as reinterpreting the "carnal" strand of Christian corporeal imaginaries. But rather than representing it as relating divinity and humanity, Merleau-Ponty conceives of flesh as the intertwining of bodies and the "flesh of the world." Chapter 4 explicates his philosophy, in which bodies are constituted by their material relationships.

Merleau-Ponty's appeals to flesh have been controversial. Prominent continental thinkers like Gilles Deleuze, Jacques Derrida, and Jean-Luc Nancy have strongly criticized "flesh," not because it is too mundane (as some theologians might assume), but because it is too religious. Nancy declares: "The 'passion' of the 'flesh' is finished and this is why the word body ought to succeed the word flesh."[30] Nancy's assertion is part of two related aims: assessing the influence of Christian theology on Western philosophy, on the one hand, and deconstructing ontotheology, on the other. For Michel Foucault, in contrast, "flesh" is a product of Christian discourses about sin. The contrast between these critiques of flesh—as too spiritual or too sinful—correlates with the carnal and somatic strands of corporeal imaginaries I identify in part I. A third critique of "flesh," articulated by Luce Irigaray, addresses its associations with the maternal and femininity.

The tendency to separate bodies from flesh, in the somatic strand, arises from constructions of flesh as the underlying principle and cause of sinfulness. Rather than rejecting flesh on the basis of its association with sin, I seek to revalue the disavowed traits as integral to corporeality—including its links to the material elements, its vulnerability, and changeability. A view of bodies as materially constituted in relation to the world nurtures a richer and more dynamic view of corporeality. "Flesh" accents the complex textures of those relations—their inherent multiplicity; the sedimentation of past events; the constant flow of elements in and out of bodies.

The third part of the book focuses on what I characterize as "ambivalent incarnations": the becoming flesh of social relations. All bodies are constituted in relation to the world, but they do not encounter it in the same ways. Frantz Fanon's "The Lived Experience of the Black," which I engage in chapter 6, represents the embodied effects of colonial politics. He adopts Merleau-Ponty's concept of the "corporeal schema" and shows how it breaks down under the weight of racism. Fanon also wrestles with poetic attempts to reimagine flesh in the works of Caribbean poet Aimé Césaire. Fanon finds both approaches insufficient. While I challenge Fanon's appraisal of Césaire's poetics, I rely on Fanon's descriptions of the corporeal dimensions of the experience of race for the analyses of the social-material constitution of the world, developed in chapter 7.

Fanon's powerful representations of being assaulted by racialization—wounded from without and transformed from within—point to the constitutive relationship between the materiality of flesh and social constructions of identity. Visible traits impact a body's engagement with the world. But visibility is always already shaped by the sedimentation of social arrangements. I engage Linda Martín Alcoff's philosophical work to explain the significance of social relations on perception, and thus in the constitution of corporeality.

The process of becoming that characterizes flesh entails encounters with the things in the world, described by Merleau-Ponty, as well as the materialization of social norms and practices, described in Judith Butler's work. My reading of Butler focuses on developing this argument, accentuating the consequences of her allusions to "materialization." Yet I also draw attention to the fact that social norms materialize not only in human bodies, but also in human-made physical structures and in the material elements of the world. Social arrangements enter into the constitution of the flesh of the world.

Emphasizing the social dimensions of the flesh of the world, this final part ponders the possibility of affirmative models of performativity. Butler has effectively warned against assuming that resistance to norms means being free from them. Yet the claims to shape flesh through intentional practices cannot be dismissed. And consenting to being flesh implies accepting the social obligations that emerge from our coexistence in the flesh of the world. Bodies and words are called upon to shape different capacities and other poetics of the flesh.

I
Regarding Christian Bodies

Like a ripe tumor
poetry beats painfully,
announcing the passion:
Oh crux ave, spes unica
Oh passiones tempore.
   . . .
And your body in the cross suspended.
And your body in the cross stripped:
   look at me.
I adore you, oh my savior
Who passionately reveals me
the innocence of flesh.

—Adélia Prado, "The Feast of the Body of God"

The Christian body has never been one. Starkly different bodies populate the pages of Christian texts—bodies that are debased and glorious, fragmented and extraordinarily reassembled, inconsequential and excessive. The differences are not only between bodies, but also within them. Christian thinkers have envisioned bodies as internally complex, subject to multiple forces acting within and without, connecting or separating bodies to or from one another, and fusing or sundering their ties with the world.

A multiplicity of views is already present in the New Testament sources, of course, which draw from and contest a variety of ancient ideas, many of them lost to contemporary readers. And yet the status of these texts in Western cultures has allowed them to stand on their own, even when the worlds from which they emerged have disappeared. They are read as ancient and thus strange, and as speaking to the present moment and thus even stranger. For centuries, readers have tried to step into the worlds of these texts to see themselves through their words, to shape their own bodies in the likeness of biblical ones. Analyzing Christian understandings of bodies thus takes us into realms that are both old and current, where not only concepts but also poetic sensibilities continue to be learned—and take flesh.

The Gospel of John's account of the incarnation places flesh at the center of Christian corporeal imaginaries. Its pronouncement, in the very first chapter, that "word became flesh," has proven unforgettable. But perhaps no tradition has been as influential in defining the terms of Christian discourses about the body as the Pauline corpus. Its differentiation between carnal and spiritual bodies, and its descriptions of the community as the body of Christ are widely recognized. Despite the tendency to conceive Christian flesh in Paul's terms, or because of it, here I privilege alternative depictions of flesh. For this reason, and against chronological convention, I begin by reading the Gospel of John. In the following chapter, I introduce Paul's distinctive view of the body and flesh, as I look toward Tertullian's more carnal imaginations—the focus of the third chapter of this part. In general, I try to begin with flesh and stay close to it, relying on it to orient my reading of related concepts and metaphors, and observing where flesh changes form or slips away.

The Pauline corpus and the Gospel of John represent different metaphysical assumptions, rhetorical aims, and poetic registers. Yet ever since the first Christian theologians tried to offer coherent and compelling accounts of the incarnation, these texts have inhabited a common discursive space in Christian imaginaries—as if placed side by side on the shelves of our "memory palaces" (Augustine). Thus centuries of interpretation have transformed the diverging Pauline and Johannine ideas, often conflating what were distinct concepts and terms. Tertullian's work is an early example of an interpretative strategy that combines those distinct views for its own (polemical) aims— and in the process redefines the particularities of flesh. Reading these texts side by side makes their differences visible again. It troubles the idea of an unambiguous and consistent Christian view of flesh. More straightforward views of body and flesh are certainly popular and influential. Yet I seek to emphasize these differences in early Christian sources in order to unsettle the assumed finality of some common readings and open spaces for new ones. More specifically, my aim in these readings is to reenergize Christian poetics of flesh as forgotten (or misremembered) precursors of and potential resources for contemporary discussions.

My readings are shaped by the current theoretical discussions that have prompted me to return to these texts and thus by twenty-first-century sensibilities, including popular and scientific ideas about body and materiality. I do not disavow those sensibilities. The writers of these texts wrestled with debates and cultural sensibilities of their own—and so have most of their readers. Like biblical scholar Tat-siong Benny Liew, I ask, "What if biblical materials, in separation from the question of faith or belief, turn out to have instructive bearing on some of the urgent issues facing our world today?"[1] So I approach these ancient texts to explicate but also to respond to them. And as I do so, I let their rhetorical boldness and poetic strangeness inflect my writing, hoping to be stirred by the vitality of words that proclaim a flesh capable of startling transformations.

CHAPTER 1

BECOMING FLESH
The Gospel of John

"The word became flesh" might well be the most remembered phrase of the gospels.[1] "Word" gives "became flesh" a strange appeal.[2] It joins the tangible and the intangible. It renders the real world evident and invisible. "It was thing and spirit both: the real/ world: evident, invisible," writes poet Marie Howe.[3]

"Word became flesh"—or "verb became flesh," as I first learned it—continues to attract those attempting to think about corporeality in cultures influenced by Christianity.[4] Poets and writers keep returning to this statement, even if doubtfully intrigued. "A word made flesh is seldom," Emily Dickinson observes.[5] The statement also repels those who seek to liberate their intellectual traditions from the legacy of Christian thought. They are anxious that the word would imprison the flesh, making it a mere instrument of the Christian God. The phrase represents light for some and the "darkness of religion" for others—but its influence cannot be neglected.

I remain intrigued by the peculiar vitality of flesh in this ancient text—even when the subtle movements of this flesh are often swept away by gusts of metaphysical pronouncements. I note the places where those gusts directly impact the verses I read. But I do not follow their path. Instead I keep my eyes on the intricate qualities of flesh. And I assume flesh refers to all human flesh—and more. Some might object that the gospel does not authorize such a reading, that its visions are only for its own community, delimited by its reviled others—those who do not believe, do not understand, who are Jews.[6] True. But I read with those who have read it as if it were speaking about all flesh, including their own, who have been moved and shaped by its poetics. I keep my eyes on the characterizations of flesh that disrupt, even if tentatively, the gospel's most restrictive impulses—and their ex-carnations.

Beginnings

The gospel's prologue draws from older biblical traditions, framing its account of the life of Jesus as an event of cosmic significance. It starts by turning back to the very beginning, to the point when the divine word creates—reminding readers of the creative word of God in the first chapter of the book of Genesis.

> In the beginning was the word, and the word was with God and the word was God. . . . All things came into being through the word. . . . What has come into being in the *word* was *life*, and the *life* was the *light* of all people. . . . The light shines in the darkness and the darkness did not overcome it. . . . And the *word* became *flesh* and lived among us, and we have seen its *glory*.[7]

Word, life, light, flesh, and glory . . . Rather than a description of distinct species remembered from Genesis 1—plants, birds, sea monsters—what is created is *life* itself. This life is also *light*—the first element called forth by God's word in Genesis 1. John's depiction of the light shining in darkness, neither overcome nor comprehended by darkness, evokes a statement in Genesis; namely that God "separated the light from the darkness."[8] And the link between life and light would have been familiar to readers of the Wisdom of Solomon, where Wisdom (*Sophia*), the creative principle of God, is also depicted as God's radiance.[9] But in the Gospel of John, these allusions to the creative word of God are followed by the announcement that the word became flesh. And immediately, one presumes simultaneously, the word is taking place among people and its radiance manifest as glory (*doxa*). Life, light, and glory appear as the word becomes flesh. Only in flesh. "Without ears to hear it, the Word remains unheard," Karmen MacKendrick observes, "and it seems that light too must become flesh as the very condition of its recognizability, its visibility, its shining."[10] Thus in the flesh, the creative word becomes not only audible, but also visible and touchable.

Taken by itself, cut off from the creation stories that inspired it and from the images and events that follow, "word became flesh" could be construed as a simple progression: from a first principle, word, to the flesh. Or it could be read as describing the trajectory of word as a vector that touches flesh at one point, as a tangent touches a circle, to use Karl Barth's image. Perhaps readers are supposed to draw that line, as many have. But the verses just cited describe complex relationships between multiple elements—not just word and flesh—forming an intricate pattern of images that is hardly reducible to a single line. Word, life, light, flesh, and glory converge into and swerve from one another. As the narrative progresses, the gospel adds other elements to its poetic streams—water, bread, and blood. All of these elements circulate through the gospel narrative, moving, being exchanged, and transformed.

Attending to these patterns of relationship between the multiple elements in the gospel opens possibilities for richer interpretations of its flesh. Yet it is also easy to lose sight of flesh. I have found it necessary to mark the gospel's explicit references to flesh, as stepping-stones from which to observe its movements and transformations.

Elemental Flesh

The discussion of the prologue already reveals the significance of flesh for the overarching argument of the gospel and by extension for Christian understandings of the body. In this most celebrated statement of the incarnation, there is no body (soma), only flesh (sarx). Indeed, the gospel uses the term "body" only in relation to the death of Jesus—its announcement and the descriptions of the actual event. While in this gospel body might be simply a corpse, flesh is unstable and complex. Flesh is what the word became (*egeneto*), but also what is born of the flesh: "What is born [*gegennēmenon*] of the flesh is flesh and what is born of the spirit is spirit."[11] A fixed boundary? Apparently not, or not so in any simple way, because those born of flesh are being called to be born of spirit. Thus not only does the word become flesh, but what became flesh will become spirit. The word is transformed as flesh and in the process flesh itself changes.

This is a well-known account of salvation as *theosis* (or *theopoiesis*). We remember it in Athanasius's terms, "God became man so that man can become God."[12] Contemporary commentators of the Gospel of John often glance over "flesh" and read "man."[13] Yet the distinct terms of the gospel's flesh evoke more elemental dimensions of life. The word became flesh so that flesh could become spirit—and bread.

Flesh—or *his* flesh—is also bread. Before establishing the link between bread and flesh, the gospel draws attention to the need to feed a hungry multitude.[14] It then moves to a long speech about bread and life. Note how these elements seem to twirl around each other. Jesus talks about the "bread of God" (*ho artos tou theou*) that gives life to the world, "bread of life" (*ho artos tes zoes*), and "bread that lives" (*ho artos ho zoe*).[15] The reader knows that the word is, contains, and gives life. Similarly this bread is, contains, and gives life. Indeed, the bread is the flesh that word became. In what has been aptly described as "the most shockingly sarctic language of the entire gospel," Jesus describes his flesh as bread given to be eaten. "The *bread* that I will give for the *life* of the world is my *flesh*."[16] The prologue describes the confluence of word, life, flesh; here we are invited to contemplate the convergence of flesh, life, bread.

The circuitous statements about bread and life, bread and flesh, are easily channeled into the gospel's direct assertions: "I am the living bread that came down from heaven."[17] It is tempting to take this as the *real* revelation. Why go through all the trouble of exploring the connections between bread, life, and flesh if we were given the answer to this riddle, namely that we have been talking about Jesus all along? But to skip over the images would flatten the gospel's elaborate characterizations and thus the distinctiveness of the text. Replacing the images and metaphors for a message deemed more important is, in other words, to dismiss the text's poetics, the impact of which derives from the intricate relation between the most common material elements and the strongest metaphysical assertions. The claim to be bread comes from the same Jesus who divided and multiplied bread and fish to feed a multitude. Surely, we are expected to interpret the hunger of the multitude and the food given as real. Still, readers are easily discouraged from contemplating common bread, most of all when it is said to be flesh. The text mocks a reductive reading of this passage, represented by the typically puzzled comments of the apostles, who focused only on the food that perishes. It also mocks those it problematically calls "the Jews" who focused on the bread from heaven and rejected its link to the son of Joseph. The characters represent differing views, both of which are presented as wrong. As I read them, their views are opposite sides of the same dichotomy, between this life—of common bread—and the life from heaven. And the reader may sense that the text would chastise anyone who fails to see the connection between flesh and bread, bread and life—we, the readers, who find all this material hard to digest. No wonder Rudolf Bultmann questioned the authenticity of these words.[18]

And yet the text keeps insisting on the fleshy terms of its message—proceeding only to add blood to this depiction of life: "Very, truly, I tell you," Jesus reiterates, "unless you eat the flesh of the son of the human and drink his blood, you have no life in you. . . . For my flesh is true food, and my blood is true drink. Those who eat my flesh and drink my blood abide in me, and I in them."[19] The images of Jesus dividing bread and fish merge with the distribution of his own flesh, divided and offered.

Flesh appears not as a self-contained mass, but as an element transformed as it is given. Like bread, flesh is shared, becoming part of many bodies, transformed into the very flesh of those bodies that partake from it. The exchange entails not only *his* flesh, but also the carnality of those invited to share in its life. If in the prologue word becomes flesh and appears in the midst of people—exposed—here we are invited to imagine it *in* the people—as food nurturing spiritual life.

The relevance of these verses exceeds definitions of flesh, but their strange carnal poetics is far from immaterial. The verses' offering of life has too often been received as an invitation to offer death—to all those who are not Christian, to the Jews—as a gift dependent on the exclusions of others. Those casted as spiritually dead can hardly escape embodied death. This history shall not be occluded. And we shall recall other less-known interpretations that open up the texts to give life to those who are excluded.

In 1514, Bartolomé de las Casas was already a priest when he converted, moved by seeing a connection that these verses suggest. In preparation for saying the Mass, he read in Ecclesiasticus 34, "Bread is the life of the poor." He concluded that the Eucharist could not be offered unless the Amerindians were freed. For the liberationist readers of las Casas, the bread offered in the Eucharist cannot be abstracted from the gifts of the earth and the labor that materializes in the bread. The Eucharist bread is at the same time the "substance of the Eucharistic offering" and the "fruit of common labor, exchanged among those who produce it," writes Enrique Dussel.[20] An elemental materiality connects the bodies of workers with shared bread, with consecrated bread. These are not arbitrary metaphors—bread is produced by the labor of human hands and the fecundity of the earth. Sharing consecrated bread is a practice by which Christians receive and become the body of Christ. These practices overflow the boundaries of both symbolic and economic exchange.

Representing flesh as nourishing bread does not erase its connection with death, which is also described by referring to wheat. "Very truly, I tell you, unless a grain of wheat falls into the earth and dies, it *remains just a single grain*; but if it dies, it bears much fruit."[21] The death of Jesus is an ever-present reality in this narrative, which is told from the perspective of that death, and the potential death of its readers.[22] Tat-siong Benny Liew reads flesh in John as a sign of the gospel's concern with vulnerability and death—comparable to Giorgio Agamben's notion of "bare life." For Liew this emphasis on death should be understood specifically in reference to the life of first-century Jews under colonial occupation, as "death-bound."[23] The gospel is indeed haunted by impending death. But even if death is associated with the arbitrary conditions of imperial rule, it is still described through reference to well-known material processes, the ongoing exchange between individual things or bodies and the elements of organic life. This rhetorical approach risks naturalizing or spiritualizing contingent sociopolitical systems and thus legitimizing them. But foregrounding and analyzing how contingent human systems produce death should not lead us to forget that often those systems work by exacerbating corporeal vulnerability. In other words, seeing both the possibilities of life and vulnerability to death as embedded in material processes affected but not determined by human activity invites us also to explore the variety of forces that act on human bodies. Ancient communities, such as the one that produced the Gospel of John, were especially aware of this.[24] Life and death are intertwined.

Spirit

I have been referring to elements explicitly associated with flesh. And it is customary to proceed by contrasting flesh to spirit. Surely the gospel does so in straightforward terms: "It is the spirit that gives life; the flesh is useless."[25] The statement is puzzling for a gospel that says so much about the imbrication of flesh and life. And the apparent dichotomy might be rendered even more equivocal by comparing the gospel's descriptions of spirit with those of flesh. To do so, I trace the movements of water—which at crucial moments the gospel associates with spirit.

Flesh, bread, and life are in Jesus and given by him to his followers. In the process the flesh and bread seem to mutate—flesh is bread given, bread is life, wheat dies to gives fruit, and so on. Jesus's followers are in turn transformed by these elements—they come to have life *in* them. Water exhibits similar patterns of transformation and exchange. Initially, there is no indication that water might be anything but a common element. Jesus turns water into wine at a wedding, pleasing a celebrating crowd. This is Jesus's "first sign," a revelation of his glory.[26] But transforming water into wine is a rather circuitous sign of glory. For what is the transubstantiation between such common elements supposed to reveal to those in search of the spirit? Does the fact that elsewhere in the gospel water stands for spirit give this transformation of water into wine any incarnational significance? Khalil Gibran imagines the bride deriving wisdom from the taste of wine, "The spirit of Jesus the Nazarene is better and more aged than any wine."[27] The pleasures of good wine are a sign.

Water continues to flow and change through the gospel's narrative—at times lacking and yet overabundant. At the Samaritan well, Jesus asks for water. In contrast with his role as the leader feeding a multitude, at the well we find Jesus as a thirsty traveler. He needs water; he asks for water. There is no crowd here, just one woman. But as in the later story of the feeding of the multitude, a quotidian scene of tending to corporeal need gives way to elaborate discussions about life. Jesus asserts that he is the source of "living water." But he also claims that those who drink from his water will have it within them and become *sources* of living water.[28] Similarly, at the feast of Tabernacles, Jesus says, "Let anyone who is thirsty come to me, and drink," adding, "Out of the believer's heart will flow rivers of living water."[29] The narrator here notes that Jesus is speaking of the spirit. As in the case of the speeches about bread, Jesus is, contains, and gives the water that transforms those who receive it. This spirit thus moves just like the flesh; its significance is revealed as the element is given and received.

The gestures of carnal and spiritual flow do not come to an end with Jesus's death. The motifs of flesh, blood, and water resurface at the crucifixion, when Jesus thirsts again and after drinking (wine) gives up his spirit. At this dramatic point Jesus says, "It is finished," and water and blood flow from his wounded side.

The patterns of flow and transformation traced by the movements of bread and water, flesh and blood, may account for John's peculiar descriptions of the emerging collectivity. "Those who eat my flesh and drink my blood abide in me, and I in them," Jesus says. "Abiding" is explained by means of a horticultural image. "Just as the branch cannot bear fruit by itself unless it abides in the vine, neither can you unless you abide in me."[30] Yet the logic of "you in me and me in you" is repeated throughout the gospel, where "abiding" is not invoked.[31] As it is with life, which is light, so it is with glory. Referring back to the beginning of the gospel—and through it to all beginnings—Jesus asks the father to receive the glory he had "before the world existed."[32] This glory flows toward his followers. "The glory that you have given me I have given them," prays Jesus to the father, "so that they may be one, as we are one."[33] Jesus' self-descriptions as bread, light, life—not least in his "I am" sayings—are woven with otherness. The "I am" is one and many. And while most often life appears to flow unidirectionally from the father to Jesus to the disciples and beyond, these statements suggest more intricate patterns of coexistence; Jesus is in them but they are also in Jesus.

An emphasis on exchanged and transformed flesh structures a collectivity in terms of the mutual imbrication of those who participate in it. The gospel limits its own insight by setting boundaries around the community it forms—and at times by setting up the community against "the world."[34] Still the elemental, earthy grounds on which the gospel's claims are rooted remain legible.

Fleshy Words

A description of flesh in the Gospel of John emerges from the confluence of images that cannot be easily reduced to simple equivalences or dichotomies.[35] The text produces its meaning by moving from one element to the next and back, just as does the flesh it describes. It is tempting to try to sort the elements that flow through the gospel into manageable categories—either trying to separate flesh from spirit, or literal from figurative meanings. But the text resists such order. What Stephen Moore says about water applies also to other elements in the gospel, namely that "this water is neither simply material and literal, since it is symbolic, nor fully spiritual and figurative, since it is physical. It is a spiritual material and a literal figure. Literality and figurality intermingle in the flow from Jesus' side, each containing the other, which is to say that we cannot keep the literal clearly separate from the figurative in the end."[36]

The word becomes flesh and calls flesh to become spirit; both flesh and spirit are given by Jesus, even at his death, which is also a glorification. Bread is what satiates the hunger of the multitude, and Jesus's flesh, and life. Water is what satiates the thirst of the woman at the well (and her ancestors), and what flows from Jesus's body, and life. And disciples in and beyond the gospel become sources of life. Spirit and flesh flow into each other; the figurative turns into the literal, and vice versa. Through the confluence of the literal and the symbolic, the gospel conveys the intertwining of the material and the spiritual—word and flesh, life and light, and so on. The most metaphysical statements rely on the most concrete material dimensions of corporeality, which often escape the boundaries of individual subjects. Its poetics also escape the boundaries of this theological text, appearing elsewhere, creatively transformed.

CHAPTER 2

ABANDONING FLESH
The Letters of Paul

Math. Time. Everything happy goes
to many decimal places
while flesh passes through
gradations of glory.
—Alice Fulton, "After the Angelectomy"

Flesh and glory—their relationship determines the qualities of each human body, not least for Christians shaped by Paul's words. In the Gospel of John, these terms converge at the beginning—both inherently linked to the incarnation. "We *have seen* the word's glory"—it witnesses. In the letters of Paul, the most enchanting visions of glory point to the end of times. As Fulton puts it, "flesh passes through gradations of glory." I find it impossible to fit all of Paul's references to the body into a single metaphysical system. Nonetheless, some of its features are widely recognized, such as Paul's depiction of resurrected bodies. It is built on a separation between spiritual and carnal bodies as wide as the chasm between heaven and earth. The two elements reach toward each other across a vast ontological distance. The expectation might be that flesh will become—might be becoming—spirit.[1] But ultimately "flesh and blood cannot inherit the kingdom of God."

Paul's writings are starkly different from the Gospel of John. They are chronologically earlier. They are letters that follow recognizable stylistic conventions and respond to specific concerns of the community it addresses explicitly.[2] Not surprisingly, there is a clear contrast between the didactic style of these texts and the poetics of the Gospel of John, with its multilayered imagery. There is no bread or water in the passages I read here. The imaginative aspects of Paul's writing come through most powerfully, though briefly, in his visions of the future transformation, as we shall see. And there is also the peculiar status and currency of Paul's letters. They are constantly being reinterpreted in Christian preaching and writing as well as by an ever-growing group of philosophers who do not identify with religion. The terms of the letters are all too familiar, even as their precise meaning remains elusive, shifting, controversial. All of these traits will necessarily affect my own reading and writing in this chapter.

Resurrected Bodies

The famous declaration—"flesh and blood cannot inherit the kingdom of God"—concludes Paul's discussion of the resurrection of the dead as a necessary consequence of the resurrection of Christ in 1 Corinthians 15. The key question is posed explicitly: what kind of body is a resurrected body? The answer is self-evident for Paul; one needs only to observe analogous phenomena, he says. He relies on two examples. The first case is the relationship between a seed and the plant sowed after the seed's "death."[3] It is clear, Paul offers, that "you do not sow the body (soma) that is to be, but a bare seed, perhaps of wheat or of some other grain."[4] No matter the seed, the shape of the plant seems to bear no resemblance to that of the seed. Their appearances are arbitrarily related. But the invisible truth is that "God gives it a soma just as he has chosen, and to each kind of seed its own soma."[5] Thus not only is the plant's body different from the seed's, but plants are also different from one another. The same is true for humans: the body that dies will receive a soma of its own, the form of which might be surprisingly different from its earthly seed.

In addition to the example of this marvelous and yet ubiquitous phenomenon of metamorphosis from seed to plant, Paul points to the diversity in the cosmos—differences in types of flesh, bodies, and glories. There are different types of *flesh* on earth: humans, beasts, birds, and the like. There is also a clear difference between earthly and celestial *bodies*. And just as the glories of earthly bodies are different from the glories of the celestial ones, the glories of celestial bodies differ from each other. The sun, the moon, the star—each has its own *glory*.[6]

The terminology here draws from contemporary philosophical systems. Paul's description, which combined cosmological and eschatological elements, would give some aspects of those ancient corporeal visions broader reach and longevity. As Dale Martin observes, Paul assumes a common philosophical understanding, "whereby different kinds of creatures occupy a body appropriate to its own realm and composed of substances derived from that realm."[7] Earthly creatures are composed of flesh. Heavenly entities, in contrast, are composed of *aether*, or *pneuma*, a lighter substance than the earthy one of flesh.[8] Paul's use of soma for celestial bodies is consonant with this ontological structure. All beings, from fish to stars, have "bodies," but they are clearly different types of bodies.

The image of a cosmos populated by varyingly glorious bodies inspires Paul's vision of resurrected bodies. But having accentuated the differences between them, how can the nature of heavenly bodies be deduced from that of earthly ones? Are they as different as plants from seeds? In response, Paul offers only bare contrasts, between the perishable and the imperishable, dishonor and glory, weakness and power.[9] Just as in the "burial" (*spereita*) of seeds, so too death will produce an astonishing transformation of corporeal constitution—from a natural body or natural-soul (*soma psychikos*) to a spiritual body (*soma pneumatikos*).[10]

The natural body is earthy just as the first Adam was. The association between Adam and the earth is not surprising, for it unfolds from Genesis 2:7: "God formed man [*adam*] from the dust of the ground [*adamah*], and breathed into his nostrils the breath of life; and the man became a living being"—or a "living soul," as translated in the Septuagint. But Paul's reading is hardly a simple retelling of the Genesis story. There are two Adams, Paul observes. "The first man, Adam, became a living soul [*psychen zosan*]"; the "last Adam [Christ] became a life-giving spirit [*pneuma zoopoium*]."[11] Other readers of Genesis had seen two persons emerging from its two creation stories—one spiritual (Genesis 1:27, "God created humankind in his image . . . male and female he created them"), the other physical (Genesis 2:7, "God formed man from the dust of the ground, and breathed into his nostrils the breath of life").[12] For the Jewish Hellenistic writer Philo of Alexandria, for instance, the two creation stories establish a distinction between spiritual and material bodies—and also, in consequence, between men and women. As Philo reads it, "there is a vast difference between the human being who has been molded now [in Genesis 2:7] and the one who previously came into being after the image of God." The second creation entailed molding a person as a "sense-perceptible object"—which required that such a person be "either man or woman, and by nature mortal." In contrast, the being created first (in the image of God) "is a kind of idea . . . incorporeal, neither male nor female, and is immortal by nature."[13] This reading of the creation story asserts the priority and ontological superiority of the spiritual/intellectual over the sensible. Gender difference belongs to the lower levels of being; the spiritual is neither male nor female. But the notion of spiritual androgyny slips into gender hierarchy in Philo—as it so often does in our times. "Observe that it is not the woman who cleaves to the man but conversely the man to the woman, Mind to Sense-perception," Philo states in a different text, setting up this gender difference as the framework for his ontological argument. "For when that which is superior, namely Mind, becomes one with that which is inferior, namely Sense-perception . . ." he adds, implying that man is to woman as mind is to sense-perception. When the mind becomes one with sense-perception, "it resolves itself into the order of flesh which is inferior, into sense-perception, the moving cause of the passions." Flesh, sense-perception, and the cause of passions all share this lower sphere—which is feminized—a common assumption already in antiquity.[14]

Paul's argument reflects the influences of the types of interpretation of Genesis that Philo exemplifies, and yet he also marks his differences from them.[15] The contrast that Paul is setting up is not between the qualities of human bodies before and after the creation of the sensible world, not even before and after the fall. Instead he is contrasting the man formed from soil with Christ.[16] And thus he explicitly rejects the temporal priority of the spiritual Adam—though not its ontological superiority. Paul agrees that there are two Adams, one physical and one spiritual. "But it is not the spiritual that is first, but the physical [*psychikon*], and then the spiritual." The difference between a living soul (Adam) and a life-giving spirit (Christ) corresponds to the distinction between the earthy and the heavenly bodies. "The first man was from earth, earthy; the second man is from heaven."[17] So rather than looking back to creation for the model of the ideal person, the spiritual Adam, Paul has his readers turning toward Christ. The ontological difference between the earthy and the heavenly affects human inclinations in the world. "As was the man of earth, so are those who are of earth; and as is the man of heaven, so are those who are of heaven."[18] What does it mean to be of earth? The statements could be read as just simile, where being of the earth is compared with certain human traits—implying no physical or metaphysical relation between bodies and real earth. But I would not take such images lightly. If different types of flesh correspond to different glories, an earthy body can be assumed to have traits corresponding to that realm. And the terms earth and heaven also set the direction of bodily transformation promised to followers of Christ. "Those who are of heaven" can refer to the present state of those who participate "in Christ," bearing his image—as all humans bear the image of Adam. But Paul's explanation accentuates the future orientation of the heavenly by returning at this point to the question of resurrection. In conclusion,

> What I am saying, brothers and sisters, is this:
> flesh and blood cannot inherit the kingdom of God,
> nor does the perishable inherit the imperishable.

The distinctions have been firmly established; the observed differences between types of bodies and their glories are tied to their place in the cosmos. These differences separate earthy bodies from heavenly ones, the first Adam from the last. The resurrection changes everything.

> Listen, I will tell you a mystery!
> We will not all die,
> but we will all be changed,
> in a moment,
> in the twinkling of an eye,
> at the last trumpet.[19]

The culminating event does not so much bridge the gap between the earthly and the heavenly as it changes the bodies, erasing the most evident mark of its earthy constitution—death. I can almost hear the trumpet—and tremble in anticipation of metamorphosis. Those awaited spiritual bodies overshadow in glory and permanence anything earthy and fleshy.

This is not simply a spirit/matter dualism in the modern sense of these terms—for spirit was likely regarded as a light substance.[20] However, as Martin summarizes a compelling reading of Paul's position, "the resurrected body is stripped of flesh, blood, and soul; it has nothing of the earth in it at all, being composed entirely of the celestial substance of *pneuma*."[21] The glory of resurrected bodies would correspond to that of heavenly bodies. Engberg-Pedersen interprets this differently, not as suggesting that bodies are stripped of flesh but rather that their flesh is changed. He hears in Paul's words the echoes of a Stoic idea of a final "conflagration"—"when everything in the world—including the earth and the earthly bodies—will be transformed into the single, 'uppermost' element of pneuma, which constitute the essence of God."[22] Even flesh would undergo a dramatic change, a fiery purification, after which it would no longer be flesh.

A vision of "spiritual bodies" sustained by such readings of this early Pauline letter has left lasting marks in Christian thought, with which contemporary thinkers contend. Thomas Altizer observes that in such traditions, "a foundation is established for a spiritual life and identity which is wholly dissociated from death, a resurrected life of the Spirit which simply and literally transcends sin and guilt, as Christ becomes the spiritual Adam from heaven who is totally dissociated from the physical Adam from earth and dust."[23] This pervasive interpretation of Paul's text is often assumed to represent all Christian theologies of the body. Paul's more labyrinthine descriptions of the present human condition, however, complicate the apparently straightforward structure delineated in 1 Corinthians 15.

Before resurrection, those who are baptized experience partial transformation and their constitution incorporates elements of both the earthy and the heavenly realms. "A '*psychic* man' is a person of flesh and blood—or body and soul—who has not received a portion of God's *pneuma* from above . . . an ordinary human being 'of the flesh' (1 Cor 3:1, 3:3). A 'pneumatic' man, by contrast, is a person who has received a portion of God's *pneuma*."[24] In the discussion of the present state "in Christ," soma has a different connotation than in 1 Corinthians 15. Rather than naming entities that can be either sarkic or pneumatic, soma is used here as a near equivalent to the natural and/or sarkic sphere.[25] But the distinction between sarx and pneuma remains crucial.

Flesh, Sin, and the Law

In Romans 6–7, both body and flesh are explicitly related to sin. Chapter 6 opens by claiming the benefits of Christ's death for those who are "in Christ" through baptism. To be "in Christ" entails joining him corporeally—to be baptized is to be baptized "into his death," crucified with him, "buried with him," "united with him in a resurrection." It means putting to death the old self, which is ultimately the destruction of "the body of sin"—the end of enslavement to sin.[26] But the freedom thus obtained seems to need further action, for Paul advises, "Do not let sin exercise dominion in your mortal bodies, to make you obey their passions."[27] If sin is allowed in, Paul seems to be suggesting, you will be subjected to bodily passions. Rather than being enslaved to sin, become enslaved to God.[28]

What is a "body of sin"? Any (carnal) body? The body of those who were not or had not been baptized? A body that belongs to sin, subject to evil forces? Or consenting to passions? Perhaps all of these. Tellingly, Paul's exhortation now changes its terms, from body to flesh.[29] It similarly associates flesh with sin and passions—as it relates them to "the law." What brings together these two terms—flesh and law? For Paul, a Jewish writer, this might be all too evident. As Daniel Boyarin observes, Jewish law insisted on the importance of flesh—of "procreation and kinship, symbolized by the mark in the flesh," that is, circumcision.[30] Paul's preaching of a gospel available to the gentiles could not avoid the questions of the carnal specificities of that law. And other less direct connections between prohibitions and flesh might also be at play in this argument, which is anything but simple.

The first analogy for the role of the law is a woman's obligation in marriage. A woman is bound to her husband and guilty of adultery if she were to live with another man. But if her husband dies, she is free to live with another. Therefore, her subjection to the law is temporary—only binding during the husband's lifetime. So is the converts' relationship to the law, Paul explains. The limits of analogy are evident. The believers are in the position of a woman subject to marriage. But the condition for being free to belong to Christ is the converts' own death. They "died to the law" to become bound to Christ. Still, Paul's elaboration is significantly more complex than this analogy suggests.

"While we were living in the flesh, our sinful passions . . . were at work in our members to bear fruit for death." (Like a married woman, I assume.) But now that we are in Christ we experience "the new life of the spirit."[31] The "sinful passions" that afflicted those "living in the flesh" were somehow "aroused by the law." Indeed, "if it had not been for the law, I would not have known sin."[32] The law reveals to a person his or her sins. But the example that follows brings to the fore other, more problematic dimensions. "I would not have known what it is to covet if the law had not said, 'You shall not covet.'"[33] The law is not sin, and yet sin "seizing an opportunity in the commandment, *produced* in me all kinds of covetousness." The argument has moved from a discussion of the law in general to the tenth commandment specifically. The peculiarity of the tenth commandment is that it forbids desire, rather than a particular act.[34] The example might be alluding to desire in general, rather than specifically to the desire for another's house or wife.[35] If this were the case, it would imply that the prohibition of desire produces desire—a proposition that some ancient, as well as some postmodern, thinkers would readily accept. Thus, paradoxically, the law and sin seem to reinforce each other—the law reveals sin, but it can also induce it.[36] The apparent impotence of the law to produce good actions needs further explanation. Paul's point is not that the law is evil or irrelevant; to the contrary, "the law is spiritual." The problem is in the flesh. "For we know that the law is spiritual; but I am of the flesh, sold into slavery under sin." Enslaved to sin, the flesh is the abode of sin within the body. As a consequence, Paul says,

> I do not understand my own actions. For I do not do what I want, but I do the very thing I hate. Now if I do what I do not want, I agree that the law is good. But in fact it is no longer I that do it, but sin that dwells within me. For I know that nothing good dwells within me, that is, in my flesh.[37]

This well-known passage expresses a recognizable experience; but the connection between existential anguish and flesh shall not be taken for granted. The fundamental difference between sarx and pneuma—which in the discussions of resurrection extended spatially (between earth and heaven) and temporally (between the present and the time of the resurrection)—is here seen in the tensions within the self, within the body. The mind assents to the goodness of the law, but that is not enough to produce the desired action. "For I delight in the law of God in my inmost person [*eso anthropon*], but I see in my members *another law* at war with the law of my mind, making me captive to the law of sin that dwells in my members [*melesin*]."[38] Thus "with my mind I am a slave to the law of God, but with my flesh I am a slave to the law of sin."[39] The (good) desires of the "inmost person" fight against those of the members, in the flesh.[40]

Paul's reference to the "inner person" would become a common feature of Christian (and Western) corporeal imaginaries. Paul's account of the struggles of a man to do what is good, indeed what he wants to do, seems paltry in comparison to that narrated in Augustine's *Confessions*. Augustine quotes Paul explicitly, of course: "For although a man rejoices in the law of

God, according to the inner man, what shall he do about the other law in his members that fights against the law in his mind."[41] But in the *Confessions* these struggles are so carefully examined and seductively expanded that the text seems to prove Paul's observation—that the prohibition of desire might produce the desire.[42] Whether the reader joins in feeling Augustine's pain and (painful) pleasure or becomes utterly exasperated by his obsessions (or both), one can hardly escape his affective force field. But Paul's inner human is clearly different from the modern self that would later claim it. At best, it is a slave to God, and still threatened, not always in control of its actions, not even capable of understanding itself—always wrestling with that most troubling law dwelling in the flesh.[43]

Scholars who read Paul's references to sin *in the flesh* as assuming ideas from contemporary Hellenistic Judaism, such as Philo's, explain that desires and passions were assumed to emerge from the body due to sensibility. And these were considered the sources for misguided actions, holding rationality captive.[44] For those who held this view, they argue, it would make sense to suggest that a corporeal "law" constrained rational action. Focusing on flesh would thus constrain spiritual attainments—they would presumably say. We do know that the idea of a law of sin attached to (or infecting) bodily "members" has proved its power beyond Paul's context—that even today it haunts Western imaginaries of "flesh."[45]

The associations between flesh, sin, and desire are potent and productive, even though (or because) the lines of cause and effect are unclear. Does the law reveal or produce sin? Does sin incite passions or do passions incite sin? Does sin bind flesh to the passions or do the passions of flesh bind people to sin? All these possibilities seem to be at play. Flesh and sin, like flesh and death, announce each other in Paul's writings. And the exhortation builds toward a memorable cry:

"Wretched man that I am! Who will rescue me from this body of death?"

Paul answers his own question. Christ has rescued them from a body of death. The value of that new life in Christ is accentuated by opposing it to life in the flesh: "Those who live *according to the flesh* set their minds on the flesh"; "to set the mind on the flesh is death"; "the mind that is set on the flesh is hostile to God"; "those who are in the flesh cannot please God."[46] "But you are not in the flesh."[47] Christ, who is pneuma, offers a way out of this wretched state and opens the possibility for living otherwise. "You are in the pneuma, since the pneuma of God dwells in you. Anyone who does not have the pneuma of Christ does not belong to him. But if Christ is in you . . ."[48]

The Body of Christ

Being in the spirit, like being in the flesh, has implications for the physical constitution of bodies—of individual bodies and of the body formed by the collectivity of those who are "in Christ." The "body of Christ" refers not only to the flesh-and-blood body of the man-savior, but also to a spiritual entity formed by all those who are "in Christ." The body of Christ is a spiritual body.[49] The image of a collective body, where each member has its predefined role and status, was much older than Paul's letters.[50] The trope conveyed the idea that the well-being of the collective body depended on the harmonious collaboration between diverse members, each having its own function. The notion of the "*body* of Christ" implicitly attributes to the collectivity beliefs and attitudes about the individual body—notably, the porosity of its boundaries and the concerns about outside threats to its health. The body of Christ is one entity, not only functionally, in terms of division of roles, but also physically.

Paul describes this vividly in an often-cited admonition against prostitution in 1 Corinthians. "The body is meant not for fornication [*porneia*] but for the lord and the lord for the body," Paul admonishes the Corinthians, as he proceeds to explain the nature of the bond between their (present) bodies and Christ.[51] "Do you not know that your bodies are *members* [*mele*] of Christ?"[52] While being a member of Christ, the body is still subject to the laws that apply to the individual body. Do you not know that whoever is joined to [*kollomenos*] a prostitute," Paul continues, "is 'one body' with her? For it is said, 'The two shall be one flesh.'"[53] The consequences are appalling—having intercourse with a prostitute amounts to making "members of Christ the members of a prostitute."[54] Never! Paul bawls.

The phrase "the two shall be one flesh" is a citation from Genesis, offered as a commentary on the implications of the creation of Eve from Adam's rib: "That is why a man leaves his father and mother and is united to his wife, and they *become one flesh*."[55] The sexual connotations are clear, and thus the suggestion that such union might have physical (carnal) effects is unsurprising. But the spiritual bond to Christ is described using the same language; "the one who is joined to [*kollomenos*] the Lord is one spirit with him."[56]

The carnal bond created by sexual intercourse and the spiritual bond with Christ are inversely analogous. All those who are baptized are united in one spirit and their carnal unions with others pertain to the collective (spiritual) body.

The significance that this description of the collective body attributes to relations—among bodies and between bodies and spirit—reflects ancient sensibilities that "presume the permeability of human bodies, especially to spirits marked as evil and holy."[57] Bodies are seen as always subject to external agencies, always needing to negotiate with powers at least partly beyond their control. This is also true of the body of Christ. Just as an individual body must be protected, avoiding practices that would subject it to the law of sin in its members, the collective body must be protected against those members who could bring the power of sin into the body of Christ. For "the *pneuma* of Christ's body would become polluted by the corrupting presence of the sinful *sarx* represented by the body of the immoral man."[58] Each individual body is thus a potential gateway for harmful powers.

Paul's view of the collectivity as a single spiritual body leads to an emphasis on the need to protect the (collective) body from the contamination brought about by the sinful unions of individual members. And as Laura Nasrallah observes, "1 Corinthians is full of advice on the discipline and control of the individual body in relation to the 'one body'. . . . A series of corrections of individual bodily practices . . . are undergirded by the notion that one's body is not one's own, but is also part of the community."[59] The image of the multiple members becoming a single body also redefines the significance of individual social identities.[60] The many are one. "For just as the body is one and has many members, and all the members of the body, though many, are one body, so it is with Christ, too." That is, "Jews or Greeks, slaves or free," are "in the one spirit . . . all baptized into one body."[61] This proclamation is similar to the one in Galatians: "There is no longer Jew or Greek, there is no longer slave or free; there is no longer male and female. For all of you are one in Christ Jesus."[62] But the understanding of the unity of differences is explicitly linked to the constitution of a spiritual body.

The meaning of these formulations of unity in Christ is highly contested. Given that Paul also asserts the duty to behave in accordance with social hierarchies—women subject to men, the governed to the rulers, and so on— the statements cannot be meant to support the abolition of such hierarchies.[63] Life "in Christ" coexists with life in the world as it is. It is clear, however, that these questions of the status of individual identities are related to the relationship between spirit and flesh (or the body of flesh). Boyarin argues that for Paul the relationship between the particular and the universal function as an anthropological principle. The "body is particular, marked through practice as Jew or Greek, through anatomy as male or female, the spirit is universal."[64] And the logic extends also to signification: "The physical, fleshy signs of the Torah, of historical Judaism, are re-interpreted as symbols pointing to something more universal."[65] (The common description of legal interpretations according to the "spirit of the law" suggests the lasting influence of this model.)

Life in Christ, in spirit, carries the implicit reference to its opposite, life in the flesh. The phrase "according to the flesh" thus denotes specific practices condemned as "carnal"—often related to passions and appetites in general or sexual practices in particular. And it also points to the particularity of ethnic identity. Later, third-century Christian writer Tertullian—to whom I turn in the next chapter—would explain, "There are some who, because of circumcision, would have flesh and blood taken to mean Judaism."[66] Often the two meanings converge—inappropriate passions become associated with marked identities. Augustine's statement, quoting 1 Corinthians 10:18, is paradigmatic of this aspect of Christian rhetoric against carnality. "'Behold Israel according to the flesh.' This we know to be carnal Israel; but the Jews do not grasp this meaning and as a result they prove themselves indisputably carnal."[67] The argument is both about understanding and about practice—failing to understand the "real" meaning of the law, they fail to move beyond a religion of the flesh, Boyarin observes. This line of argument would be deployed against the Jews to deadly ends throughout Christian history.[68]

Describing the new (spiritual) identity in the body of Christ as universal is misleading, however, tacitly construing the particularity of the Christian as universal. For this reason, Caroline Johnson Hodge suggests, it might be more appropriate to refer to the new identity as a "new ethnicity," for which kinship is established through baptism.[69] The concerns apply also to gender. For while the images of spiritual bodies were represented as an ideal of genderless bodies, these most often imply the universalization of the masculine, or "andro-gender," Karen King observes.[70] Therefore, despite its evident appeal, the image of collectivity as a spiritual body is also challenged for its potential implication of the subordination of differences to a new identity construed as universal. The continuing influence of this image and the tensions that accompany it explain why these texts are still the site for philosophical discussions about Christian/Western universalisms.[71] The appeal of a unifying reality above corporeal particularities related to birth or ethnicity—in the name of religion or of the nation—and the tendency to imagine such reality as spiritual persist.[72]

Perplexing Radiances

In the letters of Paul, the term "body" has different moral and ontological values depending on its function within each argument. At times it is used to refer to the form of any entity—from animals to stars. The lowest and the most radiant of these entities are "bodies," which are defined by their place in the cosmos. The ontological value in this case does not depend on their being bodies, but rather on their types of "flesh." No moral valuation needs to be assumed in such descriptions. In addition to their preestablished place in cosmic hierarchies, bodies are subject to transformation in relation to external forces. They can become one with other bodies and with the spirit. Individuals of flesh and blood gathered in Christ become a collective spiritual body. In all these cases, a body is a unity. But at other times the term body is used as a synonym for "flesh" and its ambiguities.

Flesh has different meanings in this corpus. It is used neutrally when referring to the different substances of different types of bodies—humans, fish, or birds. But its association with sin is consistent and enduring.[73] The distinction between flesh and spirit is fundamental for other arguments in the letters—such as the structure of the collectivity that it endorses and the possibility of resurrection.

The constitution of bodies can change in relation to their practices and will be most radically changed in the resurrection. The spiritual bodies are not immaterial, but their qualities are different from those of carnal ones. The dream of glorious bodies freed from the weight of earthy substances and the menace of death is alluring. But their brilliance is fueled by the exhaustion of flesh.

Abandoning Flesh

CHAPTER 3

EMBRACING FLESH
Tertullian

For it is said,
All flesh is grass,
and all its glory like the flower of the grass.
The grass becomes dry and the flower dead.
—1 Peter 1:24

The earliest surviving Christian texts in Latin proclaim a carnal theology. Tertullian's doctrinal works, especially *On the Flesh of Christ* and *On the Resurrection*, expand on the Gospel of John and Paul's epistles as they boldly (and polemically) assert that God embraced the tenderness and vulnerability of flesh.[1] In the second century, Irenaeus had celebrated the capabilities of tender, earthy flesh. "The glory of God shines forth in the weakness of flesh," he wrote.[2] In Tertullian's works flesh would more vividly color his words about the incarnation.[3] "Through their shared focus on the enduring value and significance of flesh," Benjamin Dunning explains, Irenaeus and Tertullian "anticipate in important ways the shift that Patricia Cox Miller has identified as a 'material turn' in late ancient Christianity."[4]

Tertullian's role in shaping Western Christian language, his striking rhetorical style, and his use of anatomical details for theological refutation, all contribute to Tertullian being regarded as representative of Christian views of flesh.⁵ It is a controversial, when not a tendentious appointment. For Tertullian's writings on women have earned him a reputation as a misogynist, and for his writings about baptism he is considered the originator of Christian technologies for sexual control.⁶ Tertullian's name is thus associated with an affirmative incarnational theology, but also with the surveillance and control over gender roles and sexual desires. All of this is part of his legacy and all of it affects flesh.

I will not follow Tertullian's texts through all their tensions, inconsistencies, and failures. Instead I trace the affirmative images of flesh, as they unfold from the poetics of the Gospel of John and the letters of Paul—repeating, combining, and transforming their language and figures. Following my reading of the Gospel of John in chapter 1, I foreground Tertullian's descriptions of flesh as a site of relation and exchange between human bodies and between the human and the nonhuman elements. I also note some of the texts' slippages, where the theological project falters and the theologian betrays his teaching. But my aim is neither to excuse nor to condemn him. The ancient theologian is not the object of my reading, but rather a Christian poetics of flesh with potentialities and dangers well beyond Tertullian's aims.

Births

Tertullian turns to flesh in response to the debates of his time. The spiritual nature of Christ is not in question, Tertullian says in passing.⁷ But Christ's flesh troubles his opponents. Such theological misgivings are inextricable from, and perhaps a symptom of, their attitudes toward their own flesh. For the incarnation is divine love for flesh, and welcoming that love implies accepting the dishonor of flesh. Tertullian's view is but one of the ways in which Christians addressed the challenging implications of the incarnation. "Ancient theologians frequently, and notoriously, tried to cleanse Christ of the embarrassing effects of so much messy contact with carnality—birth, death, and all the passionate travails that lay between," Virginia Burrus explains. "Equally frequently, however, they positively rejoice in the scandal of divine incarnation, thrilling at the shame of a flesh that was always already dying and also always already becoming divine."⁸ They sought to transform humiliation, not by avoiding it, but rather by defiantly claiming vulnerability. Tertullian performs the scandalous joys in writing. Rather than downplaying his opponents' disgust for flesh, he repeatedly intensifies it, only to move ever more deeply and ardently toward flesh—to the depths of its origins in the womb.

Denying the flesh of Christ is both the reason and the effect of denials of his birth. Tertullian connects the rejection of Christ's flesh by those he calls "heretics" to their rejection of Christ's birth. In order to deny the flesh of Christ they denied his nativity; in order to deny his nativity they denied his flesh.[9] For of course, "there is no nativity without flesh, and no flesh without nativity." Tertullian counters that Jesus's flesh is human flesh like theirs. Tertullian's argument for Jesus's birth is also about his opponents' attitudes toward their own births. Thus Tertullian guides his readers to contemplate not only Jesus's birth, but also their own births. He represents their most negative views in stark terms, as if daring them to realize the implications of such views for the incarnation.[10] "Come now," he charges sarcastically,

> Beginning then with that nativity you so strongly object to, orate, attack now, the nastinesses of genital elements in the womb, the filthy curdling of moisture and blood, and of the flesh to be for nine months nourished on that same mire. Draw a picture of the womb getting daily more unmanageable, heavy, self-concerned, safe not even in sleep, uncertain in the whims of dislikes and appetites.[11]

The reactions to birth were visceral and so is the rhetoric that Tertullian deploys in response. The statement helps us identify the carnal traits that produce disgust: filthy, unruly, desirous. Yet, far from simply agreeing with his opponents, Tertullian is citing their words against them. Rejecting Jesus's flesh as unworthy implies rejecting their own flesh. But how can they distance themselves from their own birth? "Painting a vivid scene of gestation and birth, Tertullian performatively invokes the abjection of flesh, even as he skillfully displaces the defensive affect of shame onto others."[12] Those who are ashamed of flesh are put to shame.

For Tertullian, what is at stake is nothing less than the possibility for love. "You hate a man during his birth," Tertullian reprimands his opponents, "how can you love any man?"[13] In contrast, Christ loved the person, and "along with the man he loved also his nativity."[14] As we observed before, John declared that what is born of flesh is flesh, only to call the all-too-fleshly audience to be born of the spirit. Now Tertullian calls his audience to embrace their birth in the flesh.

Yet the performance is hardly stable; it produces mixed reactions in Tertullian's readers. Modern readers are often repulsed. The text is written "with repellant plainness," says one; "showing pathological delight in assembling

Embracing Flesh 45

the least attractive elements," complains another; "showing an obscene interest in the physical constitution of Mary," says a troubled third.[15] In other words: it is disgusting! To incite these reactions might have been the very purpose of the passage. Whether contemporary readers would identify such language with their own affects toward flesh and be emboldened by a view of a Christ who exposes himself to humiliation is a different question. Some would strive for attitudes toward flesh that provoke no embarrassment. Tertullian seemed to have struggled too, for at times he is seen slipping; rather than shaming those who are ashamed of flesh he shames women who are not ashamed enough to cover themselves.[16] And the pattern tends to replay itself through history. Emphasizing what is felt as troublesome about flesh can be a strategy to intensify the significance of embracing it. But it often incites a different response—the projection of those traits onto others.

Earthy Flesh

Turning to nativity and the womb attaches flesh securely to the human—which for Tertullian is inescapably gendered. This emphasis is also apparent in Tertullian's appeal to the creation. Whereas John's narrative returns to the creation of *life* itself, Tertullian, like Paul, reads the incarnation through the creation of Adam. The humanity of Adam is defined in its relation to the earth. Irenaeus had already developed an earthy reading of the Genesis story through Romans 5:19. "For, just as through the disobedience of one man who was fashioned first from untilled earth many were made sinners and lost life, so it was fitting also through the obedience of the one man who was born first of the virgin, that many may be just and receive salvation."[17] Tertullian follows and expands on Irenaeus's interpretation. Just as Adam was created out of "virgin" earth—"subjected by no human labor, not yet subdued by planting"—the second Adam "was likewise from earth (that is, flesh)." The "virgin earth" is replaced by "virgin flesh," "not yet unsealed to generation." From it the second Adam is "brought forth by God to be a life-giving spirit."[18] Tertullian's hermeneutical maneuvers are elaborate, built on problematic gender assumptions that cannot quite sustain his project, as we will see. But a crucial incarnational principle is emerging here. The fact that Christ is called Adam already implies his earthy origins—and his earthiness, his fleshiness.[19]

The images shift when Tertullian returns to the moment of creation in *Resurrection*. There he contemplates God in the act of bringing forth the first Adam. Clay, a "paltry thing," "came into God's hands—*whatever they may be.*" Speaking as one caught in the remembrance of love received, he admits, "it would have been blessed enough had it been no more than touched." Blessed enough if that clay had "at once taken form and fashion at the touch of God." But the clay received still more, as it was worked upon by God's hands, touched, broken off the lump, kneaded, and molded.[20] As Tertullian is transported to the beginning by the passions of his theological labors, he imagines God transported to the future by God's own labor of love.

> Recollect that God was wholly concerned with it and intent upon it, with hand, mind, work, counsel, wisdom, providence, and especially with that affection which prescribed its features. For whatever expression the clay took upon it, the thought was of Christ who was to become man (which the clay was) and of the word who was to become flesh (which at that time the earth was).[21]

Note the spacing between man and flesh-earth. Flesh and earth are what the word will become. The earthy image so lovingly shaped is not only touched and formed by God's hands, but also transformed by God's breath. "Flesh blossomed out of clay," and even as that clay emerged "glorious from God's hands," flesh was even more glorious having received the breath of God.[22] This breath was fiery, "competent as it were to bake clay into a different quality, into flesh as though into earthenware."[23] The strength of the vessel does not erase its origins in clay. Thus Paul's description of believers as earthenware becomes an illustration of continuity between earth and flesh, despite differences in appearance of qualities.[24]

Flesh witnesses to its origins. Flesh carries within it the traces of its beginnings in another—memories of primordial contact. The loving touch of God's hands as he shapes the earth is never forgotten. But neither is the mother's womb to which the flesh was once firmly attached. The flesh "carries with it some part of the body from which it is torn," Tertullian writes. It even bears traces of others who shaped *her* flesh. "The flesh of Christ adheres not only to Mary, but also to David through Mary and to Jesse through David."[25] And thus the flesh weaves connections between humans—Mary's flesh carrying all of them, even as the genealogies remember only fathers' names. And flesh also establishes bonds beyond these human filiations—through the earth from which they were formed.[26]

Tertullian's claim that this body of ours "certainly testifies its own origins," expands from allusions to past history toward observable traits that extend far and deep. From earth comes flesh; from water, blood.

> Now, although there is a difference in the appearance of qualities . . . yet, after all, what is blood but red fluid? What is flesh but earth in a special form? Consider the respective qualities—of the muscles as clods, of the bones as stones, the mammillary glands as a kind of pebbles. Look upon the close junctions of the nerves as propagations of roots, and the branching courses of the veins as winding rivulets, and the down (which covers us) as moss, and the hair as grass, and the very treasures of marrow within our bones as ores of flesh.[27]

Flesh is so many forms of earth.

Life and Death

Witnessing to an earthy origin are not only the details of anatomical shapes and the constitution of the earthy vase, but also specific human experiences: hunger and thirst, weeping and trembling, pouring out blood. These are all experiences of vulnerability, which Tertullian had already linked to birth. For "nothing dies except what is born,"[28] he observed. But also, conversely, "dying itself belongs to the flesh, because to it living belongs."[29] Indeed birth and death are always intertwined. To assert the reality of Christ's death entails admitting that he had that to which living belongs. This flesh is that thing— "suffused with blood, built with bones, interwoven with nerves, entwined in veins." Yet that facticity does not make it a mere object—as it is also this flesh that "*knew* how to be born and how to die."[30] Still it is human flesh: vital and mortal.

Weakness does not just issue from the womb; it is already found at the beginning, in the earthiness of flesh. "Dust thou are; and to dust thou shall return" echoes through *On the Resurrection*. And inasmuch as vulnerability is an intrinsic aspect of flesh, part of Adam's constitution, it is not simply the result of the fall.[31] Nor is vulnerability to be simply opposed. For the weakness of flesh is simultaneously the source of pride, hope, and even pleasure.[32] At every turn and with every example, Tertullian invokes the fragility of flesh and he rejoices in its blessedness.[33]

Mortality becomes a proof of the resurrection of the flesh, for only what dies can experience resurrection. But the signs of resurrection are not confined to the end of times. All around the world death and rebirth mark the rhythms of everyday life.

> Day dies into night and is on every side buried in darkness. The beauty of the world puts on mourning, its every substance is blackened. All things are squalid, silent, numb. . . . Such lamentation is there for the light that is lost. And yet again the same light, entire and whole, together with its adornment and endowment, together with the sun, revives for the whole world, slaying its own death, the night, stripping off its funeral-trappings, the darkness, becoming heir to its own self, until night also revives herself also with her own appurtenance.[34]

Tertullian poetically describes what is both familiar and marvelous—the "rekindling" of stars every morning, the "return home" of constellations, the "refurbishing of the mirrors of the moon," the "clothing" of the trees, the new colors of flowers, and dead seeds seeing the light again. The "whole creation is recurrent"[35]—and so is human flesh. In Burrus's words, in the resurrection, the power of God is less "a power exercised over or against nature than one inhering in the nature of flesh's eternal becoming."[36]

What is flesh but earth? Tertullian asked. And yet, despite the continuity between earth and flesh, he must also claim an asymmetry between humanity and the rest of the world in order to explain his belief that only humans will enjoy the resurrection. The difference is starkly stated and yet subtly undermined. While the world was created by the word, Adam was created both by the word and by the hands of God. The word is shared by all creation, divine touch enjoyed exclusively by humans.[37] Thus things are inferior to humans, he concludes. But when it comes to proving the resurrection, it is the habits of the nonhuman world that serve as guide and exemplar. The fact that "all things begin when they have ceased" and "nothing perishes except with a view to salvation" constitutes testimony of the resurrection of the flesh.

Body, Flesh, and Spirit

Flesh is distinct from body, and even more clearly from spirit—in both cases the distinctions keep flesh human and thus blessed. By emphasizing flesh, Tertullian counters claims that Christ's body was only apparent or of a different kind than other human bodies. Tertullian insists that Christ's flesh was not spiritual, not composed of soul, not of a stellar substance, not imaginary.[38] Most often flesh means earthy, as we have seen. The difference and proximity between flesh (caro) and body (corpus) in Tertullian's works, as Jerome Alexandre explains, corresponds to that between sarx and soma. Caro, like sarx, refers to the materiality of flesh—a "substance" in Tertullian's thought. Corpus, like soma, designated corporeality as seen from the outside.[39] He associates the body—as a totality of organized parts—with Paul's influential image of community as the body of Christ, as articulated in 1 Corinthians.

The boundary between flesh and spirit may seem quite predictable, but Tertullian ingeniously (if inconsistently) shifts the weight of both Paul's and John's versions of that relation. As we saw before, Paul turns to Genesis to establish a qualitative difference between Adam, an earthy man, and Christ, a man from heaven. For Paul, the "image of the earthy" is the inheritance from Adam; the image of the man of heaven, of spirit, is what can be received from Christ—referring to the resurrected Christ. This contrast structures Paul's moral distinction between "those who are earthy" and those who are of heaven. It also frames his eschatological vision, for "flesh and blood cannot inherit the kingdom." Whether Paul's description of the distance between the natural (earthy) body and the spiritual body is interpreted existentially, ontologically, or eschatologically, the argument rests on a clear distinction between the two poles. Tertullian asserts the contrasts as starkly as Paul does. But Tertullian's task is to prove that the "image of the earth" establishes the connection between Adam and Christ. Thus the affective charge of the terms must shift. The flesh of the incarnation is *like* Adam's, and thus like all human flesh: earthy.

Tertullian seems to be aware of the apparent tension between his words and Paul's description of Christ, the last Adam, as heavenly or as a life-giving spirit. So he clarifies this by correcting other readings of the Pauline text. "This passage . . . has nothing to do with any difference of substance" between Christ's flesh and human flesh, but rather between spirit and flesh, Tertullian claims. The celestial substance refers only to Christ's spirit—not to his flesh. So much so that those whom the text compares to Christ "evidently become celestial—by the Spirit, of course—even in this 'earthy flesh.'"[40] Guarding the distinction between flesh and spirit allows Tertullian to protect the reality of Christ's flesh. Even if the spirit reaches the heavens, Christ's flesh remains grounded on earth and thus linked to all humans. And it is this bond of earthy flesh between Christ and humanity that opens the possibilities for heavenly life—in the flesh.

In the treatise *On the Resurrection*, Tertullian returns to this Pauline passage and offers multiple points of correction. First, Paul asserts the resurrection, and by definition, Tertullian argues, "resurrection is of the same substance as the death was."[41] Since Christ died in the flesh his resurrection necessarily means that he arose in the flesh.[42] Second, some flesh is kept out of the kingdom of God (not precluded from resurrection) "on account of guilt, not of substance."[43] Furthermore, when the Gospel of John states (with Tertullian's gloss) that "it is the spirit that quickeneth unto the kingdom of God: the flesh profiteth nothing," it is simply to stress that the resurrection required the spirit as well.

Tertullian then addresses Paul's argument about the different types of flesh and different types of glory, insisting that it should not be interpreted ontologically, as proposing that resurrected bodies will be of a different substance. To do so would be to "thrust out all flesh and blood in general from the kingdom of God."[44] To the contrary, he argues, in Christ flesh and blood have already seized the kingdom of God.[45] Tertullian's statement is literally the opposite of Paul's! He further justifies it by reading Paul figuratively—a peculiar strategy for a writer so adamant that flesh means common flesh (not spiritual, not of soul, not stellar), and so inclined to offer realistic, anatomically precise descriptions of flesh.[46] Paul argues that there are different types of *flesh* on earth: humans, beasts, birds, and the like.[47] Tertullian claims that the flesh of man refers to God's true servants; the flesh of cattle to the heathen; birds to martyrs; fishes to "those for whom the water of baptism suffices." Similarly with the glories: the sun is God; the moon is Christ; the stars the seed of Abraham. Thus the Pauline scale of being—dangerously close to that of Tertullian's "heretics"—is reduced to differences between *human* beings and thus refers only to their relative ranking. Tertullian's reading does away with the different types of flesh; it is all one flesh.

Tertullian fastens to flesh a wide variety of references to soul and spirit. Paul stated that the earthy man was first, in order to claim a distinct role for Christ, the man from heaven. For Tertullian, the priority of the earthy man proves the significance of flesh. "The first man Adam was flesh and not soul, and afterwards was made into a living soul," he repeats. And if Christ is called the last Adam, it is "because he is man," and he is a man "because he is flesh and not because he is soul." Thus one must conclude, he argues, that Paul distinguishes between the "soul-informed body" (*corpus animale*) and "spirit-informed body" (*corpus spiritale*) "within the same flesh."[48] Two "bodies" coexist in one and the same flesh.

Similarly, the Gospel of John's statement, "What is born of flesh is flesh; what is born of spirit is spirit," does not present two opposing alternatives, but refers to two aspects of the same person. Tertullian challenges those who assert that Christ is spirit and deny his being flesh. Accepting one of the propositions, he counters, entails accepting also the other: Christ is born of flesh *and* of spirit. To be born of spirit implies to be born of flesh. The gospel's claim that the word was *not* born of the will of the flesh nor of the will of man he also reads in this light. Drawing from a common account of conception, he argued that the "will of flesh" refers to a man's seed. In the particular case of Jesus's conception, there is no human father.[49] God's will replaces the man's seed. "It was not feasible to be born of human seed, lest, if he were wholly son of man, he should not be the Son of God."[50] Mary contributes the flesh. Having received God's spirit, "he received from the Virgin that body which he did bring forth from the Virgin."[51] Therefore, it can be said that "it was out of flesh that the Word was made flesh."[52]

The two elements are joined in one man. "Thus the official record of both substances represents him as both man and God: on the one hand born, on the other not born: on the one hand fleshly, on the other spiritual: on the one hand weak, on the other exceeding strong: on the one hand dying, on the other living."[53] In an effort to counter the spiritualization of Christ's flesh, flesh and spirit are set apart through a series of recognizable dichotomies. Predictably, flesh is feminized—an easy association if woman is defined as a flesh-producing womb.

But the hermeneutical strategy finds its limits whenever the relationship between flesh and spirit gets attached to a seemingly stable dichotomy—in this case that of gender difference. Tertullian's point is that *everyone* emerges from fleshy slush—not just *some* humans, not just women. And this necessity of human birth implies for him the undeniability of Christ's flesh. Therefore, in Tertullian's argument, to undermine the necessary link between humanity and flesh is also to undermine the reality of the incarnation. Inasmuch as the feminization of flesh makes flesh more defining of women than men, it debilitates the link between flesh and humanity, and thus risks weakening the argument for the incarnation.

Tertullian's arguments about Christian practices betray this tendency to displace flesh onto women—and, more startlingly, to deploy the term as almost equivalent to sin. Flesh opposes spirit. Or is it that, despite his claims to the contrary, Tertullian imagines different types of flesh—a difference rejected for fishes and birds, but assumed for female flesh and male flesh?[54] Can gender divide what he otherwise saw bound together in the creation and incarnation?

The long-term effects of the gender rift appear not only in instructions for Christian behavior, but also in matters of doctrine. Fleshliness is easily confined to a lesser side of Christ's nature. Later Christians would restate this gendered structure, at times to propose a natural link between women's vulnerability and Jesus's suffering flesh, at other times to assert the importance of calling God "father"—claiming that the male seed is also the *essence* of the child, and thus only a father could contribute the fundamental nature of Christ.[55] Such claims threaten to break the very connection between Christ's flesh and all human flesh. If flesh becomes an inessential element, this weakens the whole project by opening the door for questioning the need for Christ's flesh. Construing flesh as characteristic of some humans more than others undermines Tertullian's argument: unless you can embrace your own flesh, and its beginnings in the flesh of another, you cannot love other fleshly beings—nor can you understand the incarnation.

The unity of flesh and spirit produces very different challenges than its radical opposition. The soul is saved by means of the flesh, Tertullian argues. This implies not only that humans are saved by the work of Christ, but also that such work has profound implications for Christian corporeal practices. No soul can be saved except in the flesh. It is the flesh that is washed, anointed, signed, "overshadowed by the imposition of hands," fed with the body of Christ, and so on—the very means by which the soul becomes closer to God. Asserting the significance of flesh for salvation implies also, for Tertullian, that it is the locus of spiritual discipline and reform.[56] This construction of flesh as the site of formation is precisely the point of concern for Foucault, as we will see. Ironically, such regimes have often aimed at controlling and eventually taking leave of one's flesh.

The visions of flesh in the Gospel of John and in Tertullian's writings are ambivalent. Flesh is not simply good in any of these texts. (Is it ever?) And flesh is not simply another name for sin in the Pauline corpus—although it is readily seen that way. For good reasons many Christians have dreamt of

Embracing Flesh 53

being liberated from flesh—by shedding it or by radically transforming it—in order to become purely luminous bodies, light and transparent. But other visions of carnality survive alongside that one, where flesh retains its opacity and weight, even as it connects vastly different things—not only human communities, but also earth, water, and bread. This opacity is most accentuated where flesh seems to be most visible or touchable—as bread or earth—and we can no longer decide whether the language is figurative or literal. Its opacity is not the obscurity of a closed container, but a quality of what cannot be predetermined, because it remains open to change through participation and confluence.

Christian flesh is notoriously susceptible to metamorphosis. Its transformations link humanity to the earth, even if flesh also travels all the way from earth to heaven and back. Definitions of flesh are no more stable than the thing they try to define. But through the multiplicity of interpretative substitutions, displacements, and conflations, some of its features persist. The images and terms witness (opaquely and ambivalently) to its Christian origins in earth, word, or womb.

Tertullian's work offers fleeting glimpses of a poetics of flesh unshackled from gender dualisms—at times even crossing the boundaries of the human. Those descriptions are full of passion—a piece of common clay caressed by a loving God; a human body envisioned as displaying in its forms the memories of the earth from which it comes; the whole world dressed in mourning as the day ends. The cosmic scope of the metaphors allows flesh to be inflected with a love that could hardly be derived from the social hierarchies in which the texts are embedded. Poetic excesses, no doubt. And yet what would a theology of flesh be if it renounced envisioning what it cannot grasp? Still if the flesh so loved were not the very flesh that makes humans vulnerable, such poetic gestures would have little to offer to those wrestling with their own fragility and passions, seeking to love others likewise susceptible to fragility and passions. Unless carnality is described as an inescapable aspect of all bodies, allusions to flesh tempt us to hide, or reject and project onto others, any traces of weakness, corruptibility, constraints. For "it is hard to be green and take your turn as flesh," as poet Kay Ryan writes in "Green behind the Ears."[57] It is hard. But avoiding the vulnerability—the humiliations to which it exposes us—is even harder.

II

The Philosophers' (Christian) Flesh

How can we take ideas like those of history, subjectivity, incarnation, and positive finitude away from Christianity in order to attribute them to a "universal" reason with no birthplace?

—Maurice Merleau-Ponty, "Everywhere and Nowhere"

Flesh reappears in European philosophy in the mid-twentieth century. It carries with it sediments of a long history of Christian interpretations. The world's changing universalisms and gender hierarchies are complexly intertwined with flesh. Ethnicities old and new have been marked as inappropriately bound to carnality. The extreme violence of two modern wars and the colonial racialization of bodies weigh on flesh. And yet flesh finds a remarkable exponent in Maurice Merleau-Ponty.

Merleau-Ponty articulates an incarnational poetics to reorient philosophy toward the world, to foster bonds of love and responsibility between human beings. He transformed received notions of flesh to represent the relationships that shape human bodies. Flesh has to be as worldly as ever in this corporeal ontology. It nonetheless retains memories of its previous contacts with Christian poetics. At times flesh flickers with glory.

Objections to the philosophical retrieval of flesh are wide-ranging. Is "flesh" just a name for Christian projections of sin onto corporeality, devised for judging, shaping, and controlling desire? Is "flesh" just "spirit" in disguise, used to legitimize claims of absolute knowledge? The contrast between these concerns corresponds to the divergence between views of corporeality inspired by the Pauline corpus and by the Gospel of John introduced in part I.

The third critique that I present in this part is not particular to Christianity, but reflects feminist concerns. Does "flesh" merely appropriate the role of the mother's womb, in order to disavow sexual difference? I hinted at this potential problem in the discussion of Tertullian's work, and here I return to it as it appears in more recent debates about "flesh" to highlight the dangers of accepting uncritically that ancient tendency to treat flesh as femininity.

Noticing the different Christian models that inform current uses of flesh, I evaluate and respond to the critiques with theological specificity. Most importantly, I seek to more clearly identify features of Christian flesh that can nourish a contemporary poetics of corporeality.

As I address these postmodern critiques of flesh, I do not deny its ties to Christian imaginaries. I concur with Merleau-Ponty's position that to reduce philosophy to a negation of God (or of theology) would be to renounce the obligations of thinking.[1] Philosophy is committed to critical negation—as Christianity is committed to the destruction of (ritual or conceptual) idols. The conceptions that conceal or restrain the life-giving potential of flesh are to be denounced and deconstructed. The critiques in this part perform such deconstructions. Yet there are deep longings in these negations, affirmations to be brought to fruition. Negations are "only the beginning of attention, a seriousness"—which leads us to explore the world in wonder, to describe it faithfully.[2]

This part focuses on flesh as dynamic relation between the body and the world. "Flesh," Merleau-Ponty argued, is a coiling over of the sensing and the sensed, of the body and the world, never returning to the same. The approach I adopt here assumes similar patterns—the theological and the philosophical reach toward each other, coil over each other, but they come apart, changing each other, never becoming the same. My readings of Christian texts in part I were already caught in these movements; they were a response, shaped by reaching forward toward the proposals and debates that I present in this part, and thus toward worlds vastly different from that of the ancient texts. When I wrote above that histories of wars, gender hierarchies, and colonial domination weigh on flesh I meant that they have produced destructive accounts of flesh. I also meant that they have hurt flesh—human flesh, worldly flesh. Envisioning flesh differently, writing it otherwise, I seek to call attention to the harms it has produced and imagine other possibilities for carnal living. So this part also reaches forward to part III—to the ways identities mark bodies and shape the flesh of the world, to social words and their ambivalent incarnations.

CHAPTER 4

INCARNATE PHILOSOPHY

My flesh overflows and fertilizes the world;
the world overflows and my body receives it.
—Rubem Alves, *I Believe in the Resurrection of the Body*

Flesh flowing between bodies and the world—thus liberation theologian Rubem Alves summarizes a Christian view of the body based on the incarnation.[1] God's desire to be a body inspires his celebration of corporeality—of human compassion, gardens, and poetry. He calls his readers to remember the Christian dogma in order to renew their commitments to justice and hope. The incarnational philosophy on which this chapter focuses is more subdued. There are no appeals to God's desire or divinely embraced bodies. It proclaims the complete emptying of God. And still a Christian poetics subtly shapes its carnal imagination.

Merleau-Ponty's full elaboration of "flesh" emerges only in his last work. But it is hardly an afterthought, for the notion of flesh brings together and reshapes ideas and sensibilities that had concerned him since his early writings.[2] In those early texts, the pressures of political concerns immediately following the Second World War converge with a turn to the world that had been inspired by Christian thinkers, notably Gabriel Marcel. Merleau-Ponty saw in the Christian incarnation possibilities for new ways of thinking grounded in human sensibility and committed to justice in the world. His influential work on phenomenology of perception was also an investigation of embodied engagements with the world. Gradually, the idea of carnality overflows the assumed boundaries of the individual body, as it opens to the sensible world. In his posthumously published *The Visible and the Invisible*, flesh figures as the most basic ontological category, with which he explains the relationships between the world, bodies, and the cultures that they create.

This chapter traces the unfolding of Merleau-Ponty's philosophy from discussions of the incarnation, to the body, to flesh. His discussion of the incarnation articulates theologically a shift of orientation from the heavens to the world and elaborates its epistemological and ethical implications. As I read it, Merleau-Ponty's early articulation of the significance of the incarnation makes explicit Christian themes and concerns that are just assumed in his later works. The incarnation implies for Merleau-Ponty a change in the way of conceiving the self, from a subjective interiority to an embodied relation to the world. The second section of this chapter describes the body as a relation to things and to other bodies. The discussion of the body-in-the-world creates a bridge between the discussion of the incarnation in the previous section and the engagement with flesh that follows it. From the body-in-the-world I move to the flesh—what ties bodies and the world. In closing, I move to the world of culture, where flesh and language interlace.

This chapter marks a transition from Christian explications of the incarnation to an ontology of flesh. I tease out the resonances with Christian tropes throughout, even as I embrace the commitment to ground this flesh more firmly in worldly experiences. I also introduce here concepts and ideas on which I rely for my arguments about social identities in part III. The "corporeal schema," the role of the visible body, and the production of imaginary bodies are crucial for my elucidation of the influence of social hierarchies on the constitution of flesh.

Incarnation

Asked to address the contributions of the "philosophy of existence" in 1959, Merleau-Ponty argued that it "is primarily explicable by the importance . . . of *incarnation*."[3] He turns to Christian philosopher Gabriel Marcel in order to explain this idea.

Marcel's *Metaphysical Journal* had opposed the representation of the body as object with its celebrated statement, "I am my body." This proposition was not simply about the body, Merleau-Ponty submits, but more generally about the sensible world. He explains that the turn to the body implies that sensible things are brought to the center of philosophical analysis. "Through the perception we have of them, things are given to us in the flesh—carnally, *leibhaftig*."[4] In the philosophy of existence, the theme of the incarnation motivates a shift in the *object* of study, to focus on the body and the sensible world, and also a new understanding of the role of the *subject* of the philosophical inquiry. The incarnation was "a style of philosophizing."[5] It entailed abandoning the illusion of gazing at the world as if from the outside, seeing things as objects, to instead conceive the philosopher as engaged in the very problems with which she wrestles. Because the thinker is "caught up in the matter" she examines, Marcel described this philosophical task as a concern with "mysteries." Marcel gave these mysteries a religious accent, Merleau-Ponty observes.[6] But he suggests that "such a strange sort of knowledge" was already implied in the turn to the sensible world.[7] To him, perception of the world is always enigmatic.

Merleau-Ponty's retrospective assessment describes existentialism as an innovation that presupposed the turn to the incarnation developed in the philosophy of existence. But there are significant changes in Sartre's existentialism. "Incarnation" becomes "situation" and "the mystery of being becomes in some respects a limpid mystery," he observes.[8] In this description, Merleau-Ponty signals the difference between existentialism and his own philosophical trajectory, which would continue to investigate the implications of an orientation toward the sensible and emphasize its irreducible mystery.

Merleau-Ponty offered his own interpretation of the incarnation focusing on its consequences for Christian commitments to social justice in "Faith and Good Faith."[9] The essay opens by lambasting Catholicism as an institution for its inconsistent stance in relation to social problems. He is not content, however, to locate the problem solely in the contingencies of institutional history, to regard the failures of the church as accidental. "There must be an ambiguity in Catholicism as a spiritual way of life to correspond to its ambiguity as a social phenomenon."[10] The source of the ambiguity, he suggests, is nothing less than an incoherent view of God.

Christianity holds on to "a belief in both an interior and an exterior God," Merleau-Ponty argues.[11] The interior God dwells in the "inner man." We already encountered this inner man in Paul's letters, where it was identified as the site of the law of God at war with another law in the "members."

Merleau-Ponty traces the idea of an interior God inside the inner man to Augustine.[12] By naming Augustine and Luther, Merleau-Ponty is pointing to the continuities between their ideas of an inner man, the notions of subjectivity of his Christian contemporaries, and modern philosophies of the self associated with Descartes. There are important differences between these models, of course.[13] But his main contention is that a belief in an interior God—a divinity that dwells in the inner man—orients life away from the world.[14]

The notion of an interior God implies the possibility of an immediate access to truth in the self. "Whether God is the model according to which my spirit was created or whether I experience and, so to speak, *touch* God when I become conscious of myself as spirit, God is in any case on the side of the subject rather than on the side of the world."[15] Merleau-Ponty is referring to Christian notions of *imago Dei* and the "spiritual senses," respectively, both of which may construe interiority as a site of immediacy. God is imagined as clarity and light, and is ultimately indistinguishable from the interior self where it is found, and which it founds. In this model, one is obedient to God by assenting to the subject's will and this makes faith necessarily good faith.

While this interior God is conceived as immediately accessible to the individual who turns inward, it is detached from and unaffected by the world in general. It is always already complete and absolute. No human action or worldly strife would affect this God's perfection. Because it knows everything from the beginning, for this God things and persons are just "*visible* objects."[16]

"The incarnation changes everything."[17]

In the incarnation, God is externalized, Merleau-Ponty asserts.[18] The transformation is complete. The incarnation is a divine emptying without reserve. "God is no longer in Heaven but in human society and communication," Merleau-Ponty says.[19] God shall not be sought in the heavens, but in the world. This entails a reorientation of life as well as a reconceptualization of God.

The incarnate God is *not* a self-contained perfection, outside of or unmoved by the world. God is *in* the world. But this mode of presence does not imply immediacy. Indeed, neither "presence" nor "absence" seems to be an appropriate term to talk about knowledge of an incarnate God. Instead it entails pondering the implications of living in the flesh, guided by our experience and knowledge of the sensible world. No knowledge of the sensible is ever absolute, unmediated, or devoid of mystery. In the incarnation, the divine mystery is not the effect of distance or separation, but rather of God becoming flesh.

God is not a source of positive knowledge. The task for human beings is "no longer a matter of rediscovering the transparence of God outside the world but a matter of entering body and soul into an enigmatic life, the obscurities of which cannot be dissipated."[20] It is the obscurities of the world that point to God. Entering into that life means acknowledging that our complete being is caught up in that very world. All our knowledge of the world is embodied knowledge and it is necessarily entangled in the world of which it is part. There would be no knowledge without bodies and no bodies without their constitutive relations to the world.

Christians claim that the incarnate God was *seen* and left words and memories in the sensible world. These words and memories do not give access to God directly. Engaging their meaning always requires "commentary and interpretation of that ambiguous message whose energy is never exhausted."[21] Hence, the paradigmatic genre of the gospels' teachings is the parable. Merleau-Ponty does not elaborate on the significance of parables or why he considers them particularly appropriate for knowledge of the incarnate God. But these reasons may be deduced from his philosophy of language. Merleau-Ponty highlights the links between communication and perception and challenges the tendency to separate meaning from the specific words that express it.[22] The parable accentuates these connections. Rather than communicating through abstract concepts, a parable foregrounds lived experiences. The message of the parable depends on the story it tells. Speaking of the sower and the seeds, a fig tree, the birds of heaven, laborers of a vineyard—these parables appeal to specific modes of work, communal expectations, features of local geography. They invite the listeners to participate in the process of meaning making, which is always open-ended. Inasmuch as it draws attention to the emergence of knowledge through engagements with the sensible world, engagements that are necessarily situated and constitutive of the knower, the parable exemplifies the qualities of embodied knowledge.

The sensible world is both familiar and enigmatic. Knowing it entails faith. "Each of our perceptions is an act of faith in that it affirms more than we strictly know, since objects are inexhaustible and our information limited."[23] Faith does not belong to a realm outside or beyond sensible experience, but is rather implicit in it. And yet it also exceeds it. "Faith" names an "unreserved commitment which is never completely justified" which is part of all knowing. It is necessary for life, and "enters the picture as soon as we leave the realm of pure geometrical ideas and have to deal with the existing world."[24] This observation is not intended to undermine commitments because they cannot be fully or permanently justified, but to stress that all commitments are subject to critique. Religion and ethics are intricately linked, and they both entail deep commitments that assume no absolute certainty and thus admit critique as essential.[25]

Embracing the doctrine of the incarnation as a complete emptying of God means grounding ontology, epistemology, and ethics in the material world. But Merleau-Ponty concludes that Christianity does not follow the incarnation in all its consequences. Christianity is satisfied neither with an exterior nor an interior God, moving inconsistently between the two. Christianity continues to cling to an "infinite Knowledge" that has "already settled everything" and undermines its central teaching: "Love changes into cruelty, the reconciliation of men with each other and with the world will come to naught." Ultimately, "the Incarnation turns into suffering because it is incomplete."[26] The incompletion stems from the Christian attachment to the religion of absolute, detached knowledge, its insistence in looking for God in the heavens. "God will not fully have come to the earth," Merleau-Ponty states unexpectedly, adopting a prophetic tone, "until the Church feels the same obligation toward other men as it does toward its own ministers, toward the houses of Guernica as toward its own temples."[27] Here the "incarnation" is more than God's self-emptying action; it denotes also a possibility yet to be realized in the world—a self-emptying of Christians/Christianity toward the world.

Merleau-Ponty's reading of the incarnation as the *complete* emptying of God pushes the boundaries set by authoritative Christian interpretations—moving beyond Christianity itself. But claiming that the incarnation changes the orientation of embodied human life is hardly unorthodox. Merleau-Ponty scholar Emmanuel de Saint Aubert's summation of the implications of Merleau-Ponty's work captures this point of continuity with classic Christian teaching: "It is as if it were necessary for God to become incarnate for human beings to understand who they are, to help human beings live," he writes. "As if a carnal God were needed for human beings to consent to being flesh."[28] The statement echoes ancient theologies discussed in previous chapters, where the incarnation was invoked as the model and warrant for human transformation. Consenting to being flesh implies an ethical as much as a religious commitment. Sometimes the invitation points in the opposite direction than the incarnation, albeit through winding paths—to be born of the spirit, to assume spiritual bodies. At other points the invitation is to follow Christ into the flesh, also through winding and hesitant paths—to love nativity itself. For Merleau-Ponty also, fidelity to the incarnation is "consenting to being flesh," which implies humility about knowledge and ethical obligation toward others.

Body-in-the-World

Philosophical notions of subjectivity produce their own versions of the inner man. Self-consciousness is assumed as the precondition and the commanding agent of all engagements with the world. This is the "detached" subject of Kant and Descartes, Merleau-Ponty argues, while pointing back to Augustine.[29] Challenging this conception of subjectivity and consciousness, Merleau-Ponty seeks a new understanding of the subject open to the world. This project requires attending to the materiality of bodies. This is more than asserting, "I am my body." The "body" must be reconceived, for the term often names a mere material version of the inner man—a self-contained and detachable entity. The body that interests Merleau-Ponty is dynamic and malleable, always being shaped in and by the world.

To be a body is "to be tied to a certain world."[30] The body is tied to the things it perceives, the objects it uses, and to other human bodies. To study these relations Merleau-Ponty draws from psychology, psychoanalysis, and neurology, in addition to philosophy. His writing is often styled as scientific observation; he guides his readers through slow and attentive observations of bodily experiences of movement and perception. As a result, these discussions may seem far removed from the theological disquisitions I just presented. But the analyses of corporeal experiences lead Merleau-Ponty to inquire about the grounds of intercorporeal relations. In the ontological discussions about what makes these relationships possible we encounter different uses of "incarnation." Before addressing these broad questions, however, I contemplate a single body as it moves in the world.

BODIES AND OBJECTS

To understand the body as dynamically constituted in relation to the world implies looking beyond the body as an object—as a collection of cells contained within my skin or the physical contours of my body. For this Merleau-Ponty relies on the concept of "corporeal schema."[31] The body schema is a functional model of the body—not necessarily the body seen by others, but that through which I act in the world. The corporeal schema is subject to transformation, even when my empirical body seems to be the same. The concept guides Merleau-Ponty's understanding of habits and the modification of corporeal boundaries through the movement of bodies in space.

A commonly used example of the difference between the objective body and the corporeal schema is that of a patient experiencing a phantom limb—where the experienced body includes sensations from a part of the body that is no longer ("objectively") there. A patient's objective body and her knowledge of it are clearly different from the body as she experiences it.[32] Her corporeal schema has not been modified according to her new morphology. Contrastingly, when a blind person uses a walking stick as if it were part of his sensing body he demonstrates a successful transformation of his corporeal schema to include the walking stick. But these are just extreme examples of more ubiquitous phenomena.

The concept of corporeal schema helps us to understand the development of other abilities as well. A woman becomes so accustomed to wearing her hat, Merleau-Ponty observes, that she moves as if it were a part of her body. A pianist moves his fingers, his whole body, toward the piano to produce heartfelt music, without ever needing to picture the location of the keys in his mind. He expresses himself through the piano. Twenty-first-century examples of the inclusion of objects in a person's body schema would include the uses of mobile electronic devices. What allows a person to perform these quotidian tasks efficiently is the capacity for corporeal transformations, the malleability of the functional body in relation to specific needs and activities. Instead of being a purely cognitive skill, the acquisition of habits entails the "rearrangement and renewal of the corporeal schema."[33] We do not simply think differently, our bodies work differently.

The movements of the body in the world gradually reshape the body—not only its capacities, but also its structure—increasing some abilities, limiting others. It is as if the rearrangements of the corporeal schema left their marks in a person's body, traces of the history of a person's engagements with the world. The marks of our daily labor are relatively legible from our appearance—the hunched back of a scholar, the strong arms of a construction worker, the absence of fingerprints on a packer's fingers.[34] All these visible transformations can only suggest the many other invisible ones. Our particular practices also shape unseen aspects of our corporeality, through the secretion of hormones or the operation of our cells, for instance, as we will see in chapter 5.

Looking beyond the specific examples to theorize the broader conditions that make them possible, Merleau-Ponty turns to images that suggest vital material processes. "To get used to a hat, a car, or a stick is to be *transplanted* into them," he states. And conversely, "to *incorporate* them into the bulk of our body." And these dynamic processes reveal broader features of human existence, to which Merleau-Ponty keeps returning. "Habit expresses our *power of dilating* our being-in-the-world."[35] Moving toward the world, being transplanted into things and incorporating them, displaces the boundaries of the functional body and ties the body to its world.

INTERCORPOREAL ENGAGEMENTS

Just as my corporeal schema is shaped by my interactions with things, it is also formed by my interactions with other human beings. My experience of my body is always related to other bodies—from the first sensations of touch and nourishment to later senses of my body as my own and as seen by others.[36] Theorizing these intercorporeal bonds requires relational models of both the body and the psyche. Rather than thinking of the body as an agglomerate of internal sensations, it must be understood as a corporeal schema, Merleau-Ponty argues. And rather than conceiving the psyche as a closed system, a series of states of consciousness, it should be understood as a consciousness turned toward the world.[37]

Merleau-Ponty draws from child psychology and psychoanalysis to explore specifically the relationship between the body as a site of sensations and the body as seen by others. Turning to early stages of child development allows Merleau-Ponty to analyze preconceptual bonds between human beings—such as nourishment or a parent's touch and gaze—which precede more mature forms of cognition, such as mental representations of bodies. The intercorporeal bond is thus placed at the very beginning, as a precondition for any experience of the individual body. The corporeal capacities displayed in these early relations are the basis for the ongoing processes of identification and appropriation between the self and other bodies.

Merleau-Ponty describes three stages in the development of a child's experience of her body: beginning with a phase prior to the distinction between self and other, proceeding to the mirror stage, then to mature views of her body as her own and clearly separate from other bodies. In the first phase of a child's development, the child does not yet have a visual image of herself or a clear sense of her body as individual and separate from the world. Instead, there is "an anonymous collectivity, an undifferentiated group life."[38] The baby experiences the other's presence or absence through its effects on her bodily sensations. This early stage, however, is not one of isolation in a world of internal sensations. The baby's ability to imitate gestures—to smile in response to her father's smile—constitutes evidence of the existence of modes of intercorporeal engagement even at this stage. Because at this stage the child lacks a clear sense of the boundaries between her body and those of others—thus not having a sense of the body as *hers*—the response to the parent's smile cannot be interpreted as an imitation of a visual image. Instead, the child adopts or appropriates another's conduct in her own body. When a baby smiles in response to her father's smile, she is reproducing the gestures of another body in her own body. This capacity must be understood as a transformation of the corporeal schema, Merleau-Ponty concludes.[39]

I noted before that Merleau-Ponty used images of "transplantation" and "incorporation" to describe the rearrangements of the corporeal schema. He similarly describes the appropriation of gestures using intercorporeal images, as a "postural *impregnation* of my own body by the conducts I witness."[40] When the baby smiles at her father's smile, she takes in and feels a smile in her own body. She is incorporating in her body what she receives visually. This process of "impregnation" prepares the child for developing the ability to understand another person's gestures.

The initial phase of indistinction between the child's body and the world—an "initial community"—gradually gives way to individuality. This entails the "objectification of one's own body" as well as the "constitution" of the other's difference.[41] Distinguishing between self and others makes true perception possible. But the transition toward segregation and distinction is not a straight progression; Merleau-Ponty insists that the process "is never completely finished."[42] The body will always bear the traces of its emergence from an anonymous collectivity—though only as an openness toward otherness, toward alterity.

The transition to individuality is facilitated by the child's acquisition of a visual image of her body. Until the moment when the specular image arises, the child's body is a strongly felt but confused reality. The identification with a mirror image implies replacing that diffused and fragmented sense of her body with a coherent visual image. This shift is not simply a matter of understanding. The mirror stage produces a "transformation of the subject," which has lasting affective repercussions.[43] In recognizing her image in the mirror the child learns that there can be a viewpoint taken on her. The child notices that she is *visible*, to herself and to others.

The "new personality" that emerges from the passage to the "specular I" leads to alienation from the introceptive self, from the lived me. "I am no longer what I felt myself, immediately, to be; I am that image that is offered by the mirror. To use Lacan's terms, I am 'captured, caught up' by my spatial image." This link between the self and the visual image transforms the child's relation to her corporeal sensibility. "Thereupon I leave the reality of my lived *me* in order to refer myself constantly to the *ideal, fictitious, or imaginary* me, of which the specular image is the first outline."[44] Acquiring a visual image of myself makes self-observation possible and thus a new mode of relationship to myself, to my body. But self-contemplation is also associated with the view that others have of my body, and thus a visual body image is inherently linked to *imagining* how others see me. It makes possible the construction of an ideal image of myself. This ideal image, Merleau-Ponty observes, "would henceforth be either explicitly posited or simply implied by everything I see each minute."[45] We are entering the realm of social representations.

The mechanisms that Merleau-Ponty describes affect all human beings. But the effects of our visible bodies are different depending on the meanings given to each by the societies in which we live. The alienation experienced during the mirror stage is a general phenomenon, even though he considers it only an initial step toward broader dynamics that ultimately shape a person's relation to social representations. "I am torn from myself, and the image in the mirror prepares me for another still more serious alienation, which will be the alienation by others." The source of that sense of alienation is the realization that "others have only an exterior image of me, which is analogous to the one seen in the mirror. Consequently others tear me away from my immediate inwardness much more surely than will the mirror."[46] The violence of this description, and its references to "inwardness," require clarification. The "lived me" can hardly be conceived in terms of an original or natural self-isolation—a view that Merleau-Ponty constantly challenges, emphasizing that before the mirror stage the child's experience of her body is not contained within the boundaries of her skin. She feels her body as she feels her mother's presence or absence. If there is any suggestion of "immediacy" in these analyses, it must presuppose that constitutive relationality experienced through unorganized bodily sensations. The development is not from an interior self to a relational one, but from undifferentiation between self and other to a more structured relation that ushers in the possibility of sensing my body as my own. From the "beginning" the lived me is turned toward the world. But inasmuch as experiencing my body as mine requires awareness of an exterior image of my body, my experience of my body is always already entwined with images that others have of me.

Theorizing the corporeal schema shifts the focus from the "objective" body to the dynamic body-in-the-world. However, this understanding of the body as ever emerging from relational processes does not render the visible, bounded body inconsequential. For the world in relation to which the corporeal schema develops is always social. In these inter-human exchanges, the visible body is a determining factor. Even my earliest images of my body are structured in relation to the gaze of another. The sensations of my body and the other's are imbricated, and so are the cognitive representations of my own body with those of others. Perception of the world is not subsequent to self-awareness, but is part of its development.

The analogy between the other's gaze and the reflection in the mirror highlights the relationship between a foundational stage (or process) in human development and the multifarious encounters that will continue to shape a person's body image. The affective and the imaginary elements of the mirror stage, to which psychoanalysis attends, are crucial for understanding how the body image derives from and yet is not a mere copy or imprint of sensible data transmitted from the mirror to cognition. The image is already invested with affective value—the specular is already haunted by specters. This dimension of affectivity and fantasy is only accentuated when the mirrors multiply in the impossibly complex arena of social representations.

"I borrow myself from others," Merleau-Ponty says.[47] But what I borrow from others might be my own negation, as we will see in the last part of this book. Merleau-Ponty described the ability to acquire a habit as expressing our "power of dilating our being-in-the-world." The power might be severely restricted, however, by personal relations, social arrangements, and the material structures that they produce. Rather than dilating my being-in-the-world, I might find myself being constricted by it.

IN(TER)CARNATIONS

Envisioning the body-in-the-world entails wrestling with the complex connection between my body as I experience it and my body as perceived by others. For Merleau-Ponty, it is not enough to treat them as antithetical views, as Sartre does. Instead, "we must ask why there are two views of me and of my body: my body for me and my body for others, and how these two systems can exist together." The ontological questions arise at this juncture. It seems impossible to relate these views if one assumes that the body (or the psyche) is a self-enclosed entity; but the task cannot be avoided if I accept that these two views—the "for me" and the "for others"—"co-exist in *one and the same world*."[48] A common world links my body as I experience it to my body as others perceive it.

The link between the two views of my body is related to the tie between my body and the bodies of others. My body and the bodies of others "form a real system." To understand this requires "becoming conscious of what might be called 'incarnation.'"[49] Merleau-Ponty does not unpack the term's meaning in this context. Neither does incarnation figure prominently in *Phenomenology of Perception*, where it is mentioned only in passing as a broad concept referring to the "incarnation of perception," the basis of human susceptibility to "error, sickness, madness," and the idea that "existence realizes itself in the body."[50] But even in the absence of explicit references to Christianity, in Merleau-Ponty's writings the incarnation tends to appear in conjunction with assertions of our coexistence in the (same) world—although the connection is presupposed rather than explicated. For example, commenting on Edmund Husserl's work, Merleau-Ponty explains, "The reason why I am able to understand the other person's body and existence 'beginning with' the proper body . . . is that the 'I am able to' and the 'the other person exists.'" My ability to understand another human being implies also that we "belong here and now to the same world." And then he adds, as a repetition of the same idea, "that the body proper is a premonition of the other person, the *Einfühlung* and echo of my incarnation."[51] "Incarnation" alludes to the condition of my emergence, which links me to other bodies. A basic feeling of intercorporeal empathy echoes my incarnation.

I hear in these lines whispers of a Christian poetics. Clearly, the reference here is not to the Christ event that he discussed in "Faith and Good Faith." However, the connection between these two uses of the term "incarnation"—as the externalization of God and as what links my body to the other's—is not incidental. In my reading of Christian sources, I noted that the incarnation refers back to the creation and structures a vision of collective being. Tertullian uses the biblical images to emphasize the bond of flesh that runs from the creation, to the incarnation, to the present reality. For him, flesh is prior to the individual bodies. Even now, flesh remembers its origins. Alluding to the incarnation brings to mind and revaluates carnal/earthy bonds as grounds for a commitment to a shared life. These theological and ontological ideas are not explanatory systems to which I can turn to determine the mechanisms that operate in the world. They express commitments that cannot be fully justified. They are what must be presupposed for the inquiry to take place.

To be a body is to be "tied to a certain world." As it acts, the body is transplanted into things and incorporates them; it is impregnated by the gestures of other human beings; it borrows its images from others. The body is nexus and synthesis of multiple things. Much of Merleau-Ponty's analysis of these relations focuses on the dynamics and effects of movement and perception—both of which imply awareness. As the analysis of child development shows, perception plays a fundamental role in experiences of corporeality, and as we will see, considering perception is crucial for my analysis of the incarnation of social representations such as those of racialization and gendering. My body is entangled with and shaped by its images. But there are other aspects of the body's relation to the world that flow below perception. The transformations of my body caused by the water I drink, the air I breathe, or the bacteria that live in me do not require my awareness—although they do affect all corporeal processes. Merleau-Ponty's references to the incarnation, to the consequences of inhabiting one and the same world, suggest a level of relation that is not initiated by the subject. But the textures of this broader reality have yet to be addressed. Even though he consistently tried to move beyond the privilege of consciousness, *Phenomenology of Perception* started with consciousness and the body, both of which it tried to place in relation to the world. For this reason, Merleau-Ponty concludes that he must start again—with the flesh.

Flesh of the World

"That the presence of the world is precisely the presence of its flesh to my flesh, that I 'am of the world' and that I am not it, this is what is no sooner said than forgotten,"[52] Merleau-Ponty protests. In his opinion, his own works had not succeeded because they had started from the problematic of consciousness. With flesh as its focus, "L'entrelacs" begins again.

The writing in "L'entrelacs" follows the patterns of the relationships that it depicts in the overall structure of the essay as well as in the movements and turns of each of its sentences. It describes the interlacing between the body and the world, the body and the other, visibility and touch—all becoming more intricate as the essay progresses. Each description of an element of sensible experience branches out, turning into a different element, coiling back to relate it to the elements previously mentioned, incorporating what was said before, only with variations. Sentences incorporate ever more complex multiplicities, as the elements interlace: seeing and being seen, touching and being touched, touching and seeing, hearing and feeling, speaking and hearing, and so on.

"L'entrelacs" is also, and for the same reasons, an opaque and elusive text. In its circuitous statements, the patterns of flow and transformation, and its use of metaphors of flesh, light, and word, I find intriguing echoes of the Gospel of John. The text also reflects the author's interest in the "strange sense of knowledge" of the sensible, and his description of the path of knowledge as "entering body and soul into an enigmatic life, the obscurities of which cannot be dissipated." An apophatic sensibility shapes the writing—cautious about the limits of its perspectives and representations—even as it addresses what seems most accessible, two hands touching, the perception of colors, or a handshake. The writing style seems especially tailored for addressing what Merleau-Ponty describes as "both irrecusable and enigmatic." Seeing, speaking, even thinking "have a name in all languages," Merleau-Ponty explains. But "a name which in all of them also conveys significations in tufts, thickets of proper meanings and figurative meanings, so that . . . not one of these names clarifies by attributing to what it names a circumscribed signification."[53] He thus offers depictions of the manifold relationships that constitute sensible experience. And the very images offered to describe these relationships also multiply—leaves, envelopes, laps, circles, tissue, elements—they emerge, disappear, and appear again in a different form. Metaphors are sometimes said only to be unsaid. At other times predications are prefaced by multiple negations: flesh is not matter, not substance, not spirit, and so on. Merleau-Ponty describes, in another context, a desire for a "negative philosophy" modeled like a "negative theology."[54] But the apophatic gestures in "L'entrelacs" are not predominantly of negation, but rather of a multiplication of relations, images, and perspectives, as well as a persistent play of light and obscurity, visibility and invisibility.

The turn to flesh begins with observations about perception that appear, at first glance, to repeat some of the themes treated in the previous section—the relation between my body and the bodies of others, the inquiry into what links the other's body to mine. But the analyses of intercorporeal engagement place the author more consistently in the midst of what he describes. This is not the view of a *kosmostheoros*—a "sovereign gaze," which would find "things each in its own time, in its own place, as absolute individuals in a unique local and temporal disposition."[55] Instead, as one caught in the realities he analyzes, he observes, "whenever I try to understand myself the whole fabric of the perceptible world comes too."[56] Depicting that "fabric," that "flesh," is the aim of that last work.[57]

Touch and visibility reveal the imbrication of bodies in the fabric of the world. I begin with touch—with bodies touching things, reaching toward other bodies, touching each other, seeing each other. Then I move to consider what makes these possible, namely flesh—and the mysteries of a light that illuminates all flesh.

TOUCH

Touch implies proximity. Touching something requires being touched by it. In order to feel this cup I must expose my skin to its surface, as much as its surface becomes exposed to my touch.[58] I may receive its energy as it can receive mine. Touching and being touched "interlace." I can touch this cup because it is tangible, but also because I am tangible. There is "reversibility" between the hand that touches and the thing touched, Merleau-Ponty observes. And this should not be taken for granted. It implies that there is between my body and this piece of porcelain, between the particles that constitute it and my body, a certain kind of kinship. What accounts for the fact that I can experience this? That the movement of a hand over a surface enables the feelings of its textures shows that there is a relationship between them, a kind of harmony or opening of the body to the world.

The interlacing between touching and being touched occurs not only between my body and the things that I touch, but also within my body. When one of my hands touches the other, I can experience myself as both sensing and sensible. In my body, feeling and being felt are inseparable from each other. But they are still distinct experiences. Merleau-Ponty struggles to find a metaphor that appropriately conveys the relationship between these experiences as distinct yet not separable. The body sensed and the body sentient are two leaves, he says, only to unsay it. To "speak of two leaves or of layers is still to flatten and juxtapose," he worries.[59] "The body sensed and the body sentient are as the obverse and the reverse"; or two segments of one sole circular course; or slightly decentered circles. Merleau-Ponty did not settle on any of these metaphors. The key is to represent the relationship between the sensed and the sentient without recourse to the "inner man." Too often, the sensing body has been imagined as an entity in and of itself, receiving data from the sensed body. This sensing function has been attributed to the soul in Christian texts and to rationality or consciousness in modern thought. In either model, sensing capacities are separated from the world of sensible things, to which the body belongs. This makes it possible to detach the "self"—a sensing thing—from the sensed body and from the world. The sensing self is imagined as an entity *contained* in a body, *contained* in the world—like a set of Russian dolls. This logic is pervasive, and thus Merleau-Ponty keeps insisting that the sensing body and the sensed body are one and the same body.

Experiencing my body as connected to the things touched, as both touching and touched, reveals to me something about the relationship between the "objective" and "subjective" orders. It helps me understand the other person's body in its connection to the world. I can feel my body as tangible and I can also feel the body of another as tangible. Thus I must assume that the other's body, which I experience as a sensible thing, is also sentient. He is touching me when I touch him; he feels my skin when I feel his. He is, like me, an interlacement of the sensible and the sentient. He is also connected to the world, participating in the order of tangibility. We share that kinship that allows us to touch and be touched. We belong to the same world.

The basic principles that apply to touch are also true of the relationship between the seer and visible things, Merleau-Ponty contends. Properly understood—and against "common sense"—seeing is like touching. It is thus never simply surveying from outside the world or detached from it—an illusion of separability that has made vision the privileged metaphor for philosophical knowledge. Vision is "literally" a palpation with the look.[60] Seeing is enmeshed in and affected by what it sees. I do not see things naked, nor does touching them afford me absolute knowledge of them. Neither seeing nor touching implies immediacy. Seeing is situated, perspectival, in obscurity as much as in light.

The body is able to see and touch things because it is also visible and tangible. In other words, the body's visible and tangible being allows it to "participate" in the tangible, visible world.[61] Perception thus depends on conditions that exceed the perceiver and the perceived. A body's connections to things and to other bodies become the basis for a broader vision of the world. Affirming in faith more than can be strictly known, Merleau-Ponty proposes that "everything said about the sensed body pertains to the whole of the sensible of which it is part, and to the world."[62]

FLESH

Merleau-Ponty names the generality that makes possible seeing and touching "visibility" or "flesh." When focusing on vision as exemplar phenomenon, he refers to its condition of possibility as "visibility"—an important part of the project, as evidenced by the book's title, *The Visible and the Invisible*. The seer is *of* the visible. But his uses of "flesh" are no less significant. Indeed, "visibility" and "flesh" play similar roles and sometimes the differences between them disappear. "There is . . . a literal, essential identity between flesh and visibility," Merleau-Ponty tells himself in a working note.[63] This is in part because ultimately seeing and touching are not separate phenomena. Seeing and touching interlace, and flesh figures as a joining element for both. "Flesh" is the "coiling over of the visible upon the seeing body, of the tangible upon the touching body."[64] Flesh is a name for these possibilities—and more.

Flesh weaves together. Its meaning emerges only gradually in "L'entrelacs"— never fully revealed in the text, just as flesh is never wholly disclosed in the experiences that the text explores. Flesh twists and turns, constituting realities that never exhaust it.

Flesh appears first in connection to individual things. There is a flesh *of* things, but it is not a thing contained within bodies; it is not even properly a thing. It connects the perceiving body and the thing perceived. The gaze "envelops" things, "clothes them with its own flesh."[65] Flesh makes possible the "communication" between the sensing and the sensed. But the relationship it mediates is never between two self-identical, constituted things that then encounter one another. Instead, "the thickness of flesh between the seer and the thing is as constitutive for the thing of its visibility as for the seer of his corporeity."[66]

Seeing and touching—and also speaking and thinking—contribute to the world. The movements of my eyes to observe the deep red of this wine or the slow motions of my hand to feel the contours of my beloved's face, "incorporate themselves into the universe they interrogate."[67] They are given to the world. These common phenomena are evidence of a broader reality that does not originate in me or in the things I encounter. Our encounters change me; they may change much more. "Bursting forth of the mass of the body toward things," Merleau-Ponty writes, "this magical relation, this pact between them and me according to which I lend them my body in order that they inscribe upon it and give me their resemblance, this fold."[68] Flesh is this fold. I am given to a world that vastly exceeds me—and it gives itself to me.

This belonging of my body to the world is never coincidence, however. We do not become the same, nor does the world become my own. The "reversibility" between sensing and being sensed is always imminent, incessantly escaping. "Carnal adherence" is both overlapping and fission, identity and difference, segregation and openness.

In these depictions of carnal bonds I see the reappearance of some of the patterns that I noticed in the Gospel of John: flesh is transformed as it moves from one body to another, human flesh interlaces with other material elements, descriptions of flesh are elusive. In the Gospel of John, flesh is the word, what is given by the word, what others give when they partake of the flesh. In "L'entrelacs" flesh is given and received, it is always being transformed and it transforms those who participate in it. And everyone participates in it. Merleau-Ponty also uses the language of the Genesis creation story when he says that others are "flesh of my flesh."[69] Rather than interpret the well-known phrase as the foundation for a gender hierarchy, he broadens its scope beyond its sexual connotations—while retaining its affective charge. "Flesh of my flesh" is a way of declaring a desire for "intertwining" of the self-in-the-world and the world-in-the-self.[70] Saint Aubert renders Merleau-Ponty's *entrelacs* in explicitly Johannine language by describing it as a desire for the "you in me and the me in you."[71]

The multiplicity of images that Merleau-Ponty uses to describe flesh conveys the limits of all its representations. In this too Merleau-Ponty's carnal

Incarnate Philosophy 77

poetics resembles the Gospel of John—neither one of them settles on a single depiction of flesh. Indeed, they seem to elude fixity. In addition to the proliferation of terms and images, Merleau-Ponty describes it by negating specific attributes. Flesh, "one knows there is no name in traditional philosophy to designate it."[72] After this gesture toward a flesh "beyond the name," and in keeping with the genre of negative theology, we find a list of negations. "The flesh is not matter, is not mind, is not substance."

> To designate it, we should need the old term "element," in the sense it was used to speak of water, air, earth, and fire, that is, in the sense of a general thing . . . a sort of *incarnate principle* that brings a style of being wherever there is a fragment of being. The flesh is in this sense an "element" of Being.[73]

The "old term 'element'" refers to ancient (pre-Socratic) visions of the material relations between bodies and the world.[74] The interaction between the elements was considered the cause for the development of matter as much as bodily conditions and dispositions, drawing together the social and natural worlds. "The unity of things" was thus conceived as a "consequence of the plurality and harmony of their elements."[75] Aristotle too had included "flesh" in his discussion of the elements. He proposed that "just as air and water are to sight, hearing, and smell," so flesh is the "medium for that which can perceive by touch."[76] Merleau-Ponty's use of the elemental is informed by these classical sources. He also draws from his readings of Henri Bergson and Gaston Bachelard, who infuse the elemental with theological and poetic significance.

In Bergson's work, the elements are associated with the divine. Bergson's God, Merleau-Ponty explains, "is the element of joy or love in the sense that water and fire are elements. Like sentient and human beings, He is radiance, not an essence."[77] This God is not "an all-powerful being," and any "metaphysical attributes that seem to determine him are . . . negations."[78] The apophatic framing of Merleau-Ponty's definition of elemental flesh evokes this sensibility. Defining flesh as element negates the attributes one might use to determine it: matter, substance, mind, and the like. Merleau-Ponty's flesh is not a god, but an "incarnate principle." However, like Bergson's God, elemental flesh is the condition of possibility for joy or love.[79]

Whereas read against the background of Bergson's work, the elemental suggests an affinity to a certain image of divinity, in relation to Bachelard's work it highlights the link between elemental flesh and the imagination. "In order for a reverie to continue with enough persistence to produce a written work," Bachelard argues, "it must find its matter, a *material element* must give the reverie its own substance, its own law, *its specific poetics*."[80] Bachelard would explore the distinctive poetics of each element, engaging flesh in relation to the earth. (Earth is for him a type of flesh—a near inverse of Tertullian's depiction of flesh as a form of earth.) Merleau-Ponty states explicitly his debt to Bachelard's conceptualization of the elements, when he describes both being and the imaginary as "elements." They are "not objects, but fields, subdued being, non-thetic being, being before being."[81] These traits are also part of Merleau-Ponty's descriptions of flesh.

Merleau-Ponty does not circumscribe flesh to a particular mode of perception nor does he appeal to other elements.[82] Flesh links. He distinguishes it from "matter"—seeking to avert the dualisms that sneak in whenever terms such as matter, mind, spirit, and substance are used. "Flesh is not matter," he explains, "in the sense of corpuscles of being which would add up or continue on one another to form beings."[83] Flesh is not matter, if the term implies passivity or recalcitrance—requiring something else to animate it.[84] Flesh is rather "an element of Being," or "being before being." "Not a hard nucleus of being, but the softness of the flesh," he states in a course on nature, and the thought trails off. He says, unsays the said, and says it differently; he negates, interrogates, and takes imaginative leaps. Flesh cannot be circumscribed by signification; it incessantly escapes. His words point gradually and indirectly toward a poetics of elemental flesh.

IMMEMORIAL BEGINNINGS

Light appears at the beginning of "L'entrelacs," when it calls philosophy to "recommence everything."[85] It flickers through the text, faintly, between direct gazes at the touch of two hands or the vision of colors and textures, and indirect glances toward what makes touching and seeing possible. Seeing, speaking, even thinking are the "insistent reminder of a mystery as familiar as it is unexplained"—a light that, "illuminating the rest, remains at its source in obscurity."[86] A luminosity, inextricable from darkness, shines through all carnal life, "radiating everywhere and forever."[87]

Even while this light illuminates all flesh, it does not dispel obscurity. Nothing shows itself completely.[88] The visible is never free from the "invisible"; the invisible is the visible's depth and limit.[89] "One says invisible as one says immobile—not in reference to something foreign to movement, but to something which stays still."[90] Thus he speaks of "the visible and the invisible" as an alternative to Jean-Paul Sartre's "being and nothingness"—where the contrast between the terms does not entail a contradiction between them. The invisible is not of a different essence. It is not an ontological void. Indeed, Merleau-Ponty repeatedly negates the nothing: "A pattern of negations is not nothing," "the negation of nothing is essential," "life is not negativity," and so on.[91] Invisibility, obscurity, depth, are images for the indeterminacy of carnal knowing and becoming, for the irreducible otherness that marks all flesh.

The source at the beginnings of each body remains in obscurity.[92] I am formed by something I do not form.[93] I am born of the flesh of the world, by a separation from that to which I remain nonetheless open.[94] I am *of* the world—not just *in* it (as the Gospel of John proclaims). I cannot possess what relates me to the world and to myself. I cannot fully represent what forms me. Its opacity will always be woven into the fabric of flesh. My experience, my body, gives me a certain access to the flesh of the world, but it does not explain or clarify it. Merleau-Ponty states in a marginal note, "Irrepresentability is the flesh."[95] I know that I touch and that I am touched, but what makes that relationship possible remains in obscurity.

Word

Flesh and words interlace. Merleau-Ponty's descriptions of the movements and textures of this particular link remained exploratory, his language inconsistent. But his depiction of ideas as bodies proved irresistible for this theological reading. These images also inform my discussion of social identities in part III.

As in the analyses of visibility and flesh, Merleau-Ponty starts by observing particular experiences and from them ponders what makes them possible. In this case, he relates ideas to "ideality," and words to "Word." Some ideas are evidently sensible—those of literature, music, the passions. They are unknowable apart from the body; and "could not be given to us *as ideas* except in carnal experience."[96] We can develop systems to represent and explain them, to help us manage those ideas. But the explication is not the poem, the music, the feeling. Sensible ideas expressed in art or in love exist in the obscure regions of the body. But they are not produced by an isolated carnality; they are acquired through the body's encounters and exchanges with the world.

Literature, music, and the passions reveal that there is an "ideality" of flesh—as if on the other side of its "visibility." Like visibility, ideality implies a participation in something that does not belong to the individual, which joins and enfolds the individual in the world from the beginning. A primordial moment—"the first vision, the first contact, the first pleasure"—that initiates a body in sensibility, opening it to the world, also opens the dimension of ideality. The idea is a fold of ideality. And the "strict ideality in experiences of the flesh" gives rise to a "pure" ideality (which Merleau-Ponty keeps in quotations)—the realm of intelligence, culture, and knowledge.[97]

The passage from the ideality of flesh to a "pure" ideality intrigues Merleau-Ponty, and he describes it through theologically evocative images, presented in a series of repeated pictures, each time displaying additional dimensions. The first relates it to *light*, "at the joints of the opaque body and the opaque world there is a ray of generality and of light."[98] Later in the essay, he offers another description of this hinge, seen from a different angle, "My flesh and that of the world . . . involve clear zones, clearings, about which pivot their opaque zone." But this time he adds, "the primary visibility, that of the quale and of the things, does not come without a second visibility, that of the lines of force and dimensions." The second visibility derives from the first, which it structures and organizes, as a line in a drawing structures and organizes a view of the depth of the sky and the contours of a peach. The relationship between the first and second visibility is the basis for understanding the relationship between the first and second ideality that now concerns us. Yet the images are surprisingly different: "The massive flesh [does not come] without the rarefied [*subtile*] flesh, the momentary body without a *glorified* body."[99] Without warning or further explication, we witness the apparition of strange, ancient bodies—made of different types of flesh, undergoing metamorphosis.[100]

The images of subtle and glorious bodies are a distinctive feature of corporeal imaginaries inspired by the letters of Paul, as we saw in chapter 2. Merleau-Ponty was familiar with Paul Claudel's interpretation of the apostle's bodies. Claudel described the human body as capable of displaying the attributes of a glorious body. Like a spiritual body, "the human body, this body of clay" is "penetrated and penetrating," here and now. The erotic language is not incidental. Yet Claudel taps into the association of the spirit with the ability to exceed the boundaries of the individual person, while refusing to separate them from the materiality of the body. "In perception and love, the body is an organ of simultaneity and ubiquity, it is already agile like air, subtle like water or fire."[101] The relationship between the glorious and the carnal bodies may thus be imagined as similar to the relationship between elements—perhaps between flesh and air.

Merleau-Ponty had described elsewhere the process of writing fiction as the creation of "an imaginary body," one "more agile" than the author's own body.[102] His references to the subtle bodies in "L'entrelacs" pertain to the realm of ideas and are thus related to the imagination as well—but they also have broader ontological significance. The passage from massive to subtle flesh implies surpassing some of the limitations of "massive" flesh without ever becoming detached from it. Rather than proclaim the replacement of the carnal for the spiritual body, Merleau-Ponty focuses on their coexistence, interpenetration, metamorphoses. Pure ideality "is itself not without flesh," he offers.

> It is as though the visibility that animates the sensible world were to emigrate, not outside of every body, but into another *less heavy*, more *transparent* body, as though it were to change flesh, abandoning the flesh of the body for that of language, and thereby would be emancipated but not freed from every condition.[103]

A process of transformation from carnal to spiritual bodies that Paul envisioned as resurrection is here used to describe transmutations that take place here and now.[104] I envision the creation of multitudes of such bodies—like the ideal bodies to which I referred in the discussion of the mirror stage. This is not a vision of bodies abandoning their flesh at the end of time. Instead, what is being depicted are social processes. The "created generalities" of culture or knowledge "come to add to and recapture and rectify the natural generality of my body and the world"—a "miracle."[105] The metamorphosis into language produces agility, emancipation. But the process circles back. The "created generalities" of culture and language depend on flesh, but they also add to it.

The generality of language is likely what Merleau-Ponty has in mind when he refers to the "Word." The speaker "offers himself and offers every word to a universal Word," Merleau-Ponty writes. Yet the text offers only rough sketches of a view of ideas and words modeled after visibility and flesh, ending with a promissory note to look more closely at the relationship between the ideas of a mute world and the speaking world. Although the conceptual work of "L'entrelacs" was never completed, its composition evokes the Gospel of John by sounding its unmistakable opening notes—light, flesh, and word.[106]

POETICS

Art and language are nourished by our carnal experiences; they display the textures of flesh. Richard Kearney shows that for Merleau-Ponty, "diacritical" expression is, like flesh, composed of gaps, "negativities, breaches, folds, latencies, absences, silences, caesuras, lacunae, secrets, voids, crosses, furrows, blanks, abysses, elisions."[107] In the textures of expressions we can see the patterns of interlacing and "dehiscence" that shape carnal relations.[108]

Expression takes place between the sensible world and the worlds of languages. The individual act of speaking is "a fold in the immense fabric of language." Words depend on the materiality of bodies and the world that nourishes them. Likewise, meaning (*sense*) depends on the signs through which it signifies. But the writer, like the painter, is not a passive manipulator of signs—writing is "never a result," but rather a "response."

Merleau-Ponty envisions productive writing as painting. The painter, he says, works with whatever he receives—"body, life, landscapes, schools, mistresses, creditors, the police, and revolutions." These things "might suffocate painting," to be sure, but they "are also the *bread* his painting *consecrates*."[109] In this sacramental image we get another vision of transformation—from the social and material elements received in the body to expression—which similarly conveys the emergence of ideas from carnality. Just as perception implies approach and dehiscence, so does expression. Things are never presented in themselves.[110] This is the limit and the power of language. For the purpose of expression is not simply to represent what is received, what has been seen and said. "A language which only sought to reproduce things themselves would exhaust its power to teach in factual statements," Merleau-Ponty writes.[111] In expression, in the uttering of words, something new may come into being.

And this is what Merleau-Ponty seeks for philosophy. Kearney summarizes Merleau-Ponty's distinctive position: "Writing takes life to a literary style from a tacit style in sensible life itself. . . . But in taking an implicit style toward a more expressive one, the artist at the same time transfigures—or to use Merleau-Ponty's analogy, converts the bread of our quotidian life into a sacramental poetics."[112]

The traits of sensible life can be found in all language. But some forms of writing are more attentive to them, and thus more suitable for writing about flesh. Merleau-Ponty turns to art and poetry in search for lessons that can revitalize philosophy. He seeks the poets' aptitude for seeing the invisible in given forms; their commitment to see things anew and to honor the particularity of words; their attunement to disruptions, gaps, silences; their creative use of received language; the multivalent, openness of the sense of their works. "Since perception itself is never complete, since our perspectives give us a world to express and think about that envelops and exceeds those perspectives," he wonders, "why should the expression of the world be subjected to the prose of the senses or of the concept? It should be poetry."[113] Merleau-Ponty does not write poetry, but his writings on flesh weave sentences as folds, with approximations and gaps, coiling over and opening up, moving toward concepts always indirectly. And he strives for goals that poetry exemplifies for him, the attempt to "awaken and recall the sheer power of expressing" things unseen.

Merleau-Ponty's philosophy recapitulates the Christian idea of the incarnation as an obligation to turn to the world and an encouragement for consenting to becoming flesh. The ontological vision that unfolds from it carries forward epistemological and ethical commitments gathered from the incarnation. It attends to the body and the sensible world; acknowledges the limits and provisional character of all finite knowledge; affirms a world common to all of us.

Turning the gaze from the heavens to the earth, this philosophy encounters human bodies always already incarnating their worlds. As bodies are transplanted into things, incorporate the objects they use, or incarnate the gestures of other human beings, they display the malleability of their corporeal schema. Merleau-Ponty considers these phenomena as evidence of the body's power of dilating to the world. I see in them also confirmation of the susceptibility of bodies to being constricted by the world. Both the power and the vulnerability arise from our ties to the world, our flesh.

Flesh weaves bodies and the world. Flesh twists and turns, constituting realities that never exhaust it. Flesh is constitutive of my body and of the world. Yet it does not belong to me and it does not belong to you. It is an element—like water or air—on which we all depend and to which we all contribute. Because the elemental web that gives rise to and sustains my body precedes and exceeds my life, because the flesh of my body interlaces with the flesh of the world, I cannot fully represent it. Yet each of our bodies has its history, rhythms, and textures—its own way of encountering and incarnating the flesh of the world.

Bodies incarnate the world and also express ideas that emerge from and contribute to the flesh of the world. Ideas and words are produced by the body as it transforms what it receives from the social-material world. Merleau-Ponty described expression as the consecration of elements of quotidian life. He also imagined ideas emerging as luminous bodies. Flesh becomes words. Imaginative works can conjure glorified bodies to move us beyond the limits of our earthy flesh without ever separating themselves from it. Through painting or literature, ontology or theology, human creativity may strive to transform the world.

CHAPTER 5

THE ENDS OF FLESH

A carnal idea unfolds—at times dramatically, at times discreetly—from a Christian poetics of the incarnation: flesh interlaces the human body and the world. In Christian poetics divinity implicates itself with human flesh. A philosophy of flesh empties God to ground bodies firmly in the world. It unfurls this incarnational movement in the world's soil, in its flesh. And yet some thinkers worry that leaving God behind might not be enough to liberate the flesh from its Christian determinations. Flesh is by definition sinful, some of them argue. Flesh is by definition spiritual, others say. Can it be redeemed?

In this chapter I explain and respond to objections to the concept of flesh. Some of the critiques I address are directed at Christian uses of "flesh," others at Merleau-Ponty's use of the notion. I address them in dialogue with Michel Foucault, Jean-Luc Nancy, and Luce Irigaray.

Is "flesh" not a moral category, a fabrication disguised as a corporeal element for the purposes of covering over and controlling bodies? And if so, are we better off leaving the flesh to live in the body? Foucault prompts me to ask these questions. I address these concerns as critiques of modern versions of the "somatic" imaginaries I traced back to interpretations of Paul—where flesh burdens the body. Foucault's analytic approach will inform my discussion of the effects of words on living bodies, in part III.

Like Foucault's, Nancy's objections are based on the consequences of the concept of "flesh" to the treatment of human bodies. But rather than seeing "flesh" as a moral category, he focuses on its use as a metaphysical concept—like substance, essence, soul, spirit, or God—assumed to found and explain all of reality. As an "ontotheological" concept, "flesh" inevitably subordinates bodies, he adds, locating the meaning of bodies in an internal reality distinct from the body itself. These descriptions fit simplified versions of the incarnation as the process by which the spirit takes a body, but not the carnal poetics that this book seeks to develop. I explain how carnality helps me avoid the metaphysical traps that he identifies. For this I draw on the theological and philosophical resources presented thus far. Images from biology will further support my argument for retrieving flesh as an element of corporeal life in order to emphasize the effects of imperceptible processes that accumulate in our bodies.

Nancy declares the "end of the passions of the flesh." Contrastingly, Irigaray proclaims a return to the "flesh of our passions." She does so cautiously. On the one hand, she protests the absence of flesh in philosophy. On the other hand, she objects that flesh is used to replace, and thus obscure, the importance of the maternal. The main target of her critique is Merleau-Ponty, whose "flesh" exemplifies for her this assimilation of the maternal. She argues that he uses metaphors that are associated with mothers and the womb as the basis for the concept of "flesh," though he does not acknowledge this. The feminization of flesh has a long history. We encountered it already in the discussion of Tertullian's work. There I showed that attaching flesh to the womb shackles flesh to a hierarchical gender structure and forecloses the most promising insights of the incarnation, indeed eroding the grounds for Tertullian's own theology. In response to Irigaray, rather than linking flesh more firmly to the womb, I affirm Merleau-Ponty's approach, where flesh relates all life—including but by no means limited to the processes of human reproduction.

In engaging the critiques in this chapter, I am aware of the limits of treating flesh as a variable in a metaphysical formula. Surely a poetics of the flesh shall not evade assessing its assumptions and creations, for philosophical systems have ethical implications and effects. But in doing so, it is too easy to flatten flesh—occluding the instabilities, gaps, and opacity that give it its name. I identify the problem, not quite able to escape it. I hear Gayatri Chakravorty Spivak's ambiguous warning, "The desire to philosophize wrestles us to the ground, and there we lie, embraced."[1] The analytic discussions in this chapter will need to be supplemented by more capacious words and imaginaries of flesh.

Confessing Sinful Flesh

Michel Foucault's examinations of Christian flesh are part of his analyses of modern regimes of power. His uses of the category never settled and the details of his own position are shrouded in the mystery of his unpublished *Confessions of the Flesh*. We get glimpses of his evolving conceptualization of flesh scattered throughout his works. Here I focus mainly on the insights from his lectures, published as *Abnormal* and *The History of Sexuality*, volume 1. Foucault's uses of the term "flesh" are inflected by the specific Christian versions of flesh at work in the contexts he analyzes. I read them in relation to the corporeal strand of Christian corporeal imaginaries that I have traced back to the letters of Paul. Read this way, we can see how Foucault's analyses contribute to unmasking the logic and persistent influence of the idea of sinful flesh. Juxtaposing ancient understandings of flesh with modern discourses and practices also uncovers unexpected confluences between seemingly opposing discourses. The theological prepares the way for the medical reconfigurations; constructions of flesh feed discourses about instinct, for instance. Foucault's analysis of theological constructions of flesh thus illuminates the study of modern discourses of corporeality and brings attention to the impact of descriptions of flesh on the materiality of bodies.

Foucault places Tertullian at the beginning of his story of Christian flesh. "We have had sexuality since the eighteenth century, and sex since the nineteenth. What we had before then was no doubt flesh," he explains in an interview. "The basic originator of all of it was Tertullian."[2] He tells the story repeatedly—a bit differently each time, sometimes with a touch of self-mockery at his simplification of this "origin." "From the day Tertullian began saying to the Christians, 'where your chastity is concerned . . . ,'" he writes with a wink. The path that leads from Tertullian to modernity is, of course, impossibly complex—opening to multiple possible stories about the evolution of Christian thought and practice. But the way the story is told—the sharp contrast before and after Tertullian and the dramatic representation of the change—reflects Foucault's critical strategy. "He must force historical contrasts," Mark Jordan explains, "in order to unsettle the presentations of power," which tend to conceal its evolution. Foucault risks "hyperbolic history," for he is "less interested in precise firstness than in vivacity or evident significance."³ The dramatic role that Foucault gives Tertullian captures the gravity of the change in the relationship between sin and corporeality.

The story has been productive. It framed Foucault's groundbreaking analyses of the lasting effects of Christian discourses about corporeality. The story has also reproduced itself, appearing as a self-contained account of Christian flesh in contemporary philosophy. Spivak's criticism of Jean-Luc Nancy's *Corpus* is a good example of the life of the story. She writes, "Merleau-Ponty, in writing 'what we call flesh . . . has no name in any philosophy,' offers . . . nothing more than a response to the decomposed corpse of Tertullian."⁴ Nothing more is said about Tertullian; nothing else is necessary. For Tertullian has become a common name in foreign texts, his flesh inexplicably found rotting in strange lands. Tertullian appears in contemporary philosophy and his name is a metonym for Christian flesh—perhaps "the basic originator of all of it" was *Foucault*.

In Foucault's narrative of the transformations from flesh, to sex, to sexuality, Tertullian represents the historical shift from conceptions of sin—from an act of transgression against the law to something intrinsic to the body. The change is noticeable in the aims of pastoral practices. As I argued in chapter 3, Tertullian's insistence on the significance of flesh for salvation implies that flesh is also the locus of spiritual discipline and reform. In Tertullian's work on baptism, salvation is specifically defined as carnal purification. Foucault notes that purification is there no longer treated as the goal of baptism, but rather as its prerequisite. Purity must be proven before baptism can take place. And it was the body that had to provide the required evidence.⁵ The practice of examination constructs the body as an object of knowledge—and thus as a site for the exercise of power.⁶ Foucault's well-known analyses of the Christian practice of confession deal with later developments that presuppose the shifts he finds in Tertullian. The practices of examination change, developing more elaborate techniques to compel subjects to speak. The scope of confession intensifies as it expands from the monastery to all laity, making confession obligatory, with prescribed regularity and exhaustiveness.

"Flesh" is the name of the condition that these practices evaluate and manage. Readers of Foucault may recognize a pattern he examines in discourses of "sexuality" or "madness," for instance.⁷ There he observes the shifts from attention to an act—a physical encounter or an inappropriate behavior—to something else deemed, or constructed as the *cause* of an act—the identity of the homosexual or the mad person. In his examination of flesh, the change is from the sinful act conceived as a transgression of a law—mainly concerning relations to other people—to a "kind of illness that is sin's raison d'être."[8] In confession, a priest's questioning concerning the sixth commandment ("Thou shall not commit adultery") no longer focuses on its relational aspects, but on "the movements, senses, pleasures, thoughts, and desires of the penitent's body itself, whose intensity and nature is explained by the penitent himself."[9] The questioning is targeted to different parts of the body and different sensory levels. As a result, a new "code of the carnal" replaces earlier inventories of permitted and forbidden relationships.[10] Foucault also calls this regulatory standard an "anatomy of carnal pleasures" and "a cartography of the sinful body."[11]

"We are witnessing the flesh being pinned to the body."[12] "Flesh," previously used imprecisely for sins associated with the body, gets firmly attached to corporeality. In explaining this transition, Foucault adopts the language of the Christian texts he examines. He uses the term "flesh" for sins of transgression against the sixth commandment—sometimes specifically naming them "sins of the flesh." And he also refers to "flesh" as the cause of sin, the "root of all evil."[13] The shift from the first to the second of those constructions of "flesh" is what Foucault tracks.

This guilty flesh is woven from Pauline words—its distinctive patterns appear in Christian sources and Foucault's writing about them. Tertullian's demand that the body prove its purification shows the impact of the idea of guilty flesh on pastoral practices. Yet Foucault's language suggests links to even older and more familiar Christian texts. When Foucault states, "Now the sin of the flesh dwells within the body itself," I recall Romans 7. I discussed in chapter 2 Paul's enigmatic claims about the sin dwelling in the body, and specifically his observation, "I see in my members another law at war with the law of my mind, making me captive to the *law of sin that dwells* in my members."[14] It is as if in modernity we were seeing fulfilled what Paul already regarded as true: sin dwells in the flesh as its law.[15]

The ambiguous Pauline references to sin dwelling in the flesh surface in modern discourses to frame bodies as culpable. Describing body as flesh "discredits the body."[16] And defining the body as sinful flesh sets it up for rescue. Thus "making the body guilty as flesh," in turn "makes possible an analytic discourse and investigation of the body." These two parts—making the body guilty and objectifying it—are "correlative" to the new procedures for the examination of bodies.[17] Attaching a cause of sin to the body is necessary for the operation of new forms of power aimed at controlling and shaping the body.

Flesh appears as "a domain of the *exercise of power* and *objectification*."[18] Foucault does not write that flesh is "constructed," but rather that flesh "appears," to convey the elusiveness of these mechanisms of power.[19] Such ambiguities are inherent in Foucault's writing of power. As Jordan shows, "The mechanisms and sequence of the correlation of powers and objects can never be narrated straightforwardly." Power "can only be staged or revealed."[20] Referring to flesh as "constructed," as I did before, suggests a more direct cause-and-effect relation than can be claimed for these processes.

Foucault's accounts of power are elusive, unsettling the idea that power is simply repressive or clearly locatable. Paul's description of the correlation between body, flesh, sin, and law are just as perplexing as Foucault's. Recall Paul's statement, discussed in chapter 2, "While we were living in the flesh, our sinful passions, aroused by the law, were at work in our members to bear fruit for death."[21] The law incites sin, although the law is spiritual; even if the mind assents to the law, there is another law in the flesh. This is a centuries-old conundrum.

Foucault's description of the appearance of flesh in tandem with the exercise of power is not a simple repetition of Paul's account of the relationship between the law and sin, of course. But it can be read as one more chapter in the long history of the *somatic* strand of Christian conceptions of corporeality. Flesh is defined as a kind of law of sin. Tests and norms are designed to manage this sinful flesh, informing the ways bodies should be approached. That is, bodies are seen and treated as sinful flesh. But the enforcement of these norms tends to incite the very desires it condemns. Although the tactics of enforcement are modified to try to avoid inciting desire, those desires are still attributed to flesh.

Perhaps the most provocative description of the unhappy connection between body and flesh is this: "an incarnation of the body and an incorporation of the flesh [*une incarnation du corps et une incorporation de la chair*]."[22] This is a portrayal of the entanglement of the device of control (flesh) and its intended object (the body). It is not a unidirectional relation. Flesh and body get locked into each other. Ironically, the revered metaphor of the incarnation is invoked to describe the condemnation of the body, rather than its redemption. Flesh is *law made body*—the body is subjected as a body of flesh.

Who will free me from this body of sin? Paul cries in the background.

Foucault uses the terms "incarnation," "flesh," and "body" to draw on the energies the terms carry in the Christian imaginaries. But they are used for very specific and localized purposes, which are different from my own. "Flesh" for Foucault is a concept, the law of sin, which I describe as part of a "corporeal" strand in Christian thought. But in his writings, "flesh" is an apparatus. It includes not only the concept of flesh as sin, but also the descriptions of its maladies and their remedies, the norms devised for it, and the technologies used to test, manage, and enforce the norms. In contrast, the "body" is what is being occluded and managed under "flesh."

The control over the body is never absolute, however. The body resists the entrapment and sometimes "bristles against" the right of examination and the subjection to exhaustive confession.[23] The same is true for life—it is not totally absorbed into the techniques that govern and administer it. It "constantly escapes them."[24]

Some bodies, pushed too hard, resist. The situation threatened church power, and thus the problem would be entrusted to other authorities. This is how "flesh" came under the jurisdiction of medicine, Foucault argues. "What was called the 'nervous system' in the eighteenth century was a codification of the domain of the flesh."[25] He traces subsequent recodifications of flesh, until around 1850, when psychiatry "ceased being the analysis of error, delirium and illusion in order to become the analysis of all the disturbances of instinct." "Instincts" take the place of sinful flesh, or coexist with it, as another correlate of power.

"Instincts" marked then-emerging scientific constructions of race as the hidden law of the body. Discourses about psychiatric disturbances and instincts were embedded in definitions of race and "racial instincts."[26] I am tempted to say (beyond Foucault) that race *appears* in tandem with colonial forms of power, its role being akin to that of sinful flesh. Racialized peoples would become identified with flesh—as both earthiness and instinct. They were defined as objects for the examination and control of scientists, anthropologists, and religious scholars. Newly created identities were produced to name those considered as living "according to the flesh"—set up to be rescued, to be included in Western "universals." Racializing discourses are another junction of depictions of flesh, regimes of power-knowledge, and the zeal to reform bodies, along with the affective energies of their religious roots.[27]

Reading Foucault's analysis as exposing the logic of the "somatic" strand of Christian corporeality, I adapt his deconstructive argument for this book's purposes. But there are important differences between Foucault's use of "flesh" and the sense I have been discerning from John to Merleau-Ponty, on which this book builds its constructive proposal. Foucault uses the term "flesh" for an artifact of power, a discursive apparatus, and "body" for what that apparatus seeks to control. I use "flesh" to point to a vital materiality—not unlike what he calls "body." Associating flesh with material life, as I do, does not imply claiming that it is prior to or unaffected by the conceits of power-knowledge. Flesh is shaped by cultures, languages, and representations, but it is not determined by them.

I began to consider the effects of discourse on flesh in my reading of Merleau-Ponty's images of the interlacing of flesh and word. As I explained before, Merleau-Ponty describes the realm of culture and language as "adding to" the body and the world. He describes it as the creation of other types of bodies, made of a more subtle flesh. Merleau-Ponty imagines those light bodies as somewhat freer, opening spaces for new, richer carnal possibilities. Creative language and other forms of art can engage the imagination toward other forms of corporeal life. But Foucault's work alerts us to the ways disciplinary powers operate through these very capacities. Accounts of flesh—such as the ones that Foucault examines—can hinder the potentialities of corporeal life. They can occlude, trap, or manipulate flesh, turning its malleability into its liability. Ultimately, discourses about bodies—even malicious, falsifying depictions—may enter into the constitution of flesh.

Bodies are always susceptible to the exercise of power. But the susceptibility to being shaped by the world is also the basis of all life and all knowledge. I use "flesh" to name that constitutive relation to the world—a condition for corporeal survival and flourishing as well as the source of its vulnerability.

Theologies that treat flesh as a component of the body that can be confined and ultimately discarded may also interpret vulnerability and mortality as inessential. A fleshless body stands at the end of the redemptive trajectory promised to those who control flesh. Foucault articulates this vision most clearly in his reading of John Cassian's writings on chastity. "Radical mortification that allows us to live in our bodies by freeing us from the flesh," Foucault writes, ventriloquizing Cassian. And then citing him, "'Leave the flesh while remaining in the body.'"[28] This reflects a common version of the "somatic" view: abandoning the flesh culminates when the believer receives a spiritual body. The fully spiritual body would only be received at the resurrection, but Christians were encouraged to orient their lives away from carnality.

Practices of "radical mortification" have become easy targets for mocking Christian views of corporeality—particularly in popular movies. But the dream of fleshless bodies survives. It is manifest in idealized aesthetic representations of bodies and the efforts to procure bodies liberated from frailty and death. Tertullian argued that what Paul meant by "corruptibility" was simply death—and today mortality might appear as the most condemned of the "sins of the flesh."

This illusion of the possibility of a fleshless body—not always desireless, but surely pristine—is the other side of the deprecation of flesh. The malleability of flesh is embraced with the purpose of minimizing its dreaded effects in corporeal life. I am thinking not so much of church power as of capitalism, working through many industries—media, fashion, fitness, cosmetic medicine, and the like—to construct an ideal and thus desirable body, devising methods for diagnosing and correcting deviations. We are compelled to desire the impeccable bodies that these technologies offer, subject ourselves to the prescribed disciplines, and consider it our duty to persist on the path of continuous improvement. Under twenty-first-century forms of capitalist power, the self-reliant, infinitely perfectable "body" appears as a correlate of control. The images of flawless, undying bodies are on display everywhere—perhaps nowhere as explicitly as on New York's Times Square billboards. They are larger than life, radiant, undying, flat. All eyes turn to contemplate those bodies in awe. I am calling on us to think of flesh instead.

Flesh conveys corporeal qualities that we cannot afford to lose. I am not referring to "flesh" as depravity or concupiscence. This is rather flesh as a tie to a world—flesh that remembers its earthy origins, its constitutive relations to other human flesh as well as to the material elements, its malleability and feebleness. Yet I suspect these traits explain why flesh still tends to be regarded as the root of evil and associated with particular identities. If flesh is seen as binding a body to other humans and to the nonhuman, for instance, is it surprising that it is imagined as the cause of unexplainable desires and thus attributed to the queer, the primitive, the feminine? I offer this example only to suggest that problematic representations of flesh may be symptoms of disavowal of these particular elements of corporeality. These are traits that we would prefer to imagine as inessential for us, even as we project them onto others. Reclaiming the term "flesh" requires revaluating those traits—including its links to the material elements, its vulnerability and changeability—while refusing to cast them as caused by or as the cause of sin. Redeeming flesh.

Passions of the Flesh

Jean-Luc Nancy argues that flesh is a metaphysical principle in disguise. Its appearance differs depending on the discourse, but the effects are similar. Flesh may be a cipher for divine presence within the self, where one may touch God and know God fully. This immediate "touch" is a Christian invention, Nancy claims. Indeed, he argues that Christianity is "the invention of the religion of touch, of the sensible, of the immediate presence to the body and to the heart."[29] Touch and flesh are both implicated in this. When touch (and thus flesh) is imagined as a faculty of immediate presence, it can also be claimed as foundation for absolute knowledge of others and of the world. To construe flesh as a site of immediacy is to ascribe to it the capacity to overcome the limits of finite experience. It is, in other words, to describe flesh metaphysically.

Descriptions of flesh as mysterious or as depth are no less problematic, Nancy argues. For he reads such attributes as safeguarding the possibility of a site of full sense, even if it cannot be immediately reached. Whether in the far reaches of the heavens or in the depths of the soul, he objects, sense and meaning are imagined as total, absolute, complete. Such a view undermines real bodies—the bodies of those who seek understanding behind or outside their own sensibility, the bodies of those approached as objects of knowledge.

We saw similar critiques in Merleau-Ponty's work—of the "inner God" hidden in the "inner man," as well as of totalizing, disembodied, and unmediated accounts of knowledge. But while Merleau-Ponty developed a philosophy of flesh to counter those metaphysical assumptions, Nancy sees flesh as reproducing their logic—in Christianity as well as in Merleau-Ponty's work.[30] Nancy does not discuss Merleau-Ponty's work explicitly, but he implicitly criticizes his allusions to mystery as references to a concealed site of full sense. In his more explicit discussions of the incarnation, Nancy tracks the tendency to construe spirit as the sense of the body. While tracing the different ways in which flesh can function as a metaphysical foundation, Nancy identifies the risks of a carnal ontology. But the images of bodies as clarity and exposure that he suggests as an alternative to flesh seem too uniform to convey the complexities of the processes that constitute corporeal materiality.

CLARITY

The body shall not be construed as founded in an external God from which it originates and to which it returns in death. The world is "a world of bodies," Nancy insists.[31] Nothing else. The "other world" is dissolved with the death of God—as "a rotting space," a "pure concentration." But Nancy obliquely ensnares flesh in that other world whose end he proclaims. That other world, he writes, is a "crushing, lysate of bodies in the suave ineffable swarming of *this thing that has no name in any language*, this beyond of the cadaver where Tertullian . . . make[s] us *see* the end of the world."[32] The collection of images in this passage is bizarre. "This thing that has no name in any language" is a reference to Merleau-Ponty's definition of flesh: it "has no name in traditional philosophy."[33] The appearance of Tertullian—as the quintessential representative of flesh—in the same sentence assumes the continuity between their uses of flesh. Thus Merleau-Ponty and Tertullian are both treated as proponents of that something "beyond the cadaver," in the other world. But the image of a suave swarming thing seems out of place. Is Nancy's intention to make his readers acknowledge their repulsion, as Tertullian did? Or is he expressing his own disgust, siding with Tertullian's opponents? I cannot tell. Still Nancy seems to imply that Tertullian's argument of the resurrection of the flesh proves that flesh belongs with other theological concepts on that other world of God's body and of death. Nancy concludes that flesh must disappear. Flesh shall not inherit the world of bodies.

Similarly, Nancy reads "ineffability" as a veiled reference to an unnamable God who is a reserve of pure sense. Thus he interprets allusions to the mystery or depth of flesh as dependent on an otherworldly present God, a sense beyond death. He interprets Merleau-Ponty's description of flesh as something that has no name in philosophy as a theological affirmation. Nancy negates mystery, as well as other terms that may suggest ineffability—particularly depth and darkness.[34]

Bodies are not ineffable for Nancy, but they are *impenetrable*. Bodies are the limit of sense. Sense touches upon bodies but is not incarnate in them.

Thus Nancy adopts "density" as his preferred metaphor for the unassimilable nature of bodies. He rejects opacity. Bodies are "from the outset . . . in the clarity of the dawn, and everything is clear."[35] Asserting the body's clarity, Nancy dispels the opacity of flesh. Similarly, he defines bodies as extension, eliminating the depth of flesh. Against a Cartesian spirit defined as pure concentration, Nancy envisions bodies as pure extension—no inside, obscurity, beneath, or beyond.

Pushing against the tendency to found the reality of bodies in something other than being bodies, Nancy asserts their intrinsic value. Their impenetrability refutes the illusions of access to an inner truth of bodies, while accentuating their visibility and tangibility. But something is lost in this insistence on clarity and extension. For there are histories carried invisibly in corporeal materiality, traces of uncertainty and otherness constitutive of bodies and of matter.

INCARNATION

"We can in no way think the body in terms of incarnation."[36] This prohibition, repeated in various forms throughout *Corpus*, is also a testimony of its persistence in philosophical and cultural conceptions of the body. By "incarnation" Nancy means not only the Christian dogma, but also "the incarnation that is the model (itself Christian, in effect) of all our thought on the subject."[37] He summarizes the Christian version as asserting that something "without a place, without exteriority, without form, without matter (God) comes into flesh."[38] The thought of a bodyless thing taking place in flesh is a logical impossibility, he objects. And more importantly, it undermines the significance of bodies.

Nancy's critique of the incarnation is based on his understanding of "spirit" as the "sense of the body." When represented as the organ of sense, the spirit replaces the body—it functions as "the *true* body, the transfigured body."[39] Spirit is, in these models, that which being inside the body constitutes its meaning—the sense *of* the body.[40] The assumed distinction between the body and the spirit as the body's sense renders the body alien to its own sense. Therefore, Nancy concludes that the incarnation—understood as the (bodyless) spirit coming into flesh—effects disembodiment (*décorporation*).[41]

Spirit is also, more specifically, the spirit of God, which became the spirit of the Son, Nancy argues. The transmission of *spirit* from father to son is incarnation. And this implies that the Son is the body of the spirit. It is thus unlike any other body. In his discussion, Nancy circumscribes the spirit to the exchange between father and son, and the exceptional-body of the Son is no more than its temporary and incidental container. This incarnation is rather inconsequential for corporeality. It pertains an immaterial spirit confined to the body of the Son, which is unlike the "multitude of bodies, which no spirit has made or engendered."[42] This incarnation tells us nothing about real bodies.

The interpretation of the incarnation that Nancy criticizes is pervasive and influential. It is a codification of intricate Christian poetics in a handy metaphysical formulation. His objections are surely valid for dismantling those commonly assumed models. But neither the coming to flesh of an immaterial spirit nor the movement of the spirit—from father to son and back to the father—represents the complexities of incarnation.

As we have seen, the apparent simplicity of John's "Word became flesh" opens up to an array of transformations and exchanges. Nancy reads that phrase as a site of an irreducible ambivalence at the heart of the incarnation. "Word made flesh" implies both that "*caro* gives rise to the *verbum*'s glory, and true *coming*," but also, contrastingly, "that *verbum* [Logos] gives rise to the true presence and sense of *caro* [sarx]."[43] These two interpretations are entangled. The latter exemplifies the problematic of sense described above, by which spirit or Logos becomes the sense of the body—disembodying meaning. The representation of Logos as the true sense of bodies is reinforced by the priority of the distinction between Logos and sarx. "In the beginning was the Word." Nancy observes. "When one starts, one has already left the *in between*."[44] The temporal priority of the Logos sets it up as the foundation of the world of bodies.

The path that Nancy traces between the Logos and the body of the incarnation passes not only through John's Gospel, but also through Plato's cave and Aristotle's *Peri Psyche*, the first offering the images of the cave-body, the second an influential statement of "spiritual senses." The slippage in terms is understandable and perhaps unavoidable. But I return here to the ancient and overworked text of the Gospel of John to bring forward the spacing between soma and sarx, not only between Logos and sarx. As I observed before, soma does not appear in John's narrative until Jesus's death. The prologue does not portray the penetration of Logos into a body; it refers only to flesh. "What has come into being in the Logos was life, and the life was the light of the humans. . . . The light shines in the darkness." Logos *becomes* flesh, and its glory is seen. There are no wombs in this story, as Nancy rightly observes. But is it so clear that we have left the interspace of a place from which life emerges? Could it be that flesh is that in-between that gives rise to the body, where materiality and spirit are barely distinguishable?

Nancy returns to the incarnation in a later work, "*Verbum caro factum*."[45] In that essay, he focuses on the element of exposure he had identified before. While in *Corpus* he read the nativity through Plato's cave, here he asserts, "the Christian body is completely different from a body serving as an envelope (or prison, or tomb) to the soul."[46] Nancy contrasts classical interpretations of the body to Christian ones. The incarnation does not construe the body as a prison of the soul (sensible and fallen), as interiority ("body proper" or signifying), or as a pure spiritual presence. Instead, Nancy reads the creed as asserting the *becoming* flesh of the Logos. "The body is none other than the 'spirit' having exited itself."[47] The process of self-emptying to become flesh "gives man-god a [new] provenance," not simply from the divine father, but a provenance in the human body. Furthermore it gives this body "the capacity to change again into inorganic matter."[48] What is flesh but earth, Tertullian said.

Nancy's critical readings of the incarnation foreground its ambivalence. The incarnation can be understood as establishing the spirit of the father as the sense of the body. Or declaring that the spirit becomes body. The difference in its philosophical import is whether it empties or reasserts God as the foundation of the body, as the sense of the body.

Thinking corporeality through flesh, rather than "incarnation," does not assume a chronological progression. Instead it implies a nonteleological, dynamic understanding of the body-in-the-world. Yet we shall not overstate the linear temporality of the incarnation. It is true that the movements of the Logos from heaven to earth and back frame that narrative of the Gospel of John. It is also clear that "incarnation" typically suggests the integration of what was previously separated, the bridging of a chasm between heaven and earth.[49] But the separation between divinity and flesh from which the story of the incarnation begins presupposes a prior connection, not only between God and human beings, but also between human beings and the world, as we saw in chapter 1. The prologue of John returns to a beginning of all life, and its end opens toward possibilities yet to be experienced.

Tertullian takes the incarnation back to the creation of a first person, which he portrays as the separation of a body out of a still indistinct earth, to which bodies remain linked. Reading the incarnation as a repetition of other beginnings, as Christian authors have done, we see the lines of progression twist and turn, from the present to the past to the present again.[50]

The incarnation brings forth relationships that are not constrained to an exchange between father and son, common as this representation is. Flesh in the Gospel of John is distributed, transformed as it is given, and transforms those who received it. These patterns of differentiation and spacing bring divinity so very close, and restate the differences in so many ways. Rather than reasserting an incarnation as a syllogism, I focus on the circuitous paths of flesh in the Gospel of John as a model for a carnal poetics. I see a flesh that connects past and present, warping the temporal trajectory of the incarnation. Flesh is the son's body and so much more. As it is disseminated and others partake of it, flesh also blurs the boundaries of the body of the son of the human. The difference between flesh and body is generative. There are gaps and fissures in flesh itself. These traits of a carnal strand of Christian corporeal views defy representations of flesh as mere interiority or as interior depth. But these imaginaries are not metaphysical formulas; their poetics express the passion for divinity that animates them.

BARELY CONTAINED

I agree that flesh shall not be conceived as pure interiority or depth if it is to foster attention to the world of bodies and the relationships that constitute it. A flesh construed as fullness of sense—as a kernel of truth contained within a corporeal housing—in effect separates itself from the body. It also, consequently, separates the body from the world.

Nancy proposes to abandon "flesh" and offers instead images of bodies as exposure. He uses the term *ex-peau-sure*, his corporeally marked neologism (*peau* is French for "skin"). The concept highlights the body's connections to everything that surrounds it. "Expeausure" evokes sensible connections. I think about the surface of my body brushed by the breeze, touched by the warm rays of the sun, caressed by another's hands. The fragile layer of my skin also exposes my body to harm—to a violent blow, but also to a demeaning gaze or brutal words. These dangers reach my body from the exposed side of my skin—what is visible and tangible to others. For Nancy, the corporeal boundary marked by my skin is also a limit. To touch a body is to touch upon the limits of sense, he argues. I encounter the density of another's body as contact and limit—the limit of my own body but also the limit of my knowledge. The unknowability of bodies is thus figured as impenetrability, a function of their density.

Yet skin is hardly impenetrable. Discursive practices touch upon and shape my most intimate experiences—those we tend to identify with the flesh. These are not simply external exchanges. In confession as in a psychoanalytic session, speech requires the active participation of the persons shaped by it. The demand to speak may be constraining and suffocating—and its force might provoke uncontrollable corporeal responses, such as tremors, tears, and convulsions. Yet most often, we are seduced into speech. The desires thus elicited and shaped are social and corporeal—not "natural" in the sense of pre-given. And they are more than skin-deep.[51] Through language we are exposed to one another. Seeking ways to highlight the formative power of those relationships brings my attention to what happens beneath the surface of the skin, below the orders of the visible. Not a depth under the corporeal surface, but its other side, its reverse, where the visible and the invisible, speech and the unspeakable interweave.

I referred to this dimension of corporeality in my discussion of Merleau-Ponty. His analyses of movement and perception focus on the body's external contact with the world. And yet these interactions with the external world are folded into the fabric of corporeality. Objects become part of the reconstituted contours of the corporeal scheme; the smile of a parent becomes incarnate in the child's body. "Sensible ideas" are not visible, he argues, but they do emerge from the body's engagements with the world. The intertwining of the external processes and the unseen materiality of our bodies is not limited to the observable phenomena on which Merleau-Ponty's analyses rely. This folding describes also basic cellular processes by which the materiality of bodies is produced, exchanged, and transformed.

A view from a cell reveals patterns of relation, differentiation, and contingency at work in basic structures of corporeal materiality. That is not always what is conveyed in popularizations of science, where genetics is often represented as self-contained, deterministic scripts. In these representations, genetics could be mistaken for a scientific version of substance metaphysics and its essentialisms, or the "body of sense."[52] But a more careful exploration at the cellular level reveals broad networks of relationships extending in time, connecting different species, and linking the animate and the inanimate.

It is well known that we inherit our genetic makeup from our ancestors. Yet our inheritance extends more widely and leaves traces in our bodies of long evolutionary histories. Our bodies contain DNA sequences from infections that took place millions of years ago and since then have become part of our genetic makeup.[53] Ancestral bonds leave material sediments in human bodies. Some of these sediments are apparently inactive; others are active in our cells. Inasmuch as past histories affect cellular changes, they influence everyday corporeal transformations. Other entities live in us and allow us to live and become in specific ways, without ever being properly ours.[54] Communities of microbes account for up to 99 percent of the genetic information in our bodies.[55] Their "identity" depends on where I live, what I eat, what I do. It all affects the operation of my genes.[56] Simply stated, entities from our living environments may help or hinder the work of inherited genes. Even inert matter, such as manufacturing chemicals, can intervene in the functioning of genes.[57]

The picture that emerges from these examples is one in which the world coils over the body at its most fundamental level. Evolutionary histories, natural environments, cultural conventions, manufacturing practices, and the like may leave their traces in our bodies and enter into the constitution of our flesh. The metaphor of exposure represents the contact necessary for these exchanges between the body and the world, but it seems too smooth to convey the complex textures of the bodies that are woven through processes such as these—the multiplicity inherent in bodies, the sedimentation of past events, the constant flow of elements in and out of bodies. The paths traced by these exchanges and transformations twist and turn, coil in and branch out. They create zones of opacity and areas of indeterminacy.

This perspective gives new meaning to theo-poetic expressions such as "the flesh remembers its origins" or "the law becomes flesh." I want images of corporeal life that convey the effects of imperceptible processes that accumulate in our bodies, that materialize in and as our flesh. The old term "flesh" helps me imagine both the dynamic constitution of corporeal materiality at the intersection of socio-material environments as well as the persistence of their histories in the most basic structures of our bodies. Furthermore, the spacing between the terms "body" and "flesh" accentuates the difference and interdependence between the exposure that results from the location of my body *in* the world, and the coiling over by which my body is *of* the world.

Flesh comprises all the nodes created by these relationships—its folding, coiling, labyrinths. It is thus neither depth nor smooth surface. Its fabric has zones of obscurity and invisibility, which cannot be simply equated to veiled allusions to the God of pure sense. To envision such an interlacing implies revising common assumptions about materiality. In Diana Coole's reading, Merleau-Ponty was "envisaging a radically new materialism." Whereas for Descartes "matter is devoid of interiority or ontological depth," for Merleau-Ponty material existence is "folded flesh."[58] Descartes's inert matter is not devoid of religious significance, however. Its passivity is the outcome of having extracted all productivity from materiality to a God defined as substance.[59] For Merleau-Ponty, flesh is neither matter nor substance; it is not pure positivity. As he began to conceive it, Coole argues, flesh avoids both the foundationalism of metaphysics and the flattening of matter of modern science.

"Matter is an enfolding, an involution, it cannot help touching itself and in this touching it comes in contact with the infinite alterity that it is."[60] Theoretical physicist Karen Barad offers this enticing description of materiality inspired by quantum field theory. Barad's comments pertain not only to corporeal materiality, but to the world in general. "Even the smallest bits of matter are an unfathomable multitude," she adds. "Every finite being is always already threaded through with an infinite alterity differentiated through being and time."[61] This materialist ontology rejects a view of matter as passive, needing an outside power to animate it. But its relational character implies that its vitality is not fully contained in itself.

Envisioning flesh as a condition of material life implies ineffability. The weaving of flesh precedes the emergence of this body as my own. My body is here, in this world, exposed to it and yet it has traces of a past that is not my own, that I can never know.

Admitting the limit of knowledge is neither to reintroduce an all-powerful deity nor to renounce thought. "A sensitive and open thought," I hear Merleau-Ponty whispering, "should not fail to guess that there is an affirmative meaning and even a presence of spirit in this philosophical negativity."[62] Perhaps. Merleau-Ponty refused to dismiss the philosophical relevance of Christian narratives on the basis of their imaginative dimensions. And he considered the poets as best attuned to seeing the invisible in the visible. Barad also points to the need for poetic registers not as the opposite of theoretical work, but rather as that which may "lure" thinking beyond.[63] "The force of the imagination puts us in touch with the possibilities for sensing the insensible, the indeterminate."[64] A turn to corporeal materiality would turn flesh into dust if it fully dispelled ineffability, the irreducible otherness in all bodies, the indeterminacy of becoming flesh.

Carnal Fecundity

> If poetry is to reanimate the powers of creation . . . we must come to understand that the hand as well as the eye has its reveries and poetry. We must discover the power of touch.
>
> —Gaston Bachelard, *Earth and Reveries of Will*

Luce Irigaray's reading of Merleau-Ponty's flesh begins by taking us back to the beginning of "L'entrelacs." She agrees with Merleau-Ponty, we must "recommence everything and pause at the 'mystery, as familiar as it is unexplained, of a light which, illuminating the rest, remains at its source in obscurity.'"[65] But her return to that "passage through the night" aims at bringing the "material-feminine into language."[66] Her critique of Merleau-Ponty is thus part of a broader project to trace the ways in which Western philosophical traditions conceive the relation between the (always implicitly masculine) subject and the feminine.

"If traditionally, and as mother, woman represents *place* for man, such a limit means that she becomes a *thing*."[67] She appears as a womb, an envelope, a container—*his* starting point. Being his place, she is deprived of her own. In order to flourish, a woman needs to preserve her own relation to her morphology, but the masculine "nostalgia for the first dwelling," his inability to separate himself from it, results in these being taken away from her. "He contains or envelops her with walls while enveloping himself and his things with her flesh."[68] An ethics of sexual difference requires the possibility of a place for her—for "each sex, body, and flesh to inhabit."[69] "For loving partners this would be a fecundity of birth and regeneration," not reducible to the "reproduction of bodies and flesh." And this entails "the production of a new age of thought, art, poetry and language: the creation of a new poetics."[70]

Irigaray reads Merleau-Ponty's philosophy of flesh as an example of the nostalgia for the womb that robs women of their own place. She analyzes Merleau-Ponty's text for signs of this attachment, teasing out his use of images that evoke the intrauterine life. Merleau-Ponty uses images of fluidity, envelopes, and obscurity to develop his concept of flesh. While forgetting its maternal-feminine beginning, he is "moving the totality of the world into a reversion of the intrauterine adobe," she contends.[71] The absorption of the nourishing womb into a generalized flesh, the privilege of visibility, and the absence of sexual difference from his portrayals of bodies, all add to her case against Merleau-Ponty.

Reading Merleau-Ponty's references to obscurity and invisibility as allusions to the intrauterine life allows Irigaray to write the maternal-feminine into his text. This interpretive move in turn guides her critique of visibility. In order to address those critiques, I return briefly to Merleau-Ponty's account of the relation of visibility to both touch and flesh, identifying its advantages and difficulties.

Merleau-Ponty's use of visibility to name the fold between the body and the world presupposes and reframes prevalent conceptions of knowledge. In Western philosophy knowledge is often imagined as detached vision—what Merleau-Ponty refers to as the "kosmotheoros." Instead of arguing that knowledge is *not* like vision, Merleau-Ponty offers an alternative model for visibility. His embodied account of visibility shows that vision is never detached, but always already enmeshed in what is seen.[72] The gaze "envelops" things, "clothes them with its own flesh," he writes.[73] There is no vision from above.

Conceiving knowledge in a similar way implies recognizing its embeddedness in the phenomena being studied and explained. This would entail analyzing the imbrication of intellectual work in social, corporeal, and material relations. *The Visible and the Invisible* offers only openings in this direction. Other theorists have built on Merleau-Ponty's work to analyze, for instance, the interlacing between racializing worldviews, the seer, and the seen—as we will see in chapter 7. And yet Merleau-Ponty builds his argument by claiming visibility is like tactility—glossing over important distinctions between them.

When I touch I am always, *necessarily* touched by what I touch. Touching requires the interaction between two things—both of which must be tangible, Merleau-Ponty adds. But seeing seems to require more than two things or beings. In order to see, I do not need to be seen. And conversely, my visibility does not imply my capacity to see. It might be more appropriate to say that to see I must be touched, but what touches the eye is not the thing seen; it is the light that touches us both. "I see only by the touch of light," Irigaray writes.[74] Things become visible to my *human* eye as a result of my corporeal structure, but also of the environment in which I encounter them. Vision is mediated by what touches us both—light and the medium in which it travels, usually air.[75] Visibility is made possible by the interlacing of the body in the world, not only of the seer and of the seen. In Cathryn Vasseleu's interpretation, however, Merleau-Ponty circumvents the problems I just sketched. She argues that Merleau-Ponty is not "elaborating the visual domain in terms of touch or imagined contact," as other philosophers do. Instead, he "describes perception as a uniquely constituted domain in which vision and touch as well as other senses are co-extensive with each other as metonymically interrelated modes of perception."[76] Depicting "perception" or "sensibility" as the domain of interrelated modes of perception avoids overstating the parallel between visibility and tangibility. But this crucial aspect of his ontology tends to be undermined by his use of "visibility" as the all-encompassing metaphor for those interlacings.

The beginnings of life in the womb show that touch precedes and gives rise to visibility, Irigaray argues. "I am touched and enveloped by the felt even before seeing it."[77] She interprets Merleau-Ponty as privileging vision over touch and sees this tendency as a symptom of his disavowal of the maternal-feminine.[78] He has no memory "of that first event where he is enveloped-touched by a tangible invisible of which his eyes are also formed, but which he will never see."[79] The tactility that characterizes prenatal life is the beginning of visibility and the fundamental example of being enveloped in flesh—"surrounded, clothed, nourished by another body."[80] I never see what touches me and makes my seeing possible. Visibility cannot comprehend tangibility. This is true of all engagements afterward. The philosophical privilege of sight not only occludes the maternal-feminine, but also distorts perception. For "it is still possible that my look . . . disturbs the intelligence of my hand, of my touch."[81]

Writing the maternal-feminine into Merleau-Ponty's account of flesh, Irigaray gives visibility a tangible ground. And it counters the philosophical habit of discounting the significance of the maternal as a source of fecundity, by ignoring and appropriating it. Irigaray's claim is that coming to terms with maternal origins is necessary for ending masculine nostalgic attachment to the womb and thus making it possible for women to claim their own place. But making the maternal the ultimate site from which to conceive flesh helps reify the feminization of flesh, which establishes a parallel between male/female and spirit/flesh dualisms. This is clearly not Irigaray's intention. To the contrary, her statement that fecundity shall not be reduced to the production of bodies implies the broadening of the scope of carnal becoming beyond the womb. But her reading strategy ends up closing off the possibilities for such a project in Merleau-Ponty's work. I concur with Judith Butler, to the extent that "Merleau-Ponty's insistence on this prior world of flesh offers a way to disjoin the feminine from the controlling figuration of the maternal"; it may "offer bodies a way to signify outside the binary trap of mothers and men."[82]

The perilousness of the relationship between femininity and flesh extends well beyond Merleau-Ponty's philosophy. Christian discourses have contributed both to the erasure of the maternal and to the projection of carnality onto women. An example of this tendency to appropriate maternal fecundity in Christian writings is the story of the creation of the first woman out of the first man's side (Gn 2:18–24). The narrative reverses what is otherwise common knowledge: that both men and women emerge from the body of a woman. In Genesis, it is Adam who looks at the woman and exclaims,

> This at last is bone of my bones
> and flesh of my flesh;
> this one shall be called Woman,
> for out of Man this one was taken.[83]

The story frames this bond in terms of a gender hierarchy, by giving women a secondary, derivative origin. And it is the source for referring to a sexual union between a man and a woman as "becoming one flesh." "Therefore a man leaves his father and his mother and clings to his wife, and they become one flesh."[84] I referred to this Genesis phrasing cited in Paul's admonitions against porneia, in chapter 2, where it refers to the effects of illicit sexual union on the body of Christ. I also discussed Merleau-Ponty's reframing of it to assert that every other human being is flesh of my flesh. While for Merleau-Ponty the phrase still evokes images of unity and separation between different bodies, it no longer defines corporeal difference in terms of sexual categories, hierarchically related from the beginning.

The tendency to feminize flesh also has a long history in Christianity, as we saw in the analysis of Tertullian's work, in chapter 3. He referred to flesh as a form of earth and offered enticing images of its links to grass, rivers, stones, and the like. In explaining the incarnation, however, he ties flesh to gender. Describing Christ as the union of Mary's flesh and God's will was meant as a claim for the importance of flesh. But representing carnality as the contribution of women depended on and contributed to hierarchical conceptions of gender that limit the feminine to the realm of a spiritless materiality. That legacy haunts contemporary accounts of flesh. Rather than reasserting the link between flesh and womb, I seek a broader account of carnal becoming—beyond the confines of prescribed sexual identities.

A new poetics of elemental flesh attends to the broader, complex matrix of relations that ground all life. These relations are not limited to sexual difference; they encompass all materiality—human and nonhuman. Yet this poetics also needs to address the corporeal effects of social differentiations between bodies—including but not limited to sexual difference. This will be the focus of part III. Social identities enter into the constitution of the flesh of the world.

Corporeal imaginaries influenced by Christian thought are threatened by two opposing problems. Construing flesh as a law of sin condemns the body, fosters dreams of living in a fleshless body, or both. I associate this tendency with "somatic" models, because in them flesh is an extraneous element of corporeality. In contrast, "carnal" models may risk representing flesh metaphysically, as the absolute sense of the body. Both positions render flesh alien to finite bodies.

Reclaiming "flesh" does not entail denying its association with frailty or sensibility, but rather refusing to cast those traits as the cause of evil. This flesh is not an internal condition or a bundle of innate sensations. Carnal passions are neither Paul's "law dwelling in the body's members" nor the scientists' "instincts." Instead desire moves in all encounters with the world.[85] Flesh is fold, an interlacing; its passions are part of the body's relations to the world, of the desire for the you in me, and the me in you.

We are "expeaused" to others and to the world. But our skin can barely contain us. It does not protect us from others—however much we resist. Our bodies are expeaused, visible, and tangible. Flesh coils over our bodies and we are transformed.

As the elemental tissue in which we live and have our bodies, flesh overflows the visible and tangible. The interlacing of bodies and the world includes phenomena that escape even the most basic forms of perception—even sensibility as commonly understood.[86] Material exchanges between the elements and my body might be imperceptible, bypassing (human) sensibility altogether. The minerals in the air I breathe transform my body, but I cannot feel their actions as I feel the ocean breeze or see the sunlight reflected on its surface. The world shapes me without my knowledge or consent.

Touching flesh yields no unmediated sense or knowledge, however. The dynamic, evolving multiplicity of all the elements that constitute my flesh are never fully present to me. But their long histories—which are always already social and material—leave their marks in my body. The socio-material elements of my own history interlace with the sediments of my ancestral past. Indirectly, obscurely, and partially—my flesh remembers things I never knew and will never know. I can never fully grasp flesh. It is dynamic, indeterminate. Not knowing is not a weakness, I remember Glissant saying. But not wanting to sense the entanglements of our relations is. We cannot fully know it, but "we imagine it through a poetics."[87]

III
A Labyrinth of Incarnations

Society, then, is a true labyrinth of incarnations. . . .
A "labyrinth" because of a complexity that has no
discernible end or beginning, and an "incarnation"
because implicit gestural language and outward
expression are inseparable, united as man himself
is in an indissoluble bond between body and soul.

—Edward Said, "Labyrinth of Incarnations"

Words about bodies create social relations. They link bodies to one another or set boundaries between them. Words organize the world. Imaginaries of body and flesh are woven into the fabric of society—in intellectual works, cultural practices, communal spaces. These words become flesh.

Social discourses shape the world—not just represent it. Descriptions of bodies are produced at specific points in history, conceived to address the interests of particular social groups. Whether they are convincing or fantastic, judiciously or maliciously constructed, words about bodies are productive. Laws regulate the movements of peoples across national boundaries or within cities, manufacturing and environmental practices, medical experimentation and treatment, and so on. Other forms of discourse work more indirectly. Images, words, and cultural conventions teach us day after day what bodily features are significant—the color of her skin not the size of her hands, for instance. We learn what bodies are beautiful and desirable. We also learn what patterns of speech are acceptable, what food is good, and what clothing is graceful. And we act according to this knowledge. We participate in shaping our bodies and our worlds—some more intentionally than others, some with much more power than others. The discourses that structure social institutions, shape our sensibilities, and foster cultural practices work in the material world. Influencing the formation of the social and material environments in which we live, words weave the flesh of the world.

We share the same world, Merleau-Ponty insisted. But we encounter this world differently. Each of us has access to specific spaces, with particular resources and challenges. Each of us is received differently in the places we inhabit. Our encounters with the world constitute our flesh differently.

Society is a labyrinth of incarnations. The patterns of transformation and exchange that constitute flesh are dynamic and elusive, as were those depicted in the Gospel of John and in Merleau-Ponty's work. And yet social structures and hierarchies depend on the apparent stability of bodies to differentiate between them. My visible body affects which areas of the world I may inhabit and how the world reacts to my approach. The particular ways in which my *flesh* is shaped by the world depends on how my *body* is perceived in society. Part III analyzes the interlacing between these two aspects of corporeality—social identities and their changing materiality, *body* and *flesh*.

Frantz Fanon dramatizes the clash between the experienced body and its social representations. He expresses the pain produced by the looks and words of others; the puzzling metamorphoses that those interactions produced in him; the difficulties of countering racializing images and producing alternative ones. Words fell upon his body and invaded his flesh. Imaginary bodies challenged and bewildered his sense of self. These subtle bodies are as agile as those we encountered in Paul and Merleau-Ponty. But rather than embodying new corporeal capacities, these ghostly bodies threaten to destroy him—like the evil spirits that ancient Christian communities sensed and feared. Walking with Fanon, we see a world where the experienced and the fantastic bodies face each other, battle each other, cannot be easily kept apart.

A poetics of flesh must account for the effects of racialization that Fanon analyzes. It must likewise consider the effects of gendering. Words create and re-create race; they create and re-create gender. Judith Butler argues that gender is a set of social discourses and norms and that these norms "materialize." Through the repetition of acts prescribed by these norms, our bodies become gendered. Norms about gender and race implicate each other. Gender ideals are racialized. Racializing discourses promote and enforce norms about sexuality and gender. Through our acts, these social ideals become flesh. Our acts accumulate, constituting our bodies. But social forces affect our bodies in ways that precede and exceed our personal acts.

Flesh carries histories—evolutionary and also social histories. The constitution of our flesh bears the marks of our personal lives. And our flesh carries traces of the histories of our communities—marks left by the food and medicines to which communities had access, by the qualities of the air our forebears breathed, by love and joy shared, by stress or violence endured. Social hierarchies affect all these conditions. Therefore, although race and gender are not given essences, they have lasting material effects. Race and gender mark our bodies—not only as ideas projected onto our individual bodies from without, but also as forces acting in the very materiality of the worlds. Social structures form the world from which our flesh is woven.

The power of social discourses to affect corporeality is a source of anguish. It also grounds the hopes of those seeking transformation through creative language. There are great risks in such attempts to intentionally conjure other worlds, other bodies. That path can lead us to lose or even condemn flesh—imagining another world unencumbered by the weight and the pain of carnality and abandoning responsibility for the flesh of the world. Many have interpreted Paul's words, or those of his many readers, as instructing them to do precisely that, as they love and hope for bodies without flesh. But there are other possibilities for reimagining glorious bodies. Merleau-Ponty envisioned subtle bodies emerging from flesh and moving toward language. Neither free nor detached from flesh, they are a bit more agile, slightly luminous—expressions of embodied hope.

In this part I read the poets who, injured by racism, strive to conjure other bodies. These are not the negation of their racialized features, but rather their emancipation. They depict bodies they cannot yet see, with capacities they have not attained, relationships not perceived, ways of life few can dream of. Creative practices such as these are vital for redeeming flesh. Imagining bodies differently, honoring their pain and aspirations, loving the earth—to give words to longings for life-giving incarnations.

CHAPTER 6

INESCAPABLE BODIES

Colonial discourses indelibly marked conceptualizations of flesh. Constructions of racialized flesh bear resemblances to some of the theological characterizations we encountered in chapter 5. Intellectual and religious traditions had construed flesh as the underlying principle and cause of sinfulness. Since they associated sinfulness with sex, they linked flesh to sex. Foucault noted that medical discourses adopted, displaced, and transformed the shifting imaginary of flesh as "instinct." Those scientific discourses were also part of the production of colonialist knowledge and the concomitant structuring of global and local relations according to types of peoples, types of bodies. Instincts were racialized.

Flesh and race conjure each other, particularly in discourses directly affected by and responsive to the legacies of colonialism. I turn here to the work of Caribbean writers for examples of the critiques and creative rearticulations of racialized flesh. A comment by Michael Dash, a Caribbean literature scholar, captures the significance of flesh in this context. "For a long time, the Caribbean has been *trapped* in a discourse that accentuates carnality," he writes. Dash does not say explicitly what he means by "carnality." But his next sentence reveals its association with femininity. "Stereotypes of a helpless femininity have fixed the French Caribbean in a dependent relationship with the metropole. Martinique emerges as the kept woman of the

French empire."[1] Dash's statements point to the pervasiveness of "flesh" in Caribbean literatures and foreground the deep ambivalence triggered by its associations with gender, imperialism, and consequently race.

In exploring this charged literary terrain, I follow Frantz Fanon.

His essay, "The Lived Experience of the Black," included in *Black Skin, White Masks*, depicts bodily sensations and transformations produced by racialization.[2] The essay links theory to lived experience through its style as much as by explicit argumentation. It uses corporeal language to draw the reader into the experiences it describes, namely how discourses mark, wound, incite, elevate, or shatter bodies. Fanon's narrative is intimate and public, visceral and political. The body appears as both unavoidable and disruptive—a presence that threatens to undo the rational analysis of each situation. The scenes are presented in first person and tightly linked to the historical and geographical context that he addresses. He insists on the situatedness of his work: "I belong irreducibly to my time," he states from the beginning.[3] Yet his analyses overflow the specificity of his stories. As Alejandro de Oto describes it, drawing from Walter Benjamin, in Fanon's writing we encounter parables that had to become more than parables.[4]

Fanon's essay can be divided into two parts. The first part deals with European thought, referring to the work of Merleau-Ponty and more explicitly to Jean-Paul Sartre. The second part engages poets of the Négritude movement, who sought to recover African cultural values to counter and move beyond European forms of thought. Fanon cites his fellow Martinican Aimé Césaire and Senegalese Léopold Senghor. I focus mainly on his dialogue with Merleau-Ponty and Césaire. In both cases, Fanon's critiques are written as performances. He plays the characters they offer him. Then he observes the problems with embodying these identities. Fanon presents himself as the one who follows their prescriptions as well as the analyst who explains the results obtained and the conclusions to be drawn from them.

Fanon shows the inadequacies of an ontology of flesh that ignores the impact of racism. His objections disrupt the relatively harmonious unfolding of the concept of flesh. That the presence of the world's flesh to my flesh is also the presence of its hierarchies and demarcations to my body, "this is what is no sooner said than forgotten," to adapt Merleau-Ponty's statement.[5] We shall begin again.

A carnal imaginary must give a central place to social hierarchies. But reclaiming a term that carries with it sediments of colonial representations is dangerous. "Oh, it was hard, *Raza* to cleave flesh from flesh I risked us both bleeding to death," Gloria Anzaldúa writes.[6] Reading Césaire linking flesh to flesh, his flesh to the flesh of the world, Fanon feels assaulted. He fears weakness, primitivism, and sexuality are being attributed to his body. These are traits that colonialist discourses project onto racialized bodies. These projections must be recognized and challenged. But I also question associations that Fanon assumes between flesh and femininity, hypersexuality, and depravity—as well as the abjection of vulnerability. As I argued in part II, some of the characteristics that make flesh crucial for contemporary visions of corporeality are those that tend to be despised. I referred to the earthy origins of flesh, its constitutive relations to other human flesh as well as to the material elements, its malleability and feebleness. Thus rather than dismissing flesh, I reclaim it to foreground these aspects as essential to corporeality.

A poetics of the flesh thus entails not only rejecting the projection of a flesh conceived as depravity or weakness on certain bodies—bodies of women, peoples of color, nonnormative sexualities, persons with disabilities. It also calls for revaluing the affective charge of flesh and beauty of the bodies on which it has been projected. Césaire pursues this task, risking cleaving flesh to flesh. He accepts the devalued traits and transforms them poetically, envisioning carnal relations from a site of destruction, pain, and hope. For these reasons, I embrace elements of Césaire's poetry that Fanon rejected. In chapter 7, I return to Merleau-Ponty's "flesh of the world" to redescribe it in light of its unequal socio-material constitution. I let Fanon's deconstructive contributions with Merleau-Ponty's and Césaire's affirmative words reach toward each other, coil over each other, interrogate each other, and reshape flesh.

Epidermal Schemas

Fanon's references to Merleau-Ponty's work are brief and often implicit, yet indispensable. Taking seriously the productive relationship between the body and the world, Fanon shows the notion of "corporeal schema" to be insufficient to understand the constitution of bodies in a racialized world. There are other corporeal "schemas," Fanon argues, drawing Merleau-Ponty's ideas toward more robust analyses of social forces at work in the world.

Like Merleau-Ponty, Fanon envisions himself as oriented toward the world. "I came to the world imbued with the will to find meaning in things," he writes. "My spirit filled with the desire to attain the source of the world."

But this desire is at odds with the world he encounters. There he is seen as an object. "Look, a Negro!" They say. The phrase is heard at the very beginning of the essay. It is uttered before anything else is said; before the lives of Fanon and his readers began, these words were creating worlds. The statement captures, fixes, seals him into a "crushing objecthood" before any encounter with the world takes place. That is why Fanon fears that, for the racialized person, the desire to "attain the source of the world" arrives too late. A divided world rejects him.

The Martinique of Fanon's youth, a French colony, was hardly outside the reach of racializing power. Yet it is the encounter with the racializing gaze, in France, that reveals for him colonialism's most intimate, embodied dimensions. "An unfamiliar weight burdened me. The real world challenged my claims."[7] That "unfamiliar weight" did not figure in Merleau-Ponty's account of corporeality.

Fanon's critique is not a simple rejection of Merleau-Ponty's phenomenological account of the body. In fact, Fanon offers a description of movement that could have been taken from Merleau-Ponty's *Phenomenology of Perception*—suggestively incorporating elements from Merleau-Ponty's example of a person smoking at his desk.[8] "I know that if I want to smoke, I shall have to reach out my right arm and take a pack of cigarettes lying at the other end of the table. The matches, however, are in the drawer on the left, and I shall have to lean back slightly. And all these movements are made not out of habit but out of implicit knowledge."[9] The contrast between habit and knowledge in the last sentence does not precisely follow Merleau-Ponty's use of the terms. For Merleau-Ponty, "it is the body which 'understands' in the acquisition of habit," provided that "understanding" is not assumed to mean "subsuming a sense datum under an idea."[10] Habit is ultimately a type of implicit knowledge, or better, an embodied knowledge. This difference in the use of "habit" does not yet signal Fanon's distancing from Merleau-Ponty. But the differences between them can be anticipated from Merleau-Ponty's next sentence. Merleau-Ponty describes "understanding" as experiencing "*the harmony between what we aim at and what is given*, between intention and the performance."[11] Fanon's descriptions will show discordance, not harmony, between what he seeks and what he receives.

At this point in the narrative, however, Fanon's description of his movements is still consonant with Merleau-Ponty's. The account concludes as Fanon successfully leans back to smoke. This sets up the contrast that Fanon is developing. "A slow composition of my *self* as a body in the middle of a spatial and temporal world—such *seems to be the schema*. It does not impose itself on me; it is, rather, a definitive structuring of the self and of the world—definitive because it creates a real dialectic between my body and the world."[12] "Such seems to be the schema," but further analysis reveals a different schema to him—the "historico-racial schema." This other schema is *imposed*, rather than emerging from a "real dialectic" between the body and the world. The elements that constitute it are not those the scientists would commonly name—"residual sensations and perceptions primarily of a tactile, vestibular, kinesthetic, and visual character."[13] The historico-racial schema is composed of white mythologies.

Merleau-Ponty described flesh as the connective and co-constitutive *tissue* between body and things. Fanon describes a schema *woven* "out of a thousand details, anecdotes, stories."[14] A discursive force field that includes history, science, philosophy, and literature composes this other schema and imposes it on him. "Called on" into this field, the development of his corporeal schema is interrupted. The source for such difficulty is a world of legends—the myths of European superiority and the practices that support them. Fanon's body is an object and a site of fantastic projections: stories about primitivism, savagery, and biological deficiency. These stories and images hamper Fanon's attempts to relate meaningfully to the world he now inhabits. "I am responsible at the same time for my body, for my race, for my ancestors. . . . I was battered down by tom-toms, cannibalism, intellectual deficiency, fetishism, racial defects, slave-ships."[15] The weight of centuries of such stories falls—in an instant—on one person. Under that weight, the sense of a body composed organically in relation to the world, the "corporeal schema," crumbles.[16]

Merleau-Ponty's corporeal schema is an open and dynamic, yet coherent, structure of embodiment. The body expands as the subject reaches out toward the world—being "transplanted" into things and "incorporating" them. Merleau-Ponty spoke about the "power of dilating our being in the world." In contrast to this expansive power, Fanon experiences constriction. The historico-racial schema produces objectification and fragmentation. "My body was given back to me sprawled out, distorted, recolored, clad in mourning."[17] The sensations produced by such dislocations are nothing if not corporeal: "What else could it be for me but an amputation, an excision, a hemorrhage that spattered my whole body with black blood?"[18]

The movement toward the world fails to achieve its goal. There are ideas—productive ideas—that are blocking the body's access to the world. And furthermore, there is an active movement from the world against his body. Far from being lured toward the world, as Merleau-Ponty was, Fanon is threatened, even attacked by it—broken by the weight it imposes on him. A body sprawled out, distorted, recolored, clad in mourning.

Narratives of ancestral failings and historical lag that weigh on colonial bodies are codified through the naturalization of race. All the historical–mythical othering is contained in a single visual sign—skin color. Fanon speaks of an "epidermal schema" (*schema épidermique racial*).[19] He laments, "I am a slave not of the 'idea' that others have of me but of my own appearance."[20]

Race is pinned to the body. Historical myth becomes a racializing science. "In the first chapter of the history that the others have compiled for me," he recounts, "the foundation of cannibalism has been made eminently plain in order that I may not lose sight of it." The historical myth is immediately followed by a parallel story. "My chromosomes were supposed to have a few thicker or thinner genes representing cannibalism. In addition to the *sex-linked*, the scholars had now discovered the *racial-linked*." No explanation is required—just an expression of outrage: "What a shameful science!"[21]

The external sign—skin color—is explained as the *effect* of interior reality—a genetic race. The truth or "sense of the body" is thus gathered in a few chromosomes of sex and race.

Defined as race, the body is condemned and set up for rescue. In this sense, Fanon's descriptions of the racialized body are consonant with Foucault's descriptions of the body subject to spiritual direction and later to psychiatric examination. In Foucault's account, Christian flesh—treated as the cause of sin—was pinned to the body and recodified as instinct. In Fanon's narrative we see race being pinned to the racialized body as the cause of its degeneracy. Perhaps flesh was already considered the cause of race. Fanon laments, "There are times when the black man is locked into his body."[22]

Who will free me from this body of race!

Flesh of the (Other's) World

In response to the plethora of demeaning representations, poets resisting colonial representation and subjugation offered counter-descriptions of their bodies. In Aimé Césaire's poetry, we find not only a celebration of black bodies, but also a *redefinition* of blackness and a proclamation of the body's connection with the elements and with the "flesh of the world." But Fanon is also critical of Césaire's project, which he reads as adopting aspects of colonial anthropologies.

Fanon comments on Césaire's *Notebook on a Return to the Native Land*. He cites it at length and paraphrases it liberally, mimicking its style.[23] The long poem describes the poet's movement from despair at the conditions of his native land and its people to a vision of spiritual transformation. The shift entails for him recognizing alternative cultural values that his people have not been able to develop fully under colonialism. It also requires seeing the country's situation in all its precarity—the poverty, hunger, illness, and even the fragility of the earth on which he stands. He accepts as his own the degradation of the land and the failures of the people. When he finally turns to an affirmative vision for negritude, his tone is prayerful.[24] That affirmative imaginary is based on the connection of the body to the flesh of the world.

In the verses that Fanon quotes directly, Césaire pushes against European standards for greatness and praises people who are not known for their inventions or conquests, people who instead have been subjected to colonialism and Christianity. Without them, he claims, "the earth would not be the earth."[25] Thus begins Césaire's reinterpretation of "negritude."

> my negritude is not a leukoma of dead liquid over the earth's dead eye
> my negritude is neither tower nor cathedral
> it takes root in the red flesh of soil
> it takes root in the ardent flesh of the sky[26]

In these verses, Césaire interprets negritude not as an internal quality of body or a trait of these people's flesh. The "flesh" named here is the flesh of the world.

Césaire continues in praise. These people are, he says,

> truly the eldest sons of the world
> porous to all the breaths of the world
> fraternal locus for all the breaths of the world
> drainless channel for all the water of the world
> spark of the sacred fire of the World
> flesh of the flesh of the world, pulsating with the very movement
>   of the world![27]

Flesh is presented as an element, as it was in Merleau-Ponty's work. Elemental flesh is a site or means of connection with the world. The individual body is imagined as "flesh of the flesh of the world," in parallel with Merleau-Ponty's adoption of the language of Genesis to describe others as "flesh of his flesh." In the final verses, Césaire seeks to reconnect with that worldly flesh: "bind me with your vast arms of luminous clay / bind my vibration to the very navel of the world."[28] He imagines giving himself, plunging into the flesh of the world and receiving an embrace that binds him to it.[29]

Césaire describes a vast relation with the earth and its elements, but he encounters the world specifically in his native land. It is to his island that he says, "Your mud enters in the composition of my flesh."[30] Despite its references to the natural world and his uses of "negritude," Césaire's poetry can hardly be described as a naïve appeal to bonds of blood or of naturalizing race. Claiming this elemental connection with the world is furthermore the result of a struggle to overcome a colonial legacy that distances him and his people from it. Césaire's expansive affirmations of the self-world relation do not assume mastery, not even the erasure of weakness and failures. He lists negative traits systematically and follows them by repeating in liturgical fashion: "I accept this." He embraces suffering and its weakening effects, assuming responsibility for envisioning a negritude to come.

Fanon was troubled by Césaire's allusions to mythical sacrifice and mystical communion with the earth. Most of all, Fanon was disturbed by the continuity between the poet's self-portrayals and the colonial anthropologies that exoticized African cultures. Fanon was imagining the European gaze. Talk of the elements—winds, water, fire, flesh—immediately sparked fears of primitive religion, animism, and ritualized sex. And Fanon would have none of it! He aspired to be a man among men. One has to distrust "rhythm, earth-mother love, the mystic, *carnal* marriage of the group and the cosmos," he argued.[31] Indulging in such ecstatic dreams, seeking wisdom in an imagined ancestral culture, or legitimacy in a community of blood relations was to accept representations and assumptions that had to be challenged. The ideas offered as liberating were already inscribed in the European construction of Africa as exotic Other. They lead back to the mythologies about black bodies.

Fanon interprets the poet's words as alluding to sexuality, and sexuality as racialized. Fanon turns from the poet's appeals to the "spirit" of things or "flesh of the world" to a discussion of a text about sexuality in Africa. One of the scenes of transformation in Césaire's text uses sexual/fertility imagery for the encounter with the earth, in an allegory where the country is reborn to stand side by side with her lover/poet.[32] Fanon does not refer directly to it, but rather moves to anthropologies that exemplify the common link between sex and race in colonial literatures. We saw this coupling in the passage about science cited above. Such associations are part of the fabric of historico-racial discourses, where sex is portrayed as evidence of deviance and thus of race. Fanon tries to distance himself from such associations. "Black magic, primitive mentality, animism, animal eroticism, it all floods over me. All of it is typical of peoples that have not kept pace with the evolution of the human race."[33]

Colonial discourses linked flesh, race, and sex—and Fanon did too. In his view, all these stereotypes would be legitimized by the poets' claim that "for us the body is not some thing opposed to what you call the mind."[34] Fanon reacts also against the appeals to "intuition," which were common in Senghor's work, seeing in it anthropological depictions of intuition as a genetic trait of an earlier stage of human development.[35] Racialization had already categorized, assimilated, and deployed the very qualities the poets celebrated. "Every hand was a losing hand for me," he concludes.[36] "It is too late."

Ambivalent Incarnations

My mind is bent to tell of bodies changed into new forms.
—Ovid, *Metamorphoses*, book 1

Images of bodies assault Fanon everywhere. They threaten him. Even as Fanon explains the inadequacy of all these depictions of bodies, of his body, he knows they are at work in the world. His experience of his body is affected by the presence of other fantastic bodies. He expects them to appear when he sits in a movie theater, when someone looks at him—the cannibals, the primitive, the sexualized dark bodies. But these imaginary bodies do not remain simply outside of him. The weight of white mythologies distorts, dismembers, crushes his body. A body becomes infected, as "the white man injects the black with extremely dangerous foreign bodies."[37] His body also initiates transformations of its own. "Little by little, putting out pseudopodia here and there, *I secreted race*."[38]

These are incarnations of social representations. What is received through the senses becomes part of the body. I referred to similar processes in relation to Merleau-Ponty's discussion of intercorporeal engagements. Acquiring a visual image of myself makes possible the distinction between my body and those of others. But I also learn that others see me from outside. It is the beginning of a construction of an ideal image of myself. This ideal image, Merleau-Ponty observes, would become part of all interactions. I refer constantly to the *ideal, fictitious, or imaginary* me. My visual body image is thus always already entangled with a plurality of images others have of it. Maintaining the distinctions between them might be challenging and disorienting.

The visual body affects a person's relationships to the world. The seeing and the seen body belong to the same visibility, as Merleau-Ponty says. But in a world divided along racial lines, the consequences are starkly different for those whose bodies are made to bear the weight of race. "Expeausure" takes a very different meaning when it is conceived in relation to the "epidermal schema." Hierarchies of embodiment do not originate in the visual body, of course. The meanings of skin color or facial features in a given society are the effect, not the cause, of social discrimination. But cultural presuppositions shape perceptions and, through them, how a body is seen and received by the world. I return to these matters of perception in chapter 7. For now, I can simply indicate that Fanon's experiences foreground the role of perception in relationships between bodies. Some visual markers expose a body to immediate violence. Being seen can mean feeling locked inside a body, confined to objecthood, marked for rescue or destruction.

The gaze is the main mechanism through which Fanon encounters a world that negates his humanity and fends off his approach. White values are "secreted" by the masters, he writes.[39] The master's body is shaped by discriminatory habits—such as fixing someone with his gaze, looking for this or that bodily trait, keeping certain bodies at a distance. Yet the gaze stands for and reveals broader and more insidious social forces. The values that shape the racist gaze constitute other areas of the world—physically, materially. The world is shaped by its own "habits."

As a body approaches an unequally structured world it may be embraced, ignored, blocked, or poisoned by it. Its corporeal schema is rearranged accordingly. Fanon described these as the *difficulties* of developing a corporeal schema because the rearrangement it produced did not expand the capacities of his body to function in the world, but rather threatened to destroy them. In his work we see the body constituted through its relationship to a world that is always already social.

Other Subtle Bodies

Just as he diagnoses difficulties in the development of the corporeal schema, Fanon detects challenges for the development of intellectual systems. He states, "Every ontology is made unattainable in a colonized and civilized society."[40] The qualification of the context—"in a colonized and civilized society"—suggests that the difficulty is contingent. This could mean that the conditions of colonialism make it impossible to conceive or to actualize true being. In those societies, blackness is allowed as the Other of whiteness, as a negation. This does not imply foreclosing questions of being. To the contrary, to analyze the mechanism by which societies promote the flourishing of some bodies and stifle that of others is to begin exploring ontological questions. What does it mean that bodies belong to the world? How does a particular body participate in visibility; how is it sustained by the flesh of the world? Attending to these questions requires thinking of the world as socially differentiated and as producing material differences.[41]

The question of ontology is not circumscribed to evaluation of philosophical concepts, however. Thinking about *being* entails exploring the processes by which ontologies are produced. "Every ontology is a type of imagination," Merleau-Ponty writes. "Every imagination is an ontology."[42] Ontology is not a representation of pre-discursive reality. Descriptions of bodies, worlds, and their co-constitutions are creative renderings with material effects.

Césaire's work is an example of such a creative approach. His poetry depicts the relationship between bodies, worlds, and their co-constitutions imaginatively for the purpose of transformation. He sees himself as part of the world he describes and identifies the island from which comes the mud of his flesh. He expresses his pain, commitments, and aims. This mode of writing conjures visions of bodies and of the world from "shattered histories" and "shards of vocabularies," as Derek Walcott describes the work of Caribbean artists. The materials from which he creates are not pure. Some of his words had been used as tools of power by religious authorities, politicians, and scholars. These words have power. As Césaire explains in his later poem "Word," he takes into his body "vibrating words" that may also wound and kill him.[43] And yet the writing bursts forth in praise or prayer.

The poet strives to see the invisible, to express what is almost inexpressible, to call into being what is not. It is not surprising then that Césaire's writing takes on a religious aura. He uses biblical images throughout the poem. Yet I am most interested in the transformational aims of his work. Commenting on Césaire's use of Christian language and images, A. James Arnold argues, "His intention is messianic rather than specifically christic." In other words, Césaire is using the Christian ideas not to develop a vision of Christ, but rather to offer a vision of a new creation. The tenor of the poem, Arnold explains, is "related to spiritual renewal of race."[44] The poet takes into himself these powerful (and dangerous) words in order to offer a vision of flesh. He does not present that vision as an absolute, clean, or safe break from racializing ideologies. It is a transformation of ambivalent words.

At stake is not simply the liberation of a people from the bondage to a body of race, but the redemption of flesh.[45] The allusions to a communion between bodies and the flesh of the world alert us to the dangers of imagining flesh as full presence, a danger I identified in chapter 5. Césaire averts that temptation in his writing by alternating between visions of a nurturing connection with the flesh of the world and descriptions of contradictions and failures. The affirmations of racial values are punctuated by stories of pain and subjection. This vision of flesh does not expel death or weakness, nor does it found the value of bodies in supra-historical realities. Instead I read it as drawing from what the poet received—body, mud, poverty, colonial institutions, and racializing words. Things that might suffocate him become the elements that his poetry "consecrates."

To Fanon's ears, Césaire's claims to being flesh of the flesh of the earth raised suspicions of essentialism, of primitivism. But Césaire is calling his readers to *instantiate* alternative forms of relation. Dominant modes of rationality are not enough to inspire the persistence needed for "imagining a love of the earth," Édouard Glissant argues, especially when the situation is dire and when all concepts seem inadequate. This love of the earth is almost impossible, yet crucial. Thus Glissant suggests, "To oppose the disturbing affective standardization of peoples, whose *affect* has been diverted by the processes and products of international exchange, either consented to or imposed, it is necessary to renew the *visions* and *aesthetics* of relating to the earth."[46] Césaire's poetry offers a vision and aesthetics for those whose claims to the earth have been broken by slavery, colonialism, and more recent forms of power.

Caribbean thinkers have continued to wrestle with the ambiguities of flesh. There are risks in such writing. Handling dangerous "vibrating words" these texts might, and often do, propagate wounding colonialist views. But the kinds of imaginaries of flesh that Césaire models may also help redirect affects, as Glissant observes. These works might inspire intellectual and creative practices for relating flesh to the world, affirming the desires to reach toward the source of the world, to participate in earthy relations, without at any point occluding injustice, suffering, or failure.

At the end of "The Lived Experience of the Black" we find Fanon again wrestling with the options that are offered to him. He presents them as a dichotomy between mastery and humility. Previously, he had argued that the white man was always in a position of mastery in relation to the black man. But here a disabled man occupies the position of the "Other" in relation to Fanon. "The crippled veteran of the Pacific war says to my brother, 'Resign yourself to your color the way I got used to my stump; we're both victims.'"[47] Fanon rejects such a stance. "With all my strength I refuse to accept that amputation," he writes, evoking other "amputations" experienced as effects of the white gaze.[48] Fanon refuses victimhood. But he leaves the veteran in that role.

Fanon tries again to claim his right to engage in a fruitful relationship with the world. "I feel in myself a soul as immense as the world, truly a soul as deep as the deepest rivers, my chest has the power to expand without limit," he writes, evoking both Merleau-Ponty and Césaire. But he is discouraged from embracing such aspirations. "I am a master and I am advised to adopt the humility of the cripple," he objects. Implicitly, Fanon creates an opposition between the being to which he aspires—described as "mastery"—and the otherness he rejects and projects on the "cripple." Despite his own intent, however, the world will not receive him.

> Yesterday, awakening to the world, I saw the sky turn upon itself utterly and wholly. I wanted to rise, but the disemboweled silence fell back upon me, its wings paralyzed. . . . I began to weep.[49]

The will to expand toward the world is met with the threat of amputation; the move toward the sky finds it turning away. Every attempt to move toward the world fails. He weeps at a world that closes upon itself.

Responding to the sense of being trapped in a body of race, Fanon asserts the humanity that others deny him. Yet he seems to equate that humanity with the capacity for mastery. "I am my own foundation," he insists.[50] He distances himself from the perceived weakness of the "cripple." In so doing, he marks the boundaries of humanity with other bodies—the "cripple," as in other instances he does with homosexuals and women.[51] These are figures of abjection, characters onto whom societies project frailty and corruptibility. They are associated with flesh. Fanon's negative reactions to Césaire's poetry may reflect his fear of being cast, yet again, as the abject at the boundaries of humanity. He considers becoming human as an assertion of *manhood*— which typically implies occupying a position of mastery in relation to nature and flesh.

Fanon refuses the amputation, but it is not clear that he can avoid it. He desires the connection that Césaire's poetry envisions, but cannot believe in its material efficacy. He aspires to a world that would consider them all just human beings—but he fears it might be too late.

There are hints of other possibilities, however. At the end of *Black Skins, White Masks*, he turns from describing social relationships as they are to imagining what they might be. His claims to humanity extend beyond solidarity with other men of color toward a "love of man, wherever he may be."[52] The ultimate goal is the affirmation of human relationships: "to touch the other, to feel the other, to explain the other to myself."[53] Fanon closes the book in prayer.

> My final prayer:
> O my body, make me always a man who questions![54]

Others condemn his body, treating it as a body of race. Fanon asks that same body to make the man—to keep him open toward the world. The words themselves are fruitful. They put into question the objectifications of the body and reach out to touch the reader. Fanon's prayer also creates an opening toward Césaire's poem, which is also a prayer—in its words, form, and aims. The poem not only questions but transforms the ambivalent words that it utters—flesh, race, blackness. By asserting nourishing relations to the flesh of the world, it aims at inspiring intellectual and creative practices for relating flesh to flesh without occluding injustice, pain, or failure.

Interrogating the world has thus far revealed a society of labyrinthine intercorporeal transformations, of complex incarnations with no discernible end or beginning. Fanon described the effects of living in such a world with images of wounding as well as extraordinary metamorphoses. Social powers are felt as alien entities assaulting and infecting the body. But the mechanisms of power are disturbingly ordinary. They work through perception. The ways

I am seen influence the ways my body may engage the world that constitutes it. The ways I see my own body, the images against which I measure it, the ways I act based on these images also shape what I become—materially. The way I see others also changes me. There are still other processes I seldom see or think about, by which social structures, individual and collective action, materialize as the flesh of the world.

CHAPTER 7

CARNAL RELATIONS

Bodies inhabit a world shaped by social ideas and practices. Each body's visible traits, its place in prevailing social hierarchies, affects its exposure to the world—how a body is seen, heard, approached. Visible attributes thus affect how it sees, speaks, and approaches the world. These actions enter into the constitution of the flesh of the world, which in turn coils over each body and weaves its flesh. The social-material world touches upon and folds into even the tiniest element of human carnality. "The thing that arrests me," writes Adrienne Rich, "is how we are composed of molecules . . . arranged without our knowledge or consent."[1]

Social practices produce material effects that are woven in the textures of flesh. Sometimes the marks on our bodies are visible. I can see scars on the bodies of those sent to distant wars or left unprotected from violence in their own communities; the signs of malnutrition of those confined to the lowest ranks of the global economic system; the scalded skin of those exposed to radiation or toxic chemicals in their workplace. Social ideals concretized as local and global practices materialize in bodies—differentially.

There is no space or body untouched by social arrangements. Even our trivial day-to-day social interactions shape our bodies. Gradually or abruptly, flesh is always becoming flesh through relations—often without our knowledge or consent, by wars and commerce, new technologies and migrations.

This intertwining of the flesh of my body and the flesh of world is never a coincidence, however. We do not become the same, nor does the world become my own. Flesh is also shaped by our actions—even when we do not know how—by seeing, listening, or speaking, by eating or touching, by praying, dancing, or chanting. I am formed by seeing and being seen, by moving in the world, through the histories I carry in my flesh. I do not notice this. How could I? "I" is being transformed as well.

Bodies are woven by complex processes of relation and differentiation, I argued in chapter 5. Evolutionary histories, natural environments, cultural conventions, manufacturing practices, and the like may leave their traces in our bodies and enter into the constitution of our flesh. The term "flesh" conveys the inherent multiplicity, the sedimentation of past events, the constant flow of elements in and out of bodies. The exchanges and transformations between bodies and the world follow paths that twist and turn, coil in and branch out. Flesh reminds us that the boundaries between individual bodies and the world are porous, provisional, elusive.

This chapter focuses on the social dimensions of these processes, integrating social forces more explicitly in the depiction of flesh. I use the term "social-material flesh" to emphasize the intertwining of the social and material dimensions of what Merleau-Ponty calls the flesh of the world. I describe them as incarnations of social relations, taking place through perception, interactions between human beings, and the materialization of human activities in the nonhuman world.

The link between bodies and social identities can be asserted in highly problematic ways, when flesh is represented as the cause and foundation of existing social structures. I return to the critiques of biological essentialisms, to which I have referred throughout the book, in order to open the space for alternative models for the relationship between bodies and society. Moving beyond essentialist approaches, we should also beware of idealisms that might lead us to lose sight of the concrete realities of human bodies—where we encounter the devastating effects of social hierarchies, as well as the longing to transform them.

Drawing from the reading of Fanon in chapter 6, this chapter offers an analysis of the significance of seeing and being seen in society. For Merleau-Ponty seeing and being seen implied that we belong to the same world, to its visibility. Yet visibility is made possible not only by my corporeal structure, but also by the environment in which I encounter things—light and the medium in which it travels, usually air. Social conditions affect visibility as well. I discuss how social arrangements shape perception, in dialogue with Linda Martín Alcoff. By informing how we see others and our own bodies, social constructs become part of human relations, and bodies incarnate what they receive visually, not least the gestures of others.

Human beings are not passive recipients of social ideas, however. We act in relation to them. Judith Butler's description of how bodies are gendered through performative reiteration of social norms informs my discussion of how bodies are shaped as they act in a social-material world. This discussion builds on and extends the reach of Merleau-Ponty's analyses of how perception and movement shape our bodies, presented in chapter 4, by attending to the effects of restrictive social forces on the constitution of corporeality. It also shifts the language of Butler's accounts of performativity by emphasizing the materiality of "social norms"—the fact that we encounter these norms concretely in the bodies of other human beings as well as in the physical structures of the world.

The constraints imposed by societies function by guiding our acts, which shape our flesh. Our acts also affect the materiality of the nonhuman world, and this in turn affects corporeal becomings. Social norms are always *materializing* in the physical structures we build, in the elements—in air, water, and earth. In all these structures we encounter the flesh of the world—shaped by words and practices, and by things we do not see. We participate in weaving the flesh of the world—in the production, exchange, and transformation of the elements that constitute it.

Social norms may constrain corporeal becoming by restricting human action, dividing the world to distribute its riches unequally, impoverishing the earth's recourses. But there are no possibilities for corporeal flourishing without the bonds between bodies and social-material flesh. Flesh ties my body to the world; every aspect of the world constitutes the materiality of my body.

The particular ways in which I am able to interact with the world depend on how my body is perceived in society, I argued in chapter 6. Yet that body is not reducible to a position in a social system. Each body has its own rhythms and textures, traces of distant histories and ongoing habits. My flesh carries memories. "We die containing a richness of lovers and tribes, tastes we have swallowed . . . fears we have hidden in as if caves," writes Michael Ondaatje. "I wish for this to be marked on my body when I am dead."[2] Each body incarnates the world in particular ways. Each body expresses itself in ways nurtured by, yet not reducible to, the history or community that sustains its life.

Social Identities and Bodies

Race and sex are social entities, not essences. They do not identify a natural, pre-social basis for our inclinations, proclivities, or limitations—much less explain social hierarchies. But race and sex are also "most definitely physical, marked on and through the body, lived as a material experience, visible as surface phenomena, and determinant of economic and political status," Linda Martín Alcoff writes.[3] These social categories are contingent social constructions, tools of power.

The feminist arguments against biological essentialism are well known. Specific biological traits are deemed to be clear and visible evidence of "natural" differences. These differences are then treated as an unquestionable foundation for established social arrangements. Genitals are identified and granted defining significance. These visible signs—the organs labeled as "reproductive"—produce the effects of interiority through the scientific codification of sex. In other words, the truth of the body is gathered in a few chromosomes defined as sex and thus as the "sense of the body." I noted in chapter 6 a similar pattern, where the external sign (skin color) is explained as the *effect* of interior reality (a genetic race). A few chromosomes of sex and race are gathered to create the illusion of a given truth, the "sense of the body." In both cases, a complex set of social prejudices, practices, and prescriptions become naturalized by anchoring them in biology.

Against gender essentialisms, feminists argued that "one is not born a woman, but becomes one."[4] Sometimes "sex" would be related to the body while "gender" was placed firmly on the side of culture. But this split depends on assuming there is a clear boundary between the biological and the social. For instance, definitions of sexual difference based on the capacity for reproduction tend to bracket reproduction off from the material, social, and technological resources on which reproduction depends. To treat procreation as simply biological is to imagine "reproductive organs" as autonomous machines and to ignore other conditions required for the conception, development, birth, and nourishment of a child. The reproduction of human life depends on material and social structures that allow people with the capacity to produce the necessary fluids (not only eggs and sperm), to engage in sexual relations, to sustain a pregnancy (food, shelter, protection from violence and environmental threats), to support a safe delivery process (shelter, hygienic space, holding arms), and to nourish an always too vulnerable human baby. The (assumed) capacity to carry and deliver a baby does not define a woman. And furthermore, the capacity to reproduce is hardly reducible to the availability of a set of different reproductive organs.

The distinction between biological and social elements of sex has become even more complex as a result of technological advances. For example, reproductive technologies, hormone treatments, and gender-affirming (or sex-reassigning) surgery accentuate the malleability of bodies in relation to social practices—including science and technology. Scientific knowledge and medical procedures are social-material practices that transform biology in ever more fundamental ways, both visibly and functionally. Claiming that one *becomes* a woman (or a man) has not only cultural and social but also ultimately biological implications. In other words, discourses, cultural practices, and social institutions produce tangible biological effects. Cultures produce complex materializations. And those materializations in turn transform cultural views and practices. These processes cannot be addressed through metaphysical frameworks that rely on opposing culture and nature, discourse and materiality.

Assuming a locatable, stable separation between bodies and society occludes the ways in which social identities are used to control bodies. Judith Butler observes that Simone de Beauvoir challenged the assumed biological status of gender, but she did not construe gender as originating elsewhere. Gender is not simply produced by or contained in an external entity or institution. It is not "construct*ed* by a personified system."[5] Butler develops this insight drawing from Foucault's description of an apparatus of power, to which I referred in chapter 5. Gender is "the very *apparatus of production* whereby the sexes themselves are established."[6] It includes the concept of gender, the descriptions of two sexes, their maladies and their remedies, norms and the technologies to survey, manage, and enforce those norms. "Natural sex" is one of the products of this apparatus.[7] However, the discourses that invent "natural sex" define it "as 'prediscursive,' prior to culture, a politically neutral surface *on which* culture acts."[8] The definition of "sex" as *natural* conceals its *social* origin.

"Race" is the apparatus that produces *natural* race and conceals its *social* origin. The apparatus of race includes the concept of race, the descriptions of various races, their maladies and their remedies, norms and the technologies to survey, manage, and enforce those norms.

Societies produce these social categories. Yet social ideas in turn produce material realities that shape our bodies. There are multiple mechanisms by which societies do this. Social identities shape patterns of perception. They influence the implementation of laws, economic decisions, health and environmental policies, agricultural practices, zoning and construction regulations, the production of knowledge. If social hierarchies affect all these areas, we also need to explore how these affect human corporeality.

Matters of Perception

Fanon has no patience for biological essentialism, which he calls a "shameful science," as we saw in chapter 6. But he gives us other ways of thinking about the connection between bodies and social constructs by describing the experience of being seen through the epidermal schema. In these interactions, his skin color marks him as a target. The forces at work are invisible, but he experiences them in the reactions that others have to his body. He is wounded by the looks and words of others and his body produces puzzling metamorphoses. Social ideas and fantasies fell upon his body and transformed his flesh.

Social rejection can fall on a body immediately and with overwhelming force, causing immediate physical wounds or even death.[9] A body experiences being assaulted by external agents. But there are other processes where the body is transformed gradually, which Fanon depicted as metamorphoses such as the growth of pseudopodia or the secretion of race. The most insidious effects of social identities can be hard to ascertain, because they work through ordinary experiences. Stereotypes inform the ideas we have about groups of people. But socialization entails more than the transmission of intellectual ideas, more than our consciousness. Social discourses shape what we see.

Linda Martín Alcoff's analysis of social identities focuses mainly on these slow processes. She draws from Merleau-Ponty's phenomenology of perception to explore the mechanisms through which a person is shaped by living and perceiving in a world structured by racism. She advocates a "subjectivist approach," which she sees exemplified in Fanon's work, and focuses on the "microprocesses by which individual identities are formed."[10] Race should not be understood simply as "the imposition of ideology, but as part of the backdrop of practical consciousness," she argues.[11] Inasmuch as race and gendered identities are part of the ways in which I see others, "they help constitute the necessary background from which I know the world."[12]

Particular corporeal traits acquire significance through history. Racializing discourses persist as a kind of "sedimentation" that weighs on subsequent events and practices of perception.[13] The everyday acts of seeing are formed by "sedimented contextual knowledges." Indeed, "there is no perception of the visible that is not already imbued with value."[14] It is not only the *value* of what is perceived that is affected by context. The perceived *data* itself is affected by the sedimentation of social knowledge. Once race becomes encoded as a set of visible differences, it works tacitly through perception. This means that my seeing is colored by racialization, regardless of whether or not I *think* there is a biological link between phenotype and behavior or *believe* in the characteristics attributed to a given "race." What makes shaping perception such an effective mechanism for shaping the world is that it works as habits do—bypassing the slower processes of analysis and interpretation. When I acquire habits, I do not simply think differently—memorizing the location of letters on a keyboard or the functions of the controls in a car. My body works differently, performing the tasks without conscious analysis of its logic. Perception works this way too, Merleau-Ponty observes. As a habit, it "does not *consist* in interpreting" sensory data, but rather "*relieves us of the necessity*" of interpretation.[15]

Perceptual practices become habitual, shaping knowledge about self and the world in ways that appear neutral, self-evident. It is precisely the habitual character of these practices that makes them seemingly immune to intellectual challenges. "A fear of African Americans or a condescension toward Latinos is seen as simple perception of the real," Martín Alcoff explains. These observations seem "justified by the nature of things in themselves," ignoring the role of historico-cultural schemas in making such meaning appear as irrefutable.[16] I would add that seeing someone as African American or Latino reveals the effects of social histories. We have become habituated to see quickly, without thinking about it, those traits considered relevant for classifying people according to those racial categories as constructed in the United States.

Racialization works in and through practices and habits of perception. "Gazing" is performative.[17] The effects of the racializing gaze accumulate, shaping subsequent perception, which in turn impacts the levels of surveillance to which racialized bodies are exposed, the punishments imposed on them, and so on.

To change these habits it would be necessary "to make visible the practices of visibility itself, to outline the background from which our knowledge of others and of ourselves appears in relief."[18] Fanon's dramatic representation of his encounter with the racializing gaze seeks to make visible the stories and presuppositions through which those eyes see him. Philosophical analysis can likewise contribute to uncover these social practices of visibility, Martín Alcoff suggests. While Fanon exposed the effects of being seen, Martín Alcoff elaborates on how seeing affects the seer.

Vision is never detached, but always enmeshed in the world in which it sees—including the things seen and all the conditions necessary for seeing, I explained in chapter 5. Martín Alcoff relies on Merleau-Ponty's notion of intertwining to describe mechanisms by which the seer is shaped by seeing. Seeing is "our embodiment in the world," she explains. This is "the very opposite of mastery." The "self is engaged in the world—touched, felt, and seen—rather than standing above."[19] There is an ontological interdependence between being seen and seeing—as between the knower and the known. Merleau-Ponty states, "The thickness of flesh between the seer and the thing is constitutive for the thing of its visibility as for the seer of his corporeity."[20] He focuses on the ontological conditions of visibility, observing that flesh is not an obstacle between the seer and the seen but rather "their means of communication."[21] But considering social conditions of visibility foregrounds the ambiguous implications of such interlacing. Looking through historico-racial schemas changes the onlooker as well.

The intertwining of the seeing and the being seen links my experience of my body to the images that others have of it. The problem is not merely that "others have only an exterior image of me" and thus alienate me from my experienced body, as Merleau-Ponty argued. The challenge is that none of us have access to an image of our bodies or the bodies of others outside social sedimentations.

Seeing another seeing him, Fanon finds himself in a terrifying house of mirrors. Where would he turn to see himself? He begins, as we saw, with a subject peacefully turned toward the world. The expected harmony is interrupted as he sees, reflected in the other's gaze, a chaotic multiplicity of images: primitives, cannibals, hypersexual beings, animists, dark bodies moving to the rhythms of drums. He has seen those images more directly. In movies he has waited full of dread to see images of "himself." He has read the descriptions in academic texts and heard them in everyday social interactions. They are part of the common knowledge in colonial societies.[22] They had shaped the vision of those who saw him—not only how they interpreted his presence, but more fundamentally what they saw when they looked at him. Their perception changed them.

The threat that Fanon sensed was real. Being seen through the mythologies of historico-racial schema affects anyone whose body is marked negatively in society. Social fantasies pose corporeal threats to people's bodies—acting from the outside as well as from within. The forces themselves are hard to see, in most cases, invisible. Scientists can study them indirectly, by assessing their effects in institutional practices—the quality of health care received, the economic opportunities available, the exposure to environmental pollution and physical violence.[23] They also study the health effects of the fear and anxiety on those who live under threat.[24] This work is invaluable for helping us understand the labyrinths of our society. And still such research is no substitute for what Fanon expresses so powerfully—how he felt seeing himself in the eyes of another human being. Literary language, such as Fanon's, engages our imaginations at a visceral level, to help us feel what cannot be seen.

The specters of a historico-racial schema are composed through long processes by which cultural representations accumulate, fuse, and interlace. Sometimes I can see and analyze these imaginary bodies as objects. At other times they haunt me. When I see the gaze of another, social images move toward my body as if to take possession of it. In the mirror of another's eyes I see my body as if haunted by these specters. The images are and are not *of* my body, but they threaten to capture me nonetheless—affectively and physically.

Styles of the *Flesh*

> She is a certain manner of being flesh. . . . All style is a shaping of the elements of the world.
> —Merleau-Ponty, *Phenomenology of Perception*

> The body becomes . . . a mode of enacting and reenacting received gender norms which surface as so many styles of flesh.
> —Judith Butler, "Sex and Gender in Simone de Beauvoir's *Second Sex*"

Perception shapes my relationship to my social environment. Subtly and effectively, social interactions teach me how I should act in the world—how to move, speak, dress, eat, and so on. And all of these practices shape my flesh. By acting according to received social norms, I stylize my body.

These transformations entail the interaction between social forces and the creative capacities of the body to respond to its environment. Describing bodies as "reflecting" or "internalizing" social standards or stereotypes is misleading, because it suggests instead that societies act on a passive body. Body sensations and social representations are inextricable from each other. But they are not identical. I do not reflect social identities as a mirror. They are not "inscribed" on my body, as an image stamped on pliable wax. I do not "internalize" them, housing them in some "inner" self. Instead, corporeal materiality is dynamically constituted in relation to social forces.

These corporeal transformations can be described by elaborating on Merleau-Ponty's notion of corporeal schema, as the reshaping of the functional body through its active engagements with the social-material world. As we saw in chapter 4, the corporeal schema is modified in the acquisition of habits—the use of a walking stick, playing the piano, typing these words. In seeing, touching, speaking, we are also engaging with and being constituted by the world. These processes are dynamic and multidirectional; they engage the capacities of corporeal materiality. The world exerts a "remote attraction" on the body and the body responds to the world. The forces in the world "elicit from me" those reactions that would "establish the most effective balance" between us, Merleau-Ponty writes.[25] Yet the forces that elicit me, like the spaces in which my body moves, are not only physically, but also socially configured. Merleau-Ponty alluded to this, observing that "the conventions of our social group, or our set of listeners, immediately elicit from us the words, attitudes and tone which are fitting."[26] But he did not comment on how social hierarchies operate through such conventions—eliciting words, attitudes, and gestures marked by social discrimination.

Socially elicited responses have cumulative effects on the body. Empirical studies of gestures and movements provide examples of the impact of social standards on corporeal habits. Studies have shown that women tend to claim less corporeal space—occupying less area around themselves at a conference table, keeping their hand gestures closer to their bodies, shortening their stride when they walk. By restraining their movements, women reshape their corporeal schema to fit the smaller spaces that societies allot them. Posture, walking styles, hand gestures, tone of voice—all express embodied knowledge of social norms as stylization.[27] The gender-inflected enticements that lead to these habits are negative. They affect bodies differently and may constrain corporeal flourishing.

Judith Butler's notion of "performativity" offers a theoretical framework to understand such patterns of corporeal formation—and to reconceive gender accordingly. Like Merleau-Ponty, she analyzes the constitution of bodies as they act in the world. But she emphasizes the effects of social norms as constraints.

Gender is performative. This is Butler's elaboration on Simone de Beauvoir's claim "One is not born, but rather becomes, as woman." For Butler the reiteration of norms explains how one "becomes." Butler notes that, according to Beauvoir, becoming a woman is "an active process of appropriating, interpreting, and reinterpreting received cultural possibilities."[28] These interpretative processes are embodied. To be gendered entails "a purposive and appropriative set of acts, the acquisition of a skill." It means assuming "a certain corporeal style."[29]

Bodies become gendered through the repetition of acts. My acts are embodied interpretations of social norms. I interpret the limits imposed on my role at a professional meeting by restricting the physical and functional space I take, lowering my voice, asking fewer questions. The constant repetition of similarly constrained acts shapes the body. The more I act in accordance to gender norms, the more my body becomes a woman's body. These acts do not *express* the hidden truth of a natural gender. To the contrary, the stability of gender is an *effect* of my acts.

To argue that social identities are enacted, that race or gender is performative, is not to see them as a choice. We perceive and act within the rigidly regulated systems that compel particular fabrications of gender and race and punish others—even by death. Performativity is "the forced reiteration of norms."[30] Social norms limit the possibilities I can imagine and embody—constraining the ways I engage the world, enticing me to act in some ways and deterring me from others. Because my actions, desires, and therefore the constitution of my body are thus constrained, my corporeal identity seems stable. The body is "shaped by political forces with strategic interests in keeping the body bounded and constituted by the markers of sex."[31] My body appears to be the expression of a pre-given biological sex because it is tied to a socially structured world, which fosters the creation of those specific styles of flesh.

Understanding embodied identities as engagements with society implies rethinking the role of corporeal materiality. Rather than imagining "matter" as a given, Butler suggests that "materialization" is a process "that stabilizes over time to produce the effect of boundary, fixity, and surface we call matter."[32] Materiality does not precede sociality but is shaped by it. And furthermore, corporeality is formed by processes that vastly exceed the individual body.

This body that I am, at this moment, did not exist before the world that has shaped it; it did not precede the enactment of norms. My becoming is dependent on and bound to other bodies. The body emerges from its relation to the sensible world, Merleau-Ponty insists. Butler argues that the subject emerges from its social performativity. These phenomena intertwine. Butler hints at this interlacing in her reading of Merleau-Ponty. Commenting on his "L'entrelacs," she writes that flesh "is not something one has, but rather, the web in which one lives."[33] Because it is the condition of possibility of my existence, it precedes me, my body, my acts. "Something is already underway by the time we act." An action does not fully derive from a subject. And thus, it "exceeds any claim one might make to 'own' it, or to *give an account of oneself.*" Otherness and opacity are always woven in my being, in my body. While explicating Merleau-Ponty's argument, Butler is also implicating her own by echoing the title of her book, *Giving an Account of Oneself.*[34] We are thus invited to bring the social conditions of our existence to bear on the idea of flesh. "Our inability to ground ourselves is based on the fact that we are animated by others in whose hands we are born and, hopefully sustained."[35]

Being animated and sustained by others folds the capacities of other human beings into my own becoming. It links the other's dependence on the flesh of the world to the resources available to nourish my life. The organic and social dimensions of corporeality are inextricable from each other. Reading Merleau-Ponty in relation to Butler's account of the embodiment of social norms reminds us that flesh is always social-material. Recasting Butler's account of sociality in the language of flesh helps me avoid the tendency to dematerialize social norms.

The discussions of theological understandings of the incarnation in the previous parts of the book inform my approach here as well. I noted before the tendency to represent the incarnation as an event in which an immaterial principle—Logos or spirit—takes over a body. We similarly tend to imagine norms as immaterial principles that subsequently take flesh. Even while foregrounding the material effects of our engagements with the world, even while alluding to the materialization of social norms, we might still slip into conceiving norms as ideal rather than sensible—accessed intellectually even if copied materially. Imagining norms as spiritual laws coming to inhabit this or that body renders materiality passive. In contrast, I use the term "incarnation" to suggest patterns by which social-material flesh is distributed, transformed as it is given, and transforms those who participate in these processes. These incarnations do not simply reproduce sameness, do not simply copy the law. They are interpretations shaped by the unique textures and rhythms of each body.

Intercarnations

Social arrangements meet us in the bodies of others. Seeing the gaze of other human beings and hearing the cry of a child produces Fanon's body-shattering experiences. The scholarly texts and the movies in which he also encountered racialization were no less material. These artifacts were financially and politically supported by powerful empires, crafted by emissaries skilled in the practices of imperialism. He had known these ideas all along and could deconstruct them. Or so he thought. But the most vivid images in Fanon's text call attention to his encounters with others—their look, gestures, words, and their trembling bodies. Regulatory norms met him in the bodies of others who were also constituted in relation to the differentiating forces of society. We inhabit the same world. This means that the body I experience is tied to the experiences that others have of my body. I can feel empathy for others. I can incarnate the gestures and words of others. I can be wounded by them. We inhabit this world differently.

When describing bodies as constituted through the repetition of norms, Butler refers not only to words but also to acts, gestures, desires, and the like. But as Amy Hollywood shows, Butler's reliance on linguistic metaphors for describing performativity comes at the expense of other types of human practices.[36] Hollywood argues for a richer model of corporeal becoming. Performativity should account for the fact that "subjects are formed not only through the linguistic citation of norms but also by the body subject's encounters with other bodies in the world and by its practical or bodily citations."[37]

The lures and prohibitions of society reach me through others—through the ways they see me or ignore me, welcome or are threatened by my presence. By shaping the perceptual habits of the person I will encounter, societies constitute us both. I may become more "ex(peau)sed" than others.[38] And that expeausure to the demeaning gaze, interrogation, or violent strike shapes my own habits and reactions—the acts I undertake, the spaces I avoid, the possibilities I can envision.

The gestures and actions of others may thus materialize in and as our flesh. Even my cells develop "habits" meant to prepare me to confront the dangers I expect to find in my surroundings. When I feel threatened by others, my body responds. My body's adrenaline response becomes quicker the more frequently I am in danger. If these responses are too frequent, my health suffers. These social dynamics may also intervene in the functioning of my genes, scientists suggest, even affecting the health of my offspring.[39] Economic pressures that affect adults leave their marks in the bodies of their children, making them more vulnerable to illness.[40] The opposite is also true; the care of others in early stages of life helps me develop healthier patterns of response to stress. To describe these processes as biological would be reductive, for what these examples point to is the ways in which relations shape both the environment—the safety and stability of a neighborhood for me and for my caregivers—and the physical capacities of communities to sustain us. These are matters affected by politics and economics at the highest level of social organization. And yet they also pertain to the most intimate aspects of life.

Societies can strengthen or hinder our capacities to support each other's flourishing—affectively and carnally. The effects of the responses that others have to my body, and the responses that my body has to the other's reactions to my body, in turn affect my capacities to see, respond, and support others. Through habits, "I develop a pattern of existence that leans toward certain practices and that cannot tolerate others," writes Rosalyn Diprose.[41] Our freedom to give is thus "limited by the habits and capacities we have developed as well as those of the bodies with whom we dwell."[42] My capacity for empathy toward another human being echoes my own incarnation, Merleau-Ponty writes. These are capacities on which others depend for their ongoing incarnations.

No Affirmation without Survival

In her early work, Butler described performativity mainly in terms of the interaction between a body and social norms. Social relationships were implicit in her references to social norms. The possibilities of resisting the norms, she explained, emerge in the gaps between what norms prescribe and how a body interprets those norms, in the gaps between repetitions. One may strategically co-opt the power of the norm in order to deflect its effects.[43] I can, for example, (mis)appropriate imposed racial traits and turn them into positive affirmations of identity, as Césaire did. Or I can exaggerate the performance of my gender to the point that it looks like a fabrication, displaying gender precisely as performative rather than expressing an essence. These actions do not escape the norm. They are "mobilized by the law." Furthermore, even if performativity is a reiteration of norms, it is never fully successful and the results are unpredictable. There is a dynamic difference between the norm and its materialization. My repetitions of a given gesture, movement, or style can introduce difference—my hand gestures a bit wider, my stride graceless, my voice a little gruff. In time, such failures might open spaces for the emergence of new identities.

Arguing that resistance is mobilized by the law suggests, however, that all power derives from social norms. Butler's main examples of the social forces at work are pathologization, de-realization, harassment, threats of violence, violence, and criminalization. Asked about this emphasis on negative forces, she acknowledges, "I sometimes stay within a theology of lack." The reason for this might be experiential. "I tend to think that this is simply what happens when a Jewish girl with a Holocaustal psychic inheritance sits down to read philosophy at an early age." Survival could not be taken for granted. Thus the history of anti-Semitism inflects her analyses of gender and sexuality. "I wasn't sure that either my own gender or my own sexuality . . . were going to allow me to be immune from social violence of various forms."[44] This orientation gives a tragic aura to her work, as to Fanon's. "Survival is not the same as affirmation," she admits, "but there is *no affirmation without survival*."[45]

Matters of survival take precedence. There is no substitute for basic social structures of protection and economic sustenance. But inasmuch as corporeal constitution is also influenced by the encounters with others in the world, affirmative social relations can be crucial for long-term survival. While performativity does not preclude these, Butler's work tends to identify only the forces of social control. Martín Alcoff argues that Butler's reliance on psychoanalysis leads her to define subjectivity as inevitable subjection. This negative definition of subjectivity implicitly precludes positive cultural contributions to human flourishing and casts social identities as necessarily detrimental. Framed in this way, performativity does not help us understand "the way in which a public self may not match a lived self" or "the manner in which we manage to separate ourselves from our public interpellation."[46] There are other energies at work in people's social engagements, Martín Alcoff argues. The literatures written by those refusing their presumed identities represent their active contestation of those norms—distancing from social representations or clashing against them.

Butler has restated her description, offering more nuanced statements in response to these concerns. She clarifies that subjects are only partially constituted in discourse and "constituted in ways that can't quite be anticipated."[47] Performativity does not preclude the emergence of identities that differ from the imposed norms. What it challenges is the idea of a stable "inner self," a pre-social core from which subsequent action derives.[48] But these descriptions are too subdued to represent the power of affirmative practices in the constitution of bodies.[49] The accumulating effects of meeting eyes that react with love and respect to my presence, hearing words of approval, being surrounded by images that represent my body as beautiful are also part of the materialization of flesh. To account for communal processes of affirmation it seems insufficient to speak of failures in enacting the norm.

People whose bodies are marked negatively in the society in which they live intentionally seek to produce alternative models for being a body and create communities guided by them. Poetic writing is an example of a practice of creating—from "shattered histories," "shards of vocabularies," ambiguous words, and reassembled rituals—imaginative spaces for the affirmation of corporeal possibilities. These too enter into the constitution of bodies, fostering alternative visions that relativize social norms, depicting my subjection to those norms as contingent upon the situation. Demeaning images of my body will still affect me, but they compete with other images, rather than claiming universal validity. Still the power of creative practices is most effective when embraced in communities to which I may lend my body in order that it may be shaped by those visions—through words, ceremony, ritual, and practices.

Inasmuch as such communities succeed in forming the sensibilities of those who inhabit them, those visions have the power of eyes, ears, and hands capable of sustaining other bodies. Such collective spaces create constraining norms, to be sure. They are not outside the norms of society. But such collective endeavors entail more than the forced reiteration of norms. Perhaps they represent the mobilization of norms that are ignored or rejected in the broader society.

Affirmative practices do not necessarily transform the operating norms of the broader society—although it is hard to imagine the emergence of social movements without the communities that envisioned a different world in which their members could flourish. Affirmation does not protect me from the negative forces to which society exposes some bodies through the inattention of doctors, biases of teachers, or the abuse of military and police personnel. It will not give me access to material resources that I need, if my community is kept in poverty. But the creative forces of affirmative practices may strengthen my capacities to survive negative forces, when possible, to analyze and challenge them, and to support the most vulnerable.

Social-Material Flesh

The constitution of my body in relation to the social-material world entails action—reaching toward others, interpreting what I perceive, and responding. These actions involve the generative capacities of flesh. Fostering some possibilities and foreclosing others, social constraints guide those capacities to produce material results. But social forces do not work by themselves. While representing social norms as constraining forces illuminates how societies delimit corporeal flourishing, it understates the productive forces of materiality and flesh. Materiality does not yield passively to human demands. The world is shaped by human action, but not determined by it. And the world thus shaped in turn affects human action.

Theoretical physicist Karen Barad seeks to correct the tendency to imagine materiality either as a given or as an effect of human agency. She adopts and elaborates on the notion of performativity as materialization. Butler's account of performativity challenges both the priority of matter to discourse (biological essentialisms) and the representation of materiality as passive recipient of social and cultural inscriptions (constructivism). But Barad argues that by focusing on human actions, Butler's account of performativity tends to reinscribe the idea of matter as an effect of discursive practices rather than as an active participant in them.[50] Barad seeks a more precise description of the mechanisms by which biology and history intertwine. This entails, among other things, expanding the range of factors considered in the analysis of materialization.[51] We should understand all "thinking, observing, and theorizing as practices of engagement with, and as part of, the world in which we have our being."[52] And we should also consider the performativity of nonhuman materiality, the idea that "material forces actively matter to the processes of materialization."[53]

The exclusive focus on human actions limits our understanding of the mechanisms by which power affects human bodies. Addressing the principles that govern material productivity at its most fundamental levels is beyond the scope of this discussion. But it is crucial for this project to point to some of the ways in which the human and the nonhuman are implicated in the constitution of flesh.

In some cases, social practices aim directly at bodies. Examples such as medical experimentation on enslaved and colonized peoples, the mentally ill, and those imprisoned seem particularly cruel because they entailed planned, direct interaction between health professionals and those affected.[54] Yet the pervasive effects of environmental degradation can be just as deadly. Terry Tempest Williams offers her own story as an example, in an essay aptly entitled "The Clan of One-Breasted Women." She writes,

> I belong to a Clan of One-Breasted women. My mother, my grandmothers, and six aunts have all had mastectomies. Seven are dead. The two who survive have just completed rounds of chemotherapy and radiation.

"I've had my own problems," she adds. "This is my family history."[55] This medical history, written so intimately in Williams's flesh, is part of the political history of the United States. As an adult Williams decided to investigate the odd pattern of illness in her family. Most people would have assumed it was genetic, an inherited flaw. But she discovered that Utah, where her family had lived for generations, was the site of atomic testing between 1951 and 1962. It was known then that the practice was dangerous, but it was considered a matter of national security. The corporeal marks of those political decisions persisted through multiple generations.

We encounter social arrangements in the physical structures of our world. The design of facilities, tools, and physical spaces concretizes social hierarchies and structures. These things create paths of access to material resources and areas of high risk—which are unequally distributed among people. Buildings and sidewalks physically regulate the movements of bodies. Every day we encounter the definitions of "normal" forms of embodiment concretized in a stairway, a narrow door, a high countertop. Some of us barely notice how these structures regulate our social interactions and our access to services or goods. Others cannot ignore it. My friend cannot enter my house or sit at my dinner table because the building in which I live is not accessible to her.

Zoning laws and economic calculus that determine the location of a hospital, a road, or a landfill distribute the resources and risks produced by such structures. In so doing, they constitute the material qualities of local environments and the material conditions of the communities affected. Ultimately they change the flesh of those who live in their proximity. National boundaries physically separate family members from one another. The U.S.-Mexico border is an open wound, writes Gloria Anzaldúa. "The U.S-Mexican border es *una herida abierta* where the Third World grates against the first and bleeds. And before a scab forms it hemorrhages again." And that territorial wound divides peoples and her body.

> 1,950 mile-long open wound
> dividing a *pueblo*, a culture
> running down the length of my body,
> staking fence rods in my flesh,
> splits me splits me
> *me raja me raja*.[56]

There are less visible ways to restrict a person's access to the resources she needs, such as economic policies that reduce access to food. One can also track the corporeal effects of agricultural practices and commerce. The unintended consequences of the increase in consumption of quinoa in the United States is just one example. The driving force is an awareness of the nutritional value of that grain. The U.S. demand for quinoa has increased, driving its price so high that now "poorer people in Peru and Bolivia, for whom it was once a nourishing staple food, can no longer afford to eat it."[57] They have to switch to cheaper foods and there are serious concerns about malnutrition. The picture is much more complex than this. But it illustrates how a choice of food aimed at making our bodies healthy can unintentionally harm the health of other bodies.

The effects of social arrangements are not limited to the regulation of people's access to the earth's resources. The elements that compose the world are also transformed by social ideals and practices. Earth, water, and air are affected by human habits of consumption and relation—by what we eat and the ways we produce and distribute food; by how and where we build homes and workplaces and the ways we travel between them; by the wars we fight and the ways we prepare for them. These elemental transformations in turn constitute us—what we eat, where we can live, the wars sparked by limited availability of vital resources. The elements enfold in our flesh. We are not simply inscribing our laws on passive matter. As climate change dreadfully reminds us, there are forces that cannot be determined or controlled by human intentions. We are not merely *in* the world, we belong to it.

Flesh of Our Relations

The possibilities that the world opens and forecloses for me depend on how my body is seen in society. The visibility of bodies ex(peau)ses them to specific rules and expectations, different risks, unequal access to the world. All these interactions with the "external" world, with the world that sees me from the outside, are folded into the malleable fabric of my flesh. Movement and perception, but also imperceptible exchanges, materialize as our flesh. These are social-material transformations.

Flesh is dynamically constituted through all these processes of exchange and transformation—between bodies, between a body and the physical structures it inhabits, by the elements in which all bodies move and have their being. Flesh also carries memories of histories we never knew and will never know. Past encounters shaped the bodies of our ancestors, the communities that may or may not sustain our lives today, the societies in which we might be welcomed, exploited, or excluded; the world that may nourish or poison us. We are entrusted to relations wider than our bodies.

CONCLUSION

I say that poetry is flesh.
—Édouard Glissant, "Lava"

Returning to Christian texts, I have identified different corporeal imaginaries—the somatic and the carnal—that reverberate in contemporary accounts of bodies. The somatic strand represents flesh as inessential. Discarding flesh, this strand tends to reject important traits of corporeality: the earthy origins of flesh, its constitutive relations to other human flesh as well as to the material elements, its malleability and feebleness. Desiring the other's touch or the fruits of the earth opens our bodies to the world, disturbing the illusions of autonomy and self-control. We are moved by the world. And thus these somatic Christian imaginaries and the contemporary accounts that they inflect have judged carnal desires as the root of sin and of mortality. Discard desire and overcome mortality, they counsel; abandon the flesh to live in the body. And we dream of fleshless bodies freed from the weight of earthy substances, the menace of death, or the determinations of our social histories. We might not project visions of glory to the end of time. But we invent technologies to produce bodies that appear untouched by time, unmarked by race, unaffected by social-material environments. And we surround ourselves with icons of their beauty and worship them. But their brilliance is fueled by the exhaustion of flesh.

Rejecting flesh leads to the projection of carnality and its despised traits onto others. Thus flesh becomes a category of abjection. Ancient imaginaries performed their own abjections, notably of Jews and women. More recent ones deploy "flesh" to mark those perceived as failing the ideals of self-containment and mastery: women, sexual minorities, racialized peoples, those living with disabilities. The idea of a law of sin attached to bodily members has proved its power beyond the biblical context. A construct of sinful flesh replaces vital corporeality; this counterfeit is used to control the malleability of bodies. It is pinned to bodies to entrap them as bodies of sin, sex, race, or abnormality. These constructs occlude, trap, or manipulate flesh, turning its malleability into its liability.

It might be tempting to make flesh vanish. But rejection of carnality is just the other side of the system that projects it onto others. Bodies are always susceptible to the exercise of power. However, the susceptibility to being shaped by the world is also the basis of all life and all knowledge. Flesh is a constitutive relation to the world—a condition for corporeal survival and flourishing as well as the source of its vulnerability. Rather than abandon flesh to live in the body, we need to reevaluate the rejected traits of carnality—its links to the material elements, its frailty and changeability. And I find in the carnal strand of Christian imaginaries resources for this project. They offer a crucial insight: unless I can embrace my own flesh, and its beginnings in the flesh of another, I cannot love other fleshly beings—nor can I understand the incarnation. What is at stake for them is nothing less than the possibility of love.

In Christian texts, God is the initiator and model for such an embrace of flesh. Infusing earth with love, God creates. Becoming flesh, in birth and suffering, God re-creates. Christians are called to remember these stories, to see themselves in the transformations that they depict, to imitate God and be born again.

These bold claims are compromised by an attachment to the God of heavens, as a reservoir of truth, knowledge, and stability unaffected by carnality. Like Merleau-Ponty, I trust the potential of a poetics that empties itself in the world, accepting the limits of the knowledge it seeks. No knowledge of the sensible is ever absolute, unmediated, or final. All our knowledge—of self, others, of the world—is embodied and interlaced in the world of which it is part. Each of our acts is grounded in faith, for even in our everyday perception we affirm more than we strictly know, "since objects are inexhaustible and our information limited."[1] Affirming that we belong to the same world is such a commitment, one that links consenting to being flesh to ethical obligations toward others and the earth.

Turning the images of a Christian poetics of the flesh toward the world, I have sought not so much to retrieve them as to unsettle their reifications in order to let their poetics stir new imaginaries. And I strive to learn from their aptitude for describing experiences where the most mundane touches upon the inexpressible. With the images of bodies animated by an immemorial touch, divinity becoming flesh and flesh striving to become divine, or flesh that sings and shines as much as it rots and dies, I reorient here toward the socio-material world. Passionately. In this world bodies are animated, sustained, and nourished by webs of relationships (human and nonhuman) to which our lives are entrusted.

Neither the coming to flesh of an immaterial spirit nor the movement of the spirit from Father to Son and back to the Father adequately represents the complexities of incarnation. Focusing on the circuitous paths of flesh—connecting past and present, spirit and earthly elements—the incarnation brings to mind and may help us revaluate carnal/earthy bonds as grounds for a commitment to a shared life. It may remind us that the most significant events, the most loving, the most life giving, require consenting to being flesh.

What is born of flesh is flesh. And because this flesh that weaves my body is part of the flesh of the world, I can reiterate that strange statement from the Gospel of John. Bread is also flesh. A piece of bread is a materialization of relations—socioeconomic exchanges, human work, and the productive capacities of earth, water, and air. As we exchange bread we share or withhold life. Sharing bread—and also water or wine—may create communities and transform those who participate in them. Flesh is not a self-contained mass, a thing one possesses; it is not a law of sin, racial instinct, or sexual essence. It is an element transformed as it is given. Organic elements, bodies, and social arrangements intertwine in water, bread, blood, and poetry and transform each other as flesh.

I am of this world. The movements of my body, seeing and touching, speaking and thinking, constitute my body and contribute to the flesh of the world. The flesh of the world weaves the flesh of my body, beneath the surface of the skin, below the orders of the visible. Human and nonhuman forces affect me from within, at the most fundamental levels of my body. Its complex fabric is woven by multiple entities that live and act in my body, by the sedimentation of past events, the constant flow of elements in and out of it. Based on its unique rhythms and textures, its distant histories and ongoing habits, each body incarnates the world in particular ways. But the presence of the world's flesh to my flesh is also the presence of its hierarchies and demarcations to my body.

We belong to the same world, but we inhabit it differently. We perceive and are perceived differently. Social relations shape my perception of my body, the bodies of others, and the relationship between them. In this world of social representations we see ghosts, fantasies, and dreams—not only crude perceptual facts or biological data. Past histories and mythologies haunt us. What is perceived flickers with the shadows of images that are not quite there, tenuous, opaque, or excessive. The specters are not restricted to an "outside" of the body—to the other's view. They cling to people's bodies—linked to skin color, a sexual organ, or a chromosome. Through history, visible bodily traits have been construed as emerging from different types of flesh and used to justify the unequal distribution of social glories.

In a world divided along racial lines, the consequences of abiding in the flesh of the world are starkly different for people whose bodies are made to bear the weight of race. Unable to experience the power of dilating in the world, we may find that the world fends off our approach, constrains our carnality. Or it meets us with violence. The weight of centuries of racial mythologies falls on a person, and her body crumbles. Or the day-to-day encounters with these images in the eyes or words of others infect her body, induce harmful secretions and metamorphoses, produce ambivalent incarnations.

This world is a labyrinth of incarnations. To be a body is to be tied to the world, not beyond the specificities of our bodies, but through them. The visible traits of my body affect whether the world recognizes me and receives me or ignores me and wounds me. It constrains my actions—how I move or talk, what I may look at, taste, explore. Social relations leave visible marks on our bodies. Gradually societies may also shape the most fundamental elements of our corporeality. Social norms are always becoming flesh.

Social arrangements materialize in our bodies, in the physical structures we build, in the elements—in water, air, and soil as much as in flesh and blood. A poetics of flesh considers these elemental dimensions. My actions and the actions of others shape this world materially. My flesh is not like that of green grass—I may tell myself. But the fabric of flesh is not simply human. Air, water, and soil nourish my flesh and constitute it accordingly, imperceptibly, without my knowledge or consent. What is flesh but earth, in so many forms?

My actions and the actions of others may unleash forces of destruction on all of us. I see storms, plagues, and wars. The ancients may have called these forces spirits. But what we call materiality binds us together just as tightly. Still facing the world we find flesh abused, debased, shackled. This is the flesh of the incarnation.

Consenting to being flesh implies accepting the social obligations that emerge from our coexistence in the flesh of the world, analyzing social structures not as debates about ideas, positions, or power conceived in abstraction but rather as the mechanism by which societies promote the flourishing of some bodies and stifle that of others, distribute life and death. Descriptions of bodies, worlds, and their co-constitutions are creative renderings with material effects.

Flesh is worldly. It nonetheless retains memories of its previous contacts with Christian poetics. At times flesh flickers with glory. Poets, philosophers, and theorists, as much as theologians, take in ambivalent words to transform them. Still, reclaiming terms that carry with them sediments of colonial representations—"flesh," "race," "spirit"—is dangerous. But we risk taking up the words and conjuring other images and other bodies. Never forgetting injustice, suffering, or failure, such a poetics seeks to participate in earthy relations, to become flesh. There is nothing less at stake in this commitment than the possibilities of becoming for those who have been condemned by the deprecation of flesh.

This flesh is not just dust. It is not the opposite of spirit. It is not absolute clarity, a determinate thing. The qualities of flesh challenge direct explication, just as flesh is never wholly disclosed in experience. Flesh twists and turns, constituting realities that never exhaust it. Flesh comprises folds, coils, labyrinths, zones of obscurity and invisibility. It is marked by otherness. To speak of the obscurity or depth of flesh can raise suspicions of metaphysical excess, of the spiritualization of flesh. There are good reasons to worry about this for spiritualizing flesh disembodies meaning. But references to obscurity cannot be reduced to veiled appeals to a reservoir of full presence. These references point to the indeterminacy of carnal knowing and becoming, and to the irreducible otherness that marks all flesh.

A poetics of flesh deploys negations to counter reifications. But the apophatic gestures that this poetics has sought most intently are not those of negation but rather of multiplication. Describing flesh entails depicting a plurality of relations, images, and perspectives, which do not yield a smooth, uniform, or harmonious vista. Flesh displays light and obscurity, visibility and invisibility, connections and gaps. I find this poetic style in the Gospel of John, in Merleau-Ponty's later writings, and in the Caribbean poets. They convey an indeterminacy not predicated on absence, distance, or nothingness but rather on the multiplicity of a flesh that is always constituted by unpredictable interactions. The negations of flesh in Foucault and Fanon and the affirmations of Merleau-Ponty and Césaire reach toward each other, coil over each other, interrogate each other, and reshape flesh. Phenomenological observation and scientific information are woven through this book. But I do not mistake them, much less my representations of their insights, for the true flesh. The theological and the philosophical, the empirical and the imaginative, reach toward each other, coil over each other, but they come apart, changing each other, never becoming the same.

A turn to corporeal materiality would turn flesh into dust if it fully dispelled ineffability, the irreducible otherness in all bodies, the indeterminacy of becoming flesh. Writing flesh requires languages attuned to silences, disruptions, opacity, and to the complex qualities of sensation. Since flesh is always becoming, since it envelops and exceeds each one of our bodies, since our expressions emerge from it, writing flesh should be a poetics. This implies not only a style of writing but also a recognition of the limits of our knowledge and appreciation for the imaginative dimensions of thought. Such poetics does not abandon the task of learning about and from the world. It is the beginning of attention, a seriousness—which leads us to explore the world again in wonder, to describe it faithfully. We pray that our bodies may keep us open to others, to sense the entanglements of our carnal relations.

NOTES

Introduction. Both Flesh and Not

The introduction subtitle comes from David Foster Wallace's book *Both Flesh and Not* (New York: Little, Brown, 2012).

1. For the use of carnality to characterize the people of Judaism, see Daniel Boyarin, *Carnal Israel: Reading Sex in Talmudic Culture* (Berkeley: University of California Press, 1995). The book identifies examples of the association between women and carnality itself. The characterization of homosexuality as "according to the flesh" is used more explicitly in contemporary Christian rhetoric. Pope Shenouda III cites Romans 8:1, 8:5, and 8:13. The pope associates homosexuality with "carnality" because it is "an abnormality" and "against nature." He writes, "when people walked according to the lust of the flesh in the Old Testament, they received severe punishment from God." "Lust" becomes the key here: living according to flesh is living lustfully. Homosexuals live according to the flesh because "homosexual love is not love, but lust, and there is a great difference between love and lust, lust of the flesh." Pope Shenouda III, "Homosexuality and the Church: An Address to the Coptic Orthodox Priests of England," *Orthodoxy Today.org*, accessed March 15, 2015, http://www.orthodoxytoday.org/articles2/ShenoudaHomosexuality.php.

    Another source references Romans 8:13, "If you live according to the flesh, you will die." The writer describes same-sex desires as "disordered and broken"; the answer to these desires is to "kill" them. They are the result of our "sinful natures," which the author defines as "flesh." ("The Bible refers to our sinful nature as 'the flesh.'") Obedience to same-sex desires is living according to the flesh. Nick Roen, "Orienting on Homosexual Orientation," a blog post on *Desiring God*, accessed March 15, 2015, http://www.desiringgod.org/articles/orienting-on-homosexual-orientation.

2. Hélène Cixous, "Laugh of the Medusa," *Signs* 1, no. 4 (1967): 889.

3. Judith Butler, "Sex and Gender in Simone De Beauvoir's *Second Sex*," *Yale French Studies* 72 (1986): 48.
4. "Imaginary" is included in Édouard Glissant, *Poetics of Relation*, trans. Betsy Wing (Ann Arbor: University of Michigan Press, 1997), 159.
5. Derek Walcott, "The Antilles: Fragments of Epic Memory, 1992 Nobel Lecture," 69. In Derek Walcott, *What the Twilight Says: Essays* (New York: Farrar, Straus, and Giroux). Glissant's work is significantly influenced by Walcott's poetry, as Glissant explains in *Poetics of Relation*.
6. Glissant, *Poetics of Relation*. For a discussion of the relationship between poetics and the sacred in Glissant, see Mayra Rivera, "Flesh of the World: Corporeality in Relation," *Concilium* 2 (2013): 83–96.
7. Glissant, *Poetics of Relation*, 159–60. Glissant continues, "When we ask the question of what is brought into play by Relation, we arrive at that-there that cannot be split into original elements. . . . Relation has its source in these contacts and not in itself. . . . Its aim is not Being, a self-important entity that would locate its beginning in itself."
8. Glissant, *Poetics of Relation*, 154. My use of the term "entanglement" here and throughout the book is based on Glissant's use of it. Although he is aware of the scientific usages, his is primarily literary—as seen in the passages cited here. In contrast, Catherine Keller's use of "entanglement" in *Cloud of the Impossible* emerges from sustained engagement with postmodern science for a rich constructive theology of "planetary entanglement." I do not claim such knowledge of the science of entanglement, although I see important resonances between Glissant's "Relation" and Keller's cosmological vision. *Cloud of the Impossible: Negative Theology and Planetary Entanglement* (New York: Columbia University Press, 2014).
9. Glissant, *Poetics of Relation*, 154.
10. Virginia Burrus, "Seducing Theology," *Theology and Sexuality* 18, no. 2 (2013): 4.
11. For example, Carter Heyward considered "the erotic . . . our most fully embodied experience of the love of God." Carter Heyward, *Touching Our Strength: The Erotic as Power and the Love of God* (San Francisco: Harper San Francisco, 1989), 99. See also Marcella Althaus-Reid, ed., *Liberation Theology and Sexuality* (Burlington, VT: Ashgate, 2006); Gerard Loughlin, ed., *Queer Theology: Rethinking the Western Body* (Malden, MA: Blackwell, 2007); and James B. Nelson, *Body Theology* (Louisville, KY: Westminster/John Knox Press, 1992).
12. The philosophical responses to the atrocities of the Shoah deeply influenced the development of Latin American liberation thought, particularly through Dussel's engagement with Emmanuel Levinas.
13. Enrique Dussel, *El humanismo semita: Estructuras intencionales radicales del pueblo de Israel y otros semitas* (Buenos Aires: Editorial Universitaria de Buenos Aires, 1969); *El humanismo helénico* (Buenos Aires: Editorial Universitaria de Buenos Aires, 1975).
14. Grace M. Jantzen, *Becoming Divine: Towards a Feminist Philosophy of Religion* (Bloomington: Indiana University Press, 1999), 269.

15. For the feminist use of the image of the world as the body of God, see Sallie McFague, *The Body of God* (Minneapolis: Fortress Press, 1993). For recent relational ontologies see, for example, Laurel Schneider, *Beyond Monotheism: A Theology of Multiplicity* (London: Routledge, 2008) and Catherine Keller, *Cloud of the Impossible: Negative Theology and Planetary Entanglement* (New York: Columbia University Press, 2014).
16. See, for example, Angel F. Méndez-Montoya, *The Theology of Food: Eating and the Eucharist* (Malden, MA: Wiley-Blackwell, 2009); and Jennifer R. Ayres, *Good Food: Grounded Practical Theology* (Waco, TX: Baylor University Press, 2013).
17. Sharon V. Betcher, "Becoming Flesh of My Flesh: Feminist and Disability Theologies on the Edge of Posthumanist Discourse," *Journal of Feminist Studies in Religion* 26, no. 2 (2010): 107.
18. Betcher, "Becoming Flesh," 108.
19. Betcher, "Becoming Flesh," 110.
20. Sharon V. Betcher, *Spirit and the Obligation of Social Flesh: A Secular Theology for the Global City* (New York: Fordham University Press, 2013).
21. Betcher's work addresses these concerns as well. I am thus not identifying theoretical objections, but rather the different aims of our projects. Alexander G. Weheliye's *Habeas Viscus: Racializing Assemblages, Biopolitics and Black Theories of the Human* (Durham, NC: Duke University Press, 2014) offers a theory of "racializing assemblages" through an engagement with the category of flesh informed by the works of Hortense Spillers and Sylvia Wynters. Unfortunately, it was published too recently to be engaged in this book.
22. For instance, see research on lower testosterone in men raising children. Pam Belluck, "In Study, Fatherhood Leads to Drop in Testosterone," *New York Times*, September 12, 2011. New research explores not simply how genetic traits affect corporeal processes, but also how practices such as meditation, yoga, and gestures induce chemical changes in the body and ultimately shape attitudes, responses, and susceptibility to illnesses. Dana R. Carney, Amy J. C. Cuddy, and Andy J. Yap, "Power Posing: Brief Nonverbal Displays Affect Neuroendocrine Levels and Risk Tolerance," *Psychological Science* 20, no. 10 (2010): 1–6.
23. Judith Butler, "On This Occasion . . . ," in *Butler on Whitehead: On the Occasion*, ed. Roland Faber, Michael Halewood, and Deena Lin (Plymouth, UK: Lexington Books, 2012), 12. Italics mine.
24. Butler, "On This Occasion," 12.
25. There are multiple approaches gathered under "material feminisms" and "new materialisms." See, for instance, the editor's introduction to Stacy Alaimo and Susan Hekman, *Material Feminisms* (Bloomington: Indiana University Press, 2008); and Diana Coole and Samantha Frost, eds., *New Materialisms: Ontology, Agency, and Politics* (Durham, NC: Duke University Press, 2010). Still, not all scholars who contribute to these discussions agree on the appropriateness of the term "new materialism" to designate the emphasis of their works.

26. Vicky Kirby, "Introduction," in Coole and Frost, *New Materialisms*; Kirby, "Corporeal Habits: Addressing Essentialism Differently," *Hypatia* 6, no. 3 (1991): 4–27.
27. The persistent critiques of the loss of the materiality of the body in Judith Butler's works are part of this broader assessment of the shortcomings of postmodern approaches. See, for instance, Vicki Kirby, "Postructural Feminisms, Part 2: Substance Abuse: Judith Butler," in *Telling Flesh: The Substance of the Corporeal* (New York: Routledge, 1997), 101–28; Kirby, *Quantum Anthropologies: Life at Large* (Durham, NC: Duke University Press, 2011); Kirby, "Natural Convers(at) Ions: Or, What If Culture Was Really Nature All Along," in *Material Feminisms*, ed. Stacy Alaimo and Susan Hekman (Indianapolis: Indiana University Press, 2008); Karen Barad, "Posthuman Performativity: Towards an Understanding of How Matter Comes to Matter," in Alaimo and Hekman, *Material Feminisms*, 120–54; and Barad, *Meeting the Universe Halfway: Quantum Physics and the Entanglement of Matter and Meaning* (Durham, NC: Duke University Press, 2007).
28. Judith Butler, *Bodies That Matter: On the Discursive Limits of "Sex"* (New York: Routledge, 1993).
29. Nicolas Rose describes, for example, the impact of genetic testing on conceptions of communities. Changes in the criteria for identity from collective histories and shared cultural practices to biological indicators significantly transform collective self-definitions and the basis for political claims. Nikolas Rose, *The Politics of Life Itself: Biomedicine, Power, and Subjectivity in the Twenty-First Century* (Princeton, NJ: Princeton University Press, 2007).
30. Jean-Luc Nancy, *The Sense of the World* (Minneapolis: University of Minnesota Press, 1997), 149.

Part I. Regarding Christian Bodies

Epigraph cited in Vitor Westhelle, *The Scandalous God: The Use and Abuse of the Cross* (Minneapolis: Fortress Press, 2007), 33–34.
1. Benny Liew Tat-Siong, "When Margins Become Common Ground: Questions of and for Biblical Studies," in *Still at the Margins: Biblical Scholarship Fifteen Years after Voices from the Margin*, ed. R. S. Sugirtharajah (London: T and T Clark, 2008), 54.

Chapter 1. Becoming Flesh

1. The Gospel of John was likely written in Greek around the last decades of the first century in Asia Minor. The details about the community that produced the gospel remain uncertain, and the conclusions drawn from the gospel itself are a matter of scholarly debate. For a recent summary of these debates see John Ashton, *Understanding the Fourth Gospel*, 2nd ed. (New York: Oxford University Press, 2009).
2. The convention in English translations of the Bible is to capitalize "word." This practice can function to alert the reader to treat "word" as a technical term. But it can also subtly reify the tendency to privilege "word" by making that logic

appear to be part of the term itself (by means of capitalization). For why would we capitalize "word" and not "flesh"? Wanting to problematize the practice, while foregrounding these terms as ones the text defines rather than assumes, I chose not to capitalize "word"—and to make explicit the practice as part of my interpretative exercise.

3. Marie Howe, *The Kingdom of Ordinary Time: Poems* (New York: W. W. Norton, 2008).
4. The Spanish translation of the gospel (Reina Valera) retains the Septuagint's use of "verb" rather than "word" to translate the Greek *Logos*.
5. Emily Dickinson, *Poems*, vol. 1 (Raleigh, NC: Hayes Barton Press, 1955), 1788.
6. The gospel's virulent rhetoric against "the Jews" is well known. I have no intention of defending it. I do not identify with the gospel's character position for the believers either. I am most interested in Adele Reinhartz's description of her own reading strategy—one that refuses to accept either of the positions that the gospel offers to its readers as insiders or outsiders, and instead reads the texts as an active engagement. Adele Reinhartz, *Befriending the Beloved Disciple: A Jewish Reading of the Gospel of John* (London: Bloomsbury Academic, 2002).
7. John 1:3–4; 1:14, translation modified.
8. Genesis 1:4.
9. Origen noted this confluence of traditions with delight. "Now, in the same way in which we have understood that Wisdom was the beginning of the ways of God, and is said to be created, forming beforehand and containing within herself the species and beginnings of all creatures, must we understand her to be the Word of God." Origen, "De Principis (On First Principles)," in *The Ante-Nicene Fathers, Volume IV* (Grand Rapids, MI: Wm. B. Eerdmans, 1951) 2.3, 1–2. On the relationship between the Gospel of John and Wisdom literature see Elizabeth Schussler-Fiorenza, *Jesus: Miriam's Child, Sophia's Prophet* (New York: Bloomsbury Academic, 1994); and Daniel Boyarin, "The Gospel of the Memra: Jewish Binitarianism and the Prologue to John," *Harvard Theological Review* 94, no. 3 (2001): 243–84.
10. Karmen MacKendrick, *Word Made Skin: Figuring Language at the Surface of Flesh* (New York: Fordham, 2004), 26.
11. John 3:6.
12. Athanasius, *De Incarnatione* 54.3, ed. Frank L. Cross (Eugene, OR: Wipf and Stock, 2010). "Autos gar enenthropesen hina hemeis theopoiethomen"; literally, "For he was humanized so that we might be divinized."
13. See for instance, the influential work of Raymond E. Brown, *The Gospel according to John*, vol. 29, *The Anchor Bible* (New York: Doubleday, 1966), 13.
14. John 6:1–14.
15. John 6:33, 6:35, 6:51.
16. Henry Staten, "How the Spirit (Almost) Became Flesh: Gospel of John," *Representations* 41 (Winter 1993): 43. The speech about bread (in John 6) contains the most references to life in the entire gospel.
17. John 6:51.

18. Staten, "How the Spirit (Almost) Became Flesh," 42.
19. John 6:53, 55–56, translation modified.
20. Dussel, "The Bread of the Eucharist: Celebration as a Sign of Justice in the Community" in Enrique Dussel, *Beyond Philosophy: Ethics, History, Marxism, and Liberation Theology* (Lantham, MD: Rowan and Littlefield, 2003), 41. My grandmother used to kiss any piece of bread before throwing it away—a gesture of gratitude that blurred the boundaries between common bread and the host.
21. John 12:24. Note the contrast with Paul's uses of the metaphor. In 1 Corinthians 15, the carnal body is the seed that dies and thus is transformed into the spiritual body. In Romans 7:5, "living in the flesh" "bears fruits of death."
22. Tat-siong Benny Liew, "The Word of Bare Life: Workings of Death and Dream in the Fourth Gospel," in *Anatomies of the Fourth Gospel: The Past, Present, and Futures of Narraitve Criticism*, ed. Tom Thatcher and Stephen Moore (Atlanta: SBL, 2008).
23. Liew, "Word of Bare Life."
24. Cf. Denise Kimber Buell, "Imagining Human Transformation in the Context of Invisible Powers: Instrumental Agency in Second-Century Treatments of Conversion," in *Metamorphoses: Resurrection, Body and Transformative Practices in Early Christianity*, ed. Turid Karlsen Seim and Jorunn Okland (Berlin: Walter de Gruyer, 2009).
25. John 6:63.
26. John 2:11.
27. Kahlil Gibran, *Jesus, the Son of Man*, Kahlil Gibran Pocket Library (New York: Alfred A. Knopf, 1995), 37. The etymological root of "wisdom" is *Sapientia*—which means both to have wisdom and to taste; it suggests an intimate, sensory, and participatory understanding of wisdom. Ángel Méndez-Montoya interprets tasting as an "intense form of touching" that involves also judging what is good, and implies the possibility of being affected, transformed, and even destroyed. Méndez-Montoya, *Theology of Food*, 62.
28. John 4:14.
29. John 7:38.
30. John 15:14. As in the case of the bread of life, the promises of abundance for those who abide are contrasted—perhaps predicated upon—the death of those who do not. "Whoever does not abide in me is thrown away like a branch and withers; such branches are gathered, thrown into the fire, and burned" (15:6).
31. John 14:20, 17:21, 17:23.
32. John 17:5.
33. John 17:23.
34. On the strategies the Gospel of John deploys for constructing its (imagined?) community, see Tat-siong Benny Liew, *What Is Asian American Biblical Hermeneutics? Reading the New Testament* (Honolulu: University of Hawai'i Press, 2008), 34–56.
35. I am grateful to Denise Buell who suggested that these and other New Testament images, including some words about spirit, could be characterized as "fleshy words" (personal conversation).

36. Stephen D. Moore, *Poststructuralism and the New Testament: Derrida and Foucault at the Foot of the Cross* (Minneapolis: Fortress Press, 1994), 58.

Chapter 2. Abandoning Flesh

1. The relationship is more complex than these dichotomies suggest. Biblical scholars continue to argue for the need to nuance the assumed dualisms in Paul. That there is a persistent need to challenge readings of Paul as establishing a dichotomy between flesh and spirit suggests, for me, the difficulties of avoiding such readings—certainly my own difficulties.
2. Scholars estimate that the Letter to the Romans was written between 55 and 58 C.E., and 1 Corinthians between 52 and 57 C.E.
3. The motif of the sowing and the seeds was common in Jewish and early Christian texts, where it had been used to explain the resurrection. According to Asher, "Besides Christian and rabbinic parallels, the metaphor of sowing or seeds was a common one in stoic anthropogeny and was used by them to describe the generation of terrestrial humans." Jeffrey R. Asher, *Polarity and Change in 1 Corinthians 15* (Tübingen: Mihn Siebeck, 2000), 137. According to Songe-Møller, however, the use of this metaphor in Greek thought emphasized the continuity between the seed and the offspring, whereas Paul's emphasis is on their differences. Vigdis Songe-Møller, "With What Kind of Body Will They Come? Metamorphosis and the Concept of Change: From Platonic Thinking to Paul's Notion of the Resurrection of the Dead," in *Metamorphoses: Resurrection, Body, and Transformative Practices in Early Christianity*, ed. Turid K. Seim and Jorunn Økland (Berlin: Walter de Gruyter, 2009), 116.
4. 1 Cor 15:37.
5. 1 Cor 15:38.
6. 1 Cor 15:40–41.
7. Dale B. Martin, *The Corinthian Body* (New Haven, CT: Yale University, 1995), 125. See also Troels Engberg-Pedersen, *Cosmology and the Self in the Apostle Paul: The Material Spirit* (Oxford: Oxford University Press, 2010); and Asher, *Polarity and Change in 1 Corinthians 15*. "We have here a classification of the types of bodies in the cosmos that incorporates two principles: the division of a genus (bodies) into two species (celestial bodies and terrestrial bodies) and the coordination or partition of predicates under a species (either celestial or terrestrial). . . . They are classified as coordinates by their location . . . and by their characteristics: composition (as in the terrestrial flesh) and radiance (as in the celestial *doxa*)." Asher, *Polarity and Change in 1 Corinthians 15*, 105.
8. According to Engberg-Pedersen, "it is a distinctly Stoic idea that 'heavenly' bodies are also 'pneumatic' ones." Engberg-Pedersen, *Cosmology and the Self*, 28. See also Asher, *Polarity and Change in 1 Corinthians 15*; and M. R. Wright, *Cosmology in Antiquity* (London: Routledge, 1995).
9. "What exactly Paul means by doxa is controversial. . . . It is likely that the expression refers to the radiance of all the created bodies in the cosmos because they are the products of God's creative power. Nevertheless, the two types of

doxa in v. 40b are clearly opposites." Asher, *Polarity and Change in 1 Corinthians 15*, 105n.38.

10. Note that in the Gospel of John, the death of the seed means that it will no longer be alone. See discussion in chapter 1.

11. 1Cor 15:46. This approach is not unique to Paul. As Benjamin Dunning observes, "Throughout the Roman Mediterranean, ancient thinkers from a variety of philosophical and religious persuasions gravitated to cosmogonic narratives such as Plato's *Timaeus* and the Book of Genesis as crucial hermeneutical sites for working out their understandings of the human subject. (Indeed Paul's appropriation of the figure of Adam for his own theological anthropology is symptomatic of this wide-ranging interest)." Benjamin H. Dunning, *Specters of Paul: Sexual Difference in Early Christian Thought* (Philadelphia: University of Pennsylvania Press, 2011), 19.

12. The contemporary meaning of the English word "physical" does not exactly correspond to the ancient Greek terms of these interpretations, as we shall see.

13. Philo, cited by Dunning, *Specters of Paul*, 21.

14. Philo, cited by Dunning, *Specters of Paul*, 21.

15. For other ancient readings of the original androgyny in comparison with Paul see, for instance, Karen King, *The Gospel of Mary of Magdala: Jesus and the First Woman Apostle* (Santa Rosa, CA: Polebridge Press, 2003), 119–27.

16. See Dunning's discussion of the implications of Paul's interpretation of Christ through Adam for tensions about the status of gender in later Christian thought. Dunning, *Specters of Paul*.

17. 1Cor 15:47.

18. 1Cor 15:48.

19. 1Cor 15:50–52.

20. See, for instance, Engberg-Pedersen, *Cosmology and the Self*; and Martin, *Corinthian Body*.

21. Martin, *Corinthian Body*, 129. Asher disagrees with Martin's description, arguing that it is impossible to determine whether Paul meant to assert that flesh and blood would be shed off or transformed. Asher, *Polarity and Change in 1 Corinthians 15*, 156n.20. For Both Asher and Engberg-Pedersen, these texts reflect Stoic understandings of change transformation.

22. Engberg-Pedersen, *Cosmology and the Self*, 34. See also Asher, *Polarity and Change in 1 Corinthians 15*, chapter 5, "The Metaphysics of Change."

23. Thomas J. J. Altizer, "Paul and the Birth of Self-Consciousness," *Journal of the American Academy of Religion* 51, no. 3 (1983): 370.

24. Engberg-Pedersen, *Cosmology and the Self*, 104.

25. Analyzing statements in 1 Corinthians 2 and 3, in addition to Romans 7–8, Engberg-Pedersen argues, "there is at least one powerful line of thought in Paul that places the human body (soma)—together with its soul—squarely on the side of sarx." *Cosmology and the Self*, 104.

26. Rom 6:6.

27. Rom 6:12.

28. For a discussion of slavery in early Christianity and the use of its rhetoric in the Pauline letters, see Jennifer A. Glancy, *Slavery in Early Christianity* (Minneapolis: Fortress Press, 2006); and Dale B. Martin, *Slavery as Salvation: The Metaphor of Slavery in Pauline Christianity* (New Haven, CT: Yale University, 1990).
29. Rom 7.
30. Daniel Boyarin, *A Radical Jew: Paul and the Politics of Identity* (Berkeley: University of California Press, 1994), 69.
31. Rom 7:5, 7:6.
32. This discussion should be read in conjunction with Romans 5:12–14 as part of the broader argument about the status of those who had the law versus the gentiles. That argument is beyond the scope of this chapter.
33. Rom 7:7.
34. Boyarin observes that the verse of the Decalogue cited in the commandment "is the only negative commandment in the whole Torah that refers to desire and not to an action." But his interpretation focuses on the tension between the commandments to procreate and against desire, to suggest that it is the former that produces sin by provoking the violation of the latter. Boyarin, *A Radical Jew*, 163.
35. As Wasserman observes, "The example of the tenth commandment works well here because the LXX's ouk epithumeseis can easily be exploited as a command about epithumia (desire)." Emma Wasserman, *The Death of the Soul in Romans 7: Sin, Death, and the Law in Light of Hellenistic Moral Psychology* (Tübingen, Germany: Mohr Siebeck, 2008), 105.
36. Wasserman points to parallels between this relation between the law and sin in Greek sources. "Plato, Polybius, and Seneca claim that in extreme cases of immorality positive interventions such as law and punishments can inflame or incite further acts of wickedness and immorality." Wasserman, *Death of the Soul in Romans 7*, 105.
37. Rom 7:14.
38. Rom 7:23.
39. Rom 7:25, translation modified. For an illuminating analysis of an ancient view of human agency as "instrumental" to spiritual forces rather than autonomous, see Buell, "Imagining Human Transformation in the Context of Invisible Powers: Instrumental Agency in Second-Century Treatments of Conversion."
40. Given that "nothing good *dwells* in me" is explicitly said to mean "in the flesh," the following statement, "the law of sin that *dwells* in my members," can be assumed to be referring also to the flesh.
41. Augustine, *The Confessions*, trans. Philip Burton (New York: Alfred A. Knopf, 2001), 7.21.27.
42. For a delightful exploration of the incitements of Augustine's *Confessions*, see Virginia Burrus, Mark D. Jordan, and Karmen MacKendrick, *Seducing Augustine: Bodies, Desires, Confessions* (New York: Fordham University Press, 2010).
43. See chapter 4, pp. 61–62.
44. Stanley K. Stowers, *A Reading of Romans: Justice, Jews, and Gentiles* (New Haven, CT: Yale University Press, 1994); Wasserman, *Death of the Soul in Romans 7*.

45. The idea that sin is lodged in the flesh has lasted well beyond Paul. Although Augustine sometimes affirms flesh as part of God's creation, he often figures it as holding or carrying sin. In such cases, flesh is sometimes the corruptible and perishable element of the body. At other times, flesh is "a moral category" used to refer to "all kinds of sin, whether bodily or psychic." Andrea Nightingale, *Once out of Nature: Augustine on Time and the Body* (Chicago: University of Chicago Press, 2011), 213–14. Martin Luther sees sexual desire as natural and unavoidable and declares of bodies that God "wills to have his excellent handiwork honored as his divine creation, and not despised." Martin Luther, "The Estate of Marriage," in *Luther's Works: The Christian in Society*, ed. Walter I. Brandt (Philadelphia: Muhlenberg Press, 1962), 17. At the same time, the flesh works constantly against the spirit in its desires and lust, diverting people from righteousness. This becomes especially clear in Luther's exegesis of Paul, for instance, in "An Argument in the Defense of All the Articles of Dr. Martin Luther Wrongly Condemned in the Roman Bull," trans. C. M. Jacobs, in *Works of Martin Luther* (Grand Rapids, MI: Baker Book House, 1982), 25–29. Some contemporary works maintain a similar notion of flesh as fallen and inhabited by sin. See, for example, Thomas Weinandy, *In the Likeness of Sinful Flesh: An Essay on the Humanity of Christ* (Edinburgh: T and T Clark, 1993). Parts 2 and 3 of this book trace other such hauntings.
46. Rom 8:5–8.
47. Rom 8:9.
48. Rom 8:9–10.
49. The implications of envisioning the "body of Christ" as a spiritual body still spark controversy. For instance, in an entry to a blog posted in 2009, a writer criticizes Dr. Michael Horton's use of "the body of Christ." "He draws the distinction between *sarx* and *soma* in order to try to acknowledge that in some sense we are the 'body of Christ' while denying that we are the hands and feet of Christ. Soma, for Horton, is without sarx; soma is purely spiritual. But this raises serious theological problems." Bryan Cross, "Horton on Being Made 'One Flesh with Christ,'" *Called to Communion* (blog), September 27, 2009, http://www.calledtocommunion.com/2009/09/horton-on-being-made-one-flesh-with-christ.
50. Martin, *Corinthian Body*, 38–47. John K. McVay, "The Human Body as Social and Political Metaphor in Stoic Literature and Early Christian Writers," *Bulletin of the American Society of Papyrologists* 37, no. 1–4 (2000): 135–47. Stoics' conception of the collective body also assumed an ontological unity.
51. 1Cor 6:13.
52. 1Cor 6:15a.
53. 1Cor 6:16a.
54. 1Cor 6:15b.
55. Genesis 2:24.
56. 1Cor 6:17, translation modified.
57. Denise Kimber Buell, "Hauntology Meets Posthumanism: Some Payoffs for Biblical Studies," in *The Bible and Posthumanism*, ed. Jennifer L. Koosed (Atlanta: Society of Biblical Literature, 2014), 36.

58. Martin, *Corinthian Body*, 169.
59. Laura Nasrallah, *An Ecstasy of Folly: Prophecy and Authority in Early Christianity* (Cambridge, MA: Harvard Theological Studies, 2003), 80–81.
60. Nasrallah further argues that the image of the body, readily available to be deployed to assert the "hierarchy, ordering, and boundaries" in the church, the household, and the state, is used in 1 Corinthians to control practices related to spiritual gifts. Nasrallah, *An Ecstasy of Folly*, 61–94.
61. 1Cor 12:12–13.
62. Gal 3:26–29.
63. Boyarin, *Carnal Israel*, 31–60. Elizabeth Castelli, *Martyrdom and Memory: Early Christian Culture Making* (New York: Columbia University Press, 2004), 62–63. Elizabeth Schüssler Fiorenza summarizes key scholarly debates about Paul's position and concludes that scholars often argue that "Paul advocates that slave wo/men should become free and be treated as 'beloved.'" However, "the texts are so ambiguous that equally as many scholars argue that Paul insists they remain in slavery." Elisabeth Schussler Fiorenza, "Slave Wo/Men and Freedom: Some Methodological Reflections," in *Postcolonial Interventions*, ed. Tat-Siong Benny Liew (Sheffield, UK: Sheffield Phoenix Press, 2009), 127.
64. Boyarin, *Radical Jew*, 7.
65. Boyarin, *Radical Jew*, 7.
66. Tertullian, *On the Resurrection*, trans. Ernest Evans (London: SPCK, 1960), 5.25.
67. Augustine, "Tractatus adversus Judæos," vii, 9. Cited in Boyarin, *Carnal Israel*, 1.
68. For examples of this in Christian writings see Daniel Boyarin, *Unheroic Conduct: The Rise of Heterosexuality and the Invention of the Jewish Man* (Berkeley: University of California, 1997), 209–19.
69. Caroline E. Johnson Hodge, *If Sons, Then Heirs: A Study of Kinship and Ethnicity in the Letters of Paul* (Oxford: Oxford University Press, 2007), 116.
70. As Karen King explains (in response to an earlier version of Boyarin's argument), in addition to the myth of the prima androgyne, there is a second one that is also formative for notions of gender in Western cultures—"a myth in which there is only one gender, the male, females being deformed or degenerative males.... The male is the truly human and sex is degradation, even if duty should demand it for the sake of procreation.... These two myths of gender androgyne and of andro-gender ... seldom appear completely separate from each other." Karen King, "Response," in *Galatians and Gender Trouble: Primal Androgyny and the First-Century Origins of a Feminist Dilemma*, ed. Christopher Ocker (Berkeley: Center for Hermeneutical Studies, 1992).
71. Paul's universalism is specifically addressed in Alain Badiou, *Saint Paul: The Foundation of Universalism*, trans. Ray Brassier, Cultural Memory in the Present (Stanford, CA: Stanford University Press, 2003). Žižek takes up Badiou on Paul in Slavoj Žižek, *The Ticklish Subject: The Absent Centre of Political Ontology* (London: Verso, 1999), 127–70.
72. These tendencies affect debates about the status of ethnic/racial identities, but also those of sexual difference. For a discussion of the repercussions of the

tensions emerging from Paul's letters in later Christian thought about sexuality, see Dunning, *Specters of Paul*.

73. A theological controversy in 1521 illustrates the perennial discussion of the relationship between sin and flesh. Phillip Melanchton reads "flesh" as including the whole human nature, accentuating that the best in humanity was still "according to the flesh." He contrasts this view with Duns Scotus's description: "The 'tinder' is an inordinate quality of the flesh that inclines the sensitive appetite to an act which in relation to the judgment of reason is deforming and defective." Duns Scotus, In sent., lib II, d. 29.4; Philip Melanchthon, "Loci Communes Theologici," in *The Library of Christian Classics vol. 19: Melanchthon and Bucer*, ed. Wilhelm Pauck (Philadelphia: Westminster, 1969), 37.

Chapter 3. Embracing Flesh

1. Tertullian describes *On the Flesh of Christ* (*Carn. Chr.*) as a "preparatory volume" for his argument in *On the Resurrection* (*Res.*), where he proves the "substantiality" of flesh "as opposed to the emptiness of a phantasm, and vindicate[s] its humanity" (*Res.* 2.18–19). Translations are Ernest Evans's, unless noted otherwise. Tertullian, *De Carne Christi Liber (On the Flesh of Christ)*, ed. Ernest Evans (London: SPCK, 1956).

2. Irenaeus, "Against Heresies," in *Ante-Nicene Fathers Volume I*, ed. Alexander Roberts, D.D. and James Donaldson, LL.D. (Peabody, MA: Hendrickson Publishers, 1994), 5.3. Henceforth *AH*.

3. I am focusing here on the doctrinal writings, rather than on the works on Christian practices, such as *On Baptism* and *The Apparel of Women*. Some scholars draw a clear distinction between the two types of work. For instance, arguing that the instructions follow Paul more closely and tends to be less consistent and more dualistic, Jean-Claude Fredouille observes, "Mais si l'exposé de son anthropologie morale s'en ressent et paraît parfois dualité, son ontologie est foncièrement unitaire. Et c'est en fonction de celle-ci qu'il convient d'interpréter la première." Jean-Claude Fredouille, "Observations sur la terminologie anthropologique de Tertullien: Constantes et variations," in *Les pères de l'église face à la science médicale de leur temps*, ed. Véronique Boudon-Millot and Bernard Pouderon (Paris: Beauchesne Éditeur, 2005). Others argue that the texts on Christian practice reveal the intentions of Tertullian's ontology. See, for instance, Carly Daniel-Hughes, *The Salvation of the Flesh in Tertullian of Cathage: Dressing for Resurrection* (New York: Palgrave Macmillan, 2011). I do not pursue this question directly. My aim is rather to foreground the potentialities of flesh beyond (perhaps even in spite of) Tertullian, while noting the points of tension and foreclosure.

4. Dunning, *Specters of Paul*, 98.

5. Laurel Schneider argues that Tertullian's Carthaginian background, one shaped by diverse cultures and practices, influences his attempts to tempter Hellenistic skepticism toward emotional practices. Schneider, *Beyond Monotheism*.

6. Elizabeth Schussler-Fiorenza, *In Memory of Her: A Feminist Theological Reconstruction of Christian Origins* (New York: Crossroad, 1994). The charge of

misogyny is not uncontested. Tertullian's apparent approval of female prophecy raises some questions. Karen King points to the tensions in the reception of Tertullian's corpus: "Although Tertullian linked sexual differentiation inseparably to a system of hierarchical patriarchal gender roles that contemporary feminism rejects, his theology placed a high value on the body and gave marriage and childbearing positive signification, as some forms of feminism would like to do." For a summary of the debates about this point, see Dunning, *Specters of Paul*, 124–27. I treat the role that Foucault assigns Tertullian in the development of modern disciplinary practices in chapter 5.

7. *Carn. Chr.* 1.9.
8. Virginia Burrus, "An Embarrassment of the Flesh," in *Saving Shame: Martyrs, Saints, and Other Abject Subjects* (Philadelphia: University of Pennsylvania Press, 2008), 45. Burrus's analysis of the dynamics of shame, in addition to her reading of Tertullian, deeply informs my reading of Tertullian and has shaped my sensibility to the affective elements of "flesh." Burrus analyzes the representations of flesh in other Jewish and Christian sources in late antiquity in "Carnal Excess: Flesh at the Limits of Imagination," *Journal of Early Christian Studies* 17, no. 2 (Summer 2009): 247–65.
9. "Marcion was apprehensive that a belief of a fleshly body would also involve a belief of birth," Tertullian explains. Tertullian, *Adversus Marcion (Against Marcion)*, trans. Ernest Evans (Oxford, UK: Clarendon Press, 1972), 3.6.2–3.
10. These attitudes were widespread in Tertullian's context. Cf. Jennifer A. Glancy, *Corporeal Knowledge: Early Christian Bodies* (Oxford: Oxford University Press, 2010), 120–24.
11. Tertullian, *Carn. Chr.* 4.3–7. Tertullian makes a similar argument in *Against Marcion*, clearly attributing this view to his opponents. "Come then, wind up your cavils against the most sacred and reverend works of nature; inveigh against all that you are; destroy the origin of flesh and life; call the womb a sewer of the illustrious animal—in other words, the manufactory for the production of man; dilate on the impure and shameful tortures of parturition, and then of the filthy, troublesome, contemptible issues of the puerperal labour itself! But yet, after you have pulled all these things down to infamy, that you may affirm them to be unworthy of God, birth will not be worse for Him than death, infancy than the cross, punishment than nature, condemnation than the flesh." *Marc.* 11.6.
12. Burrus, "Embarrassment of the Flesh," 53. Judith Perkins similarly observes that "Tertullian acknowledges the repulsion that maternal birth processes would evoke; indeed, he uses this common reaction to dispute the legitimacy of Marcion's Christ." Judith Perkins, "The Rhetoric of the Maternal Body in the Passion of Perpetua," in *Mapping Gender in Ancient Religious Discourses*, ed. Todd C. Penner and Caroline Vander Stichele (Leiden: Brill, 2007), 318.
13. *Carn. Chr.* 4.13–14.
14. *Carn. Chr.* 4.22–23.
15. Glancy, *Corporeal Knowledge*, 85. "Tertullian arouses a strange passion in his modern-day readers," Laura Nasrallah observes. Nasrallah, *Ecstasy of Folly*, 100.

16. Daniel-Hughes, *Salvation of the Flesh*.
17. *AH* 3.18.7.
18. *Carn. Chr.* 17.22–24. The biblical reference is to 1 Corinthians 15:45.
19. Elsewhere Tertullian notes, "But remember that 'man' is properly called flesh" (*Res.* 5.34–35, translation modified).
20. *Res.* 6.7–8.
21. *Res.* 6.8–12.
22. *Res.* 7.4–5; 7.25–26.
23. *Res.* 7.13–14.
24. The references are to Romans 9:20 and 2 Corinthians 4:7. "Si nouvelle et différente soit la chair, elle conserve cependant la mémoire de son origine. En elle, la terre n'est pas détruite mais transformée; son souvenir n'est pas effacé. Une parenté, sinon la continuité d'un genus, l'unit fortement à la terre, décelable jusque dans les traits de sa nature." Jérôme Alexandre, *Une chair pour la gloire: L'anthropologie réaliste et mystique ee Tertullien* (Paris: Beauchesne Éditeur, 2001), 212.
25. *Carn. Chr.* 21.34–35.
26. According to Alexandre and Braun, flesh precedes the body in the order of creation, so that body can be considered secondary, or "accidental," in the Aristotelian sense of the term. Alexandre, *Chair pour la gloire*, 205. René Braun, "Sacralité et sainteté chez Tertullien." *Bulletin de l'Association Guillaume Budé: Lettres d'humanité* 48 (December 1989): 339–44.
27. *Carn. Chr.* 9.
28. *Carn. Chr.* 6.34–35.
29. *Res.* 7.50–51.
30. *Carn. Chr.* 5.
31. "L'imperfection du corps est moins présentée comme la conséquence dramatique du péché que comme la condition de la nature humaine. . . . Nous savons que la conception stoïcienne de l'harmonie des composantes bonnes et mauvaises de la nature atténue, chez Tertullien, la conception chrétienne des conséquences de la première faute dans l'histoire particulière du genre humaine." Alexandre, *Chair pour la gloire*, 206.
32. For instance, "Then let the flesh begin to give you pleasure [*placere*]" (*Res.* 5.18–19, translation modified). "I may but vindicate for the flesh as much as he conferred upon it who made it even then with cause for pride" (*Res.* 6.1–2).
33. Tertullian clarifies that flesh and blood are *not* corruption; they are simply subject to corruption, that is, to death. So Paul's statement that corruption will not inherit incorruption just means that death will not survive (*Res.* 51.33–46).
34. *Res.* 12.1–8.
35. *Res.* 12.21.
36. Burrus, "Embarrassment of the Flesh," 56–57.
37. This very logic elsewhere places woman, created from Adam, at a lower position, but in the doctrinal works, Tertullian focuses on the creation of man from dust. "Certainly there is a witness of this principle from the beginning itself, when the male was formed earlier, for Adam was first, and the female was

formed some considerable time later, for Eve came after" (Aristotle, *De anima*, trans. D. W. Hamlyn, Clarendon Aristotle Series [Oxford: Oxford University Press, 1993], 36.3). And given that the argument is that creation by God's hands warrants resurrection and resurrection does include women, in this interpretation Tertullian would need to make the claim of creation apply to both.

38. *Carn. Chr.* 15.14–15.
39. Alexandre, *Chair pour la gloire*, 201. Jean-Claude Fredouille similarly argues, "Entre *caro* et *corpus*, la distinction que fait Tertullien est généralment conforme à l'usage, *corpus* ayant une extension sémantique plus large que *caro*." Fredouille, "Observations sur la terminologie anthropologique de Tertullien," 324.
40. *Carn. Chr.* 8.31, translation modified.
41. *Res.* 48.33.
42. *Res.* 48.5–30.
43. *Res.* 50.10.
44. *Res.* 51.4–5.
45. *Res.* 51.15–16.
46. Tertullian makes significant use of scientific sources, but not always consistently. Glancy comments that, "Tertullian's tolerance for scientific inconsistency is compatible with the paradoxes that characterize his theology and the contrary statements that inflect his rhetoric" Glancy, *Corporeal Knowledge*, 119.
47. See the discussion of Paul's argument in chapter 2.
48. *Res.* 53.38–45. Thus flesh "must be understood . . . to be that which is both sown a soul-informed body and the spiritual body when it is raised."
49. Tertullian does not adhere to this view consistently. In *De anima* he claims that the male seed produces both the flesh and the soul. See Nasrallah, *Ecstasy of Folly*, 122–24.
50. *Carn. Chr.* 15.1–3.
51. *Carn. Chr.* 5. 12–14.
52. *Carn. Chr.* 5.17.
53. *Carn. Chr.* 5.38–40.
54. Dunning argues that the opposition in Tertullian's thought is based on the assumed penetrability of female flesh. Dunning, *Specters of Paul*, 124–50.
55. For instance, much later, Anselm argues, "it is more consistent to call the supreme Spirit father than mother, for this reason, that the first and principal cause of offspring is always in the father. For . . . it is exceedingly inconsistent that the name mother should be attached to that parent with which, for the generation of offspring, no other cause is associated, and which no other precedes" (Anselm, "Monologium," in *Proslogium; Monologium; An Appendix in Behalf of the Fool by Gaunilon; and Cur Deus Homo*, trans. Sidney Norton Deane [La Salle, IL: Open Court, 1951], LXII).
56. "It is not enough that Christian modesty seems to be true; it must be seen to be true." Daniel-Hughes, *Salvation of the Flesh*, 99.
57. Kay Ryan, "Green behind the Ears," *The Best of It: New and Selected Poems* (New York: Grove Press, 2010), 261.

Part II: The Philosophers' (Christian) Flesh

1. Maurice Merleau-Ponty, "In Praise of Philosophy," in *In Praise of Philosophy*, trans. John Wild and James M. Edie (Evanston, IL: Northwestern University Press, 1963).
2. Merleau-Ponty, "In Praise of Philosophy," 46.

Chapter 4. Incarnate Philosophy

1. Rubem Alves, *I Believe in the Resurrection of the Body* (Eugene, OR: Wipf and Stock, 1986).
2. Gilles Labelle identifies three stages in Merleau-Ponty's engagement with Christianity. In the first one, Merleau-Ponty locates himself within Christianity; the second comprises his critique of Christianity and his self-identification as an atheist. In the third stage, Labelle argues, Merleau-Ponty defines the relationship between philosophy and theology as one of endless critique. This framing is helpful to identify differences in styles throughout, but one should not overemphasize this, as Merleau-Ponty's critique of Christian thought is implicitly also a reworking of its meaning and thus of his relationship with it. Gilles Labelle, "Merleau-Ponty et le Christianisme," *Laval théologique et philosophique* 58, no. 2 (2002): 317–40.
3. Maurice Merleau-Ponty, "The Philosophy of Existence," trans. Allen S. Weiss, in *Texts and Dialogues: On Philosophy, Politics, and Culture*, ed. Hugh J. Silverman and James Barry (Amherst, NY: Humanity Books, 1992), 132. He refers to the "philosophy of existence," influenced by Husserl, Karl Jaspers, Heidegger, and Marcel, rather than "existentialism," which at the time of his lecture was associated with philosophies developed after the Second World War, particularly by Jean Paul Sartre. Merleau-Ponty, "Philosophy of Existence," 132.
4. Merleau-Ponty, "Philosophy of Existence," 132. Merleau-Ponty attributed this idea to Husserl. Derrida has challenged Merleau-Ponty's translation of Husserl's *leibhaftig* as flesh. Cf. Jacques Derrida, *On Touching—Jean-Luc Nancy*, trans. Christine Irizarry (Stanford, CA: Stanford University Press, 2005), 188ff.
5. Merleau-Ponty, "Philosophy of Existence," 133.
6. "Il n'est pas le spectateur du problème, il est pris dans l'affaire et c'est lá pour lui ce qui définit le mystère." Merleau-Ponty, "La philosophie de l'existence," *Dialogue* 5, no. 3 (1966), 313.
7. "I consider this sensible knowledge of the world completely paradoxical, in the sense that it always appears to me as already complete at the very instant that I pay attention to it. When I reflect, when I pay attention, my interior gaze bears upon my perception of things. This perception is already there." Merleau-Ponty, "Philosophy of Existence," 133.
8. Merleau-Ponty, "Philosophy of Existence," 136.
9. Maurice Merleau-Ponty, "Faith and Good Faith," in *Sense and Non-Sense* (Evanston, IL: Northwestern University Press, 1964). The essay was originally published in 1946 in *Les Temps Modernes*. Merleau-Ponty had previously argued that the devaluation of works in the Lutheran theology of justification by faith fostered a preoccupation with the relation between "each soul and its God," and

thus a turn toward the self. "From there," Merleau-Ponty explains, "one is easily led to abandon love of one's neighbor and to invest the moral functioning of society with 'authority.'" "There is perhaps not a necessary sequence here," he concedes, but the abandonment of responsibility toward society appears to be a historical fact. Merleau-Ponty, "Christianity and *Ressentiment*," in *Texts and Dialogues: On Philosophy, Politics, and Culture*, ed. Hugh Silverman and James Barry, trans. Michael B. Smith et al. (Amherst, NY: Humanity Books, 1992), 95.

10. Merleau-Ponty, "Faith and Good Faith," 173.
11. Merleau-Ponty, "Faith and Good Faith," 173.
12. Luther's reliance on Augustine's writings about the "inner man" explains why Merleau-Ponty would target both theologians in his critiques.
13. Augustine's inner man, like Paul's, is not divine. Even though Augustine is suspicious of the senses and sees the way toward God as requiring a gradual turn inward, this inner space is not identified as God. For a description of the Augustinian self in contrast to the Platonic and modern versions, see Phillip Cary, *Augustine's Invention of the Inner Self: The Legacy of a Christian Platonist* (Oxford: Oxford University Press, 2000). On the relationship between Augustine's and Descartes's self, see Stephen Philip Menn, *Descartes and Augustine* (Cambridge: Cambridge University Press, 1998).
14. Whether one claims that God dwells in the person or that the person turns inward and up to receive a revelation of God's will, the assumption is still that a person gains access to truth by turning to his isolated interiority.
15. Merleau-Ponty, "Faith and Good Faith," 174. My emphasis. I will return to these two theological ideas—the image of God and the "spiritual senses"—in the next chapter.
16. Merleau-Ponty, "Faith and Good Faith," 177. Italics in the original.
17. Merleau-Ponty, "Faith and Good Faith," 174.
18. Merleau-Ponty's description of the process follows Hegel's: this event marks a transition from the reign of the father, through the incarnation, to the reign of the spirit. "The meaning of the Pentecost is that the religion of the Father and the Son are fulfilled in the religion of the Spirit." From the outset, I note the supersessionist tone of this schema. In his later works, Merleau-Ponty would no longer adopt the logic of temporal progress implicit in this description.
19. Merleau-Ponty, "Faith and Good Faith," 177.
20. Merleau-Ponty, "Faith and Good Faith," 175. Merleau-Ponty consistently represents the soul as obscurity. "The human soul can signal God's place at the origin of the world, but it can neither see nor understand Him and cannot therefore be centered in Him." Merleau-Ponty, "Faith and Good Faith," 175.
21. Merleau-Ponty, "Faith and Good Faith," 175.
22. For a detailed exploration of the relationship between language and perception, see Richard Kearney, "Ecrire la chair: L'expression diacritique chez Merleau-Ponty," *Chiasmi International* (2013): 183–96.
23. Merleau-Ponty, "Faith and Good Faith," 179.
24. Merleau-Ponty, "Faith and Good Faith," 179.

25. Merleau-Ponty argues that the criticism of false gods, which philosophy presses to the limit, is Christianity's essence. The task never ends, for "where will one stop the criticism of idols, and where will one ever be able to say the true God actually resides?" Merleau-Ponty, "In Praise of Philosophy," 47.
26. Merleau-Ponty, "Faith and Good Faith," 177.
27. Merleau-Ponty, "Faith and Good Faith," 178.
28. Emmanuel de Saint Aubert, "'L'incarnation change tout': Merleau-Ponty critique de la 'théologie explicative,'" *Archives de Philosophie* 71, no. 3 (2008): 376. My translation.
29. "Analytical reflection believes that it can trace back the course followed by a prior constituting act and arrive, by the 'inner man'—to use Saint Augustine's expression—at a constituting power which has always been identical with that inner self." Maurice Merleau-Ponty, *Phenomenology of Perception* (New York: Routledge, 1962), xi.
30. Merleau-Ponty, *Phenomenology of Perception*, 171. I return to the "tie" in my discussion of Judith Butler.
31. Neurologists Henry Head and Gordon Morgan Holmes first described the concept in 1911.
32. This condition challenges any explanation that assumes cognition as the source of corporeal coherence, because it cannot be explained as a problem with the person's *knowledge* of the new boundaries of her body. Instead, Merleau-Ponty points toward interpretations of this phenomenon as a problem of the corporeal schema. For an assessment of Merleau-Ponty's argument for a distinction between cognitive and motor intentional activity in light of contemporary neuroscience, see Sean Dorrance Kelly, "Merleau-Ponty on the Body," *Ratio* 15 (2002): 376–91.
33. Merleau-Ponty, *Phenomenology of Perception*, 164.
34. José Carlos Santiago explains that a new time-clock system is installed at the manufacturing facility that identifies employees by their fingerprints. As he works on the setup of the system, registering employees' fingerprints, he realizes that their daily work has virtually erased their fingerprints. Others have lost part of their fingertips in occupational accidents. Personal communication.
35. Merleau-Ponty, *Phenomenology of Perception*, 166. Italics mine.
36. Merleau-Ponty capitalizes on the double meaning of *sens* (sense)—as the capacity to *perceive* something as well as the *meaning* of a concept.
37. Maurice Merleau-Ponty, "The Child's Relations with Others," in *The Primacy of Perception: And Other Essays on Phenomenological Psychology, the Philosophy of Art, History and Politics*, ed. James M. Edie (Evanston, IL: Northwestern University Press, 1964), 117.
38. Merleau-Ponty, "Child's Relations with Others," 119.
39. "If my body is to appropriate the conducts given to me visually and make them its own, it must itself be given to me not as a mass of utterly private sensations but instead by what has been called a 'postural,' or 'corporeal schema.'" Merleau-

Ponty, "Child's Relations with Others," 117. This essay was part of Merleau-Ponty's *Cours de Sorbonne*, 1950–51.
40. Merleau-Ponty, "Child's Relations with Others," 118. Italics mine. Merleau-Ponty is here adopting Henri Wallon's language. Merleau-Ponty explains, "If we are dealing with a schema, or a system, such a system would be relatively transferable from one sensory domain to the other in the case of my own body, just as it could be transferred to the domain of the other." Merleau-Ponty, "Child's Relations with Others," 118.
41. Merleau-Ponty, "Child's Relations with Others," 119.
42. Merleau-Ponty, "Child's Relations with Others," 119.
43. Merleau-Ponty, "Child's Relations with Others," 136, 38.
44. Merleau-Ponty, "Child's Relations with Others," 136. My emphasis.
45. Merleau-Ponty, "Child's Relations with Others," 136.
46. Merleau-Ponty, "Child's Relations with Others," 136.
47. Merleau-Ponty, "Philosopher and His Shadow," *Signs*, trans. Richard C. McCleary (Evanston, IL: Northwestern University Press, 1964), 159. Merleau-Ponty is here affirmatively commenting on Husserl's work.
48. Merleau-Ponty, *Phenomenology of Perception*, 121n17. Italics mine. See also "The Battle over Existentialism," in *Sense and Non-Sense* (Evanston, IL: Northwestern University Press, 1964).
49. Merleau-Ponty, "Child's Relations with Others," 120.
50. Merleau-Ponty, *Phenomenology of Perception*, 44, 143, 92. Emmanuel Saint-Aubert argues that, in his earlier works, Merleau-Ponty's use of flesh was a negative term, as it was for Sartre, a sign of alienation. Emmanuel de Saint Aubert, *Du lien des êtres aux éléments de l'être: Merleau-Ponty au tournant des années 1945–1951* (Paris: Vrin, 2004).
51. Merleau-Ponty, "Philosopher and His Shadow," *Signs*, trans. Richard C. McCleary (Evanston, IL: Northwestern University Press, 1964), 175.
52. Maurice Merleau-Ponty, *The Visible and the Invisible*, trans. Alphonso Lingis (Evanston, IL: Northwestern University Press, 1968), 127.
53. Merleau-Ponty, *Visible and the Invisible*, 130.
54. Merleau-Ponty, *Visible and the Invisible*, 179.
55. Merleau-Ponty, *Visible and the Invisible*, 113.
56. Maurice Merleau-Ponty, *Signs*, trans. Richard C. McCleary (Evanston, IL: Northwestern University Press, 1964), 15.
57. "When we say that the perceived thing is grasped . . . 'in the flesh' this is to be taken literally," Merleau-Ponty argues elsewhere. Merleau-Ponty, "Philosopher and His Shadow," 167.
58. Karen Barad notes that classical physics explains touch in terms of repulsion between electrical charges—thus revealing proximity between things, but never continuity. A new picture emerges from quantum field theory, however, where particles touch alterity, even as they touch themselves. Cf. Karen Barad, "On Touching: The Inhuman That Therefore I Am," *Differences* 25, no. 3 (2012): 206–23.

59. Merleau-Ponty, *Visible and the Invisible*, 137–38.
60. Merleau-Ponty, *Visible and the Invisible*, 134.
61. Merleau-Ponty, *Visible and the Invisible*, 134. Vision is "participation in and kinship with the visible" (138).
62. Merleau-Ponty, *Visible and the Invisible*, 138.
63. Merleau-Ponty, *Visible and the Invisible*, 134.
64. Merleau-Ponty, *Visible and the Invisible*, 146.
65. Merleau-Ponty, *Visible and the Invisible*, 131.
66. Merleau-Ponty, *Visible and the Invisible*, 135.
67. Merleau-Ponty, *Visible and the Invisible*, 133.
68. Merleau-Ponty, *Visible and the Invisible*, 146.
69. Merleau-Ponty, *Signs*, 139.
70. Merleau-Ponty, "In Praise of Philosophy," 176.
71. de Saint Aubert, "'L'incarnation change tout,'" 398.
72. Merleau-Ponty, *Visible and the Invisible*.
73. Merleau-Ponty, *Visible and the Invisible*, 139. For the influence of Gaston Bachelard on Merleau-Ponty's interpretation of the elements, see de Saint Aubert, *Du lien des êtres aux éléments de l'être*. Italics mine.
74. de Saint Aubert comments that around 1957 Merleau-Ponty showed interest in the pre-Socratic elements, but never offered a precise source on the subject. *Du lien des êtres aux éléments de l'être*, 257.
75. Elizabeth Grosz, "Irigaray and the Divine," in *Transfigurations: Theology and French Feminism*, ed. C. W. Maggie Kim, Susan M. St. Ville, and Susan M. Simonatis (Eugene, OR: Wipf and Stock, 2002), 205.
76. Aristotle, *De anima*, trans. D. W. Hamlyn, Claredon Aristotle Series (Oxford: Oxford University Press, 1993), II.423b.17ff. The "sense-organ" is for him internal, not the site of touch.
77. Merleau-Ponty, "Bergson in the Making," in *Signs*, trans. Richard C. McCleary (Evanston, IL: Northwestern University Press, 1964), 190.
78. Merleau-Ponty, "Bergson in the Making," 190.
79. de Saint Aubert, "'L'incarnation change tout,'" 397.
80. Gaston Bachelard, *Earth and the Reveries of Will: An Essay on the Imagination of Matter*, trans. Kenneth Haltman (Dallas: Dallas Institute of Publications, 2002), 3. My emphasis.
81. Merleau-Ponty, *Visible and the Invisible*, 267. Notes on "*L'imaginaire*."
82. Gale Johnson argues that Merleau-Ponty points indirectly to the elements in "Eye and Mind." Gale A. Johnson, "Desire and Invisibility in 'Eye and Mind': Some Remarks on Merleau-Ponty's Spirituality," in *Merleau-Ponty in Contemporary Perspectives*, ed. Patrick Burke and Jan Van der Veken (Dordrecht, the Netherlands: Kluwer Academic Publishers, 1993).
83. Merleau-Ponty, *Visible and the Invisible*, 139.
84. This attempt to conceive relations and their conditions of possibility in material terms while avoiding received models of "matter" shows important points of contact with the "new materialisms" of the twenty-first century. I will return

to these questions of materiality and their promise. For now, I do not translate flesh as materiality and continue to explore the dimensions of flesh that press against the edges of theology—critically, productively, and dangerously.

85. Merleau-Ponty, *Visible and the Invisible*, 130.
86. Merleau-Ponty, *Visible and the Invisible*, 130.
87. Merleau-Ponty, *Visible and the Invisible*, 142. Merleau-Ponty writes, "an anonymous visibility inhabits both of us, a vision in general, in virtue of that primordial property that belongs to the flesh, being here and now, of radiating everywhere and forever, being an individual, of being also a dimension and a universal."
88. Merleau-Ponty's main examples of this partial view—a table, a hand, a house—are things of such density and volume that one can only talk about the flat surfaces seen, like the facade of a house. Only one perspective at a time.
89. Merleau-Ponty, *Signs*, 21.
90. Merleau-Ponty, *Signs*, 21.
91. Maurice Merleau-Ponty, *Nature: Course Notes from the Collège de France* (Evanston, IL: Northwestern University Press, 2003), 238.
92. Merleau-Ponty refers to a "natal secret." He also calls it an "ontogenesis" and clarifies that this does not mean a single event at an identifiable point in time, but rather as a "suture or seam." Merleau-Ponty, *Nature*, 229.
93. Judith Butler reads Merleau-Ponty's conceptualization of a primordial touch that makes possible sensibility as a phenomenological translation of sensible theology. Judith Butler, "Merleau-Ponty and the Touch of Malebranche," in *The Cambridge Companion to Merleau-Ponty*, ed. Taylor Carman and Mark B. N. Hansen (Cambridge: Cambridge University Press, 2005).
94. The body unites us to things, Merleau-Ponty adds, "by welding to one another the two outlines of which it is made, its two laps: the sensible mass it is and the mass of the sensible wherein it is born by segregation and upon which, as seer, it remains open." Merleau-Ponty, *Visible and the Invisible*, 136. Note that this account of the emergence of the subject by segregation is consonant with and replaces the psychoanalytic one, which we discussed before.
95. Merleau-Ponty, *Visible and the Invisible*, 135.
96. Merleau-Ponty, *Visible and the Invisible*, 150.
97. Merleau-Ponty, *Visible and the Invisible*, 152.
98. Merleau-Ponty, *Visible and the Invisible*, 148, 46.
99. Merleau-Ponty, *Visible and the Invisible*, 148. Emphasis mine.
100. He had referred to the glorious bodies much earlier in "Faith and Good Faith," but the interpretation seems starkly different. "In the last analysis," he stated, "the soul is so little to be separated from the body that it will carry a radiant double of its temporal body into eternity." The invocation of these Christian images of glorious—perhaps pneumatic—bodies in the midst of that critique of a transparent God is striking. But they are still referring to the soul and eternity, which is not the case in "L'entralacs." "Faith and Good Faith," 175.
101. de Saint Aubert, *Du lien des êtres aux éléments de l'être*, 250n3. My translation.

102. Merleau-Ponty, "Indirect Language and the Voices of Silence," *Signs*, trans. Richard C. McCleary (Evanston, IL: Northwestern University Press, 1964), 76.
103. Merleau-Ponty, *Visible and the Invisible*, 153.
104. In his interdisciplinary study of the corporeal schema and the body image, Douwe Tiemersma identifies the religious imaginaries of subtle bodies as antecedents of the scientific notions of the body image. He cites a variety of notions of subtle bodies across historical periods and cultures, including those of "primitive" cultures described by Paul Ferdinand Schilder—the psychiatrist and psychoanalyst to whom the concept of "body image" is attributed. I will return to the concept of the "body image" in a subsequent chapter, in relation to sources where the religious inheritance has all but disappeared. Douwe Tiemersma, *Body Schema and Body Image: An Interdisciplinary and Philosophical Study* (Amsterdam: Swets and Zeitlinger, 1989).
105. Merleau-Ponty, *Visible and the Invisible*, 152.
106. In a note, Merleau-Ponty outlined a series in three parts: The Visible, Nature (as flesh), and Logos. Merleau-Ponty, *Visible and the Invisible*, 274. On his courses on Nature, he refers to the Logos of language and the Logos of perception, and states: "There is a Logos of the natural esthetic world, on which the Logos of language relies." *Nature*, 212.
107. Kearney, "Ecrire la chair," 183.
108. "Dehiscence," to gape or open, comes from the Latin *dehiscere*, from *de-* "away" plus *hiscere*, "begin to gape." It is one of the terms that Merleau-Ponty uses to refer to the noncoincidence between touching and being touched.
109. Merleau-Ponty, "Indirect Language and the Voices of Silence," 64.
110. "Each partial act of expression . . . recreates both the [expressive] power and the language by making us verify in the obviousness of given and received meaning the power that speaking subjects have of going beyond signs toward their meaning. Signs do not simply evoke other signs for us and so on without end, and language is not like a prison we are locked into or a guide we must blindly follow." Merleau-Ponty, "Indirect Language and the Voices of Silence," 81.
111. Merleau-Ponty, "Indirect Language and the Voices of Silence," 77.
112. Kearney, "Ecrire la chair," 191. My translation.
113. Merleau-Ponty, "Indirect Language and the Voices of Silence," 52.

Chapter 5. The Ends of Flesh

1. Gayatri Chakravorty Spivak, "Response to Jean-Luc Nancy," in *Thinking Bodies*, ed. Juliet Flower MacCannell and Laura Zakarin (Stanford, CA: Stanford University Press, 1994), 34.
2. Michel Foucault, *Power/ Knowledge: Selected Interviews and Other Writings 1972–1977* (New York: Pantheon Books, 1980), 211.
3. Mark Jordan, *Convulsing Bodies: Religion and Resistance in Foucault* (Stanford, CA: Stanford University Press, 2014), 83.
4. Spivak, "Response to Jean Luc Nancy," 21.

5. This is consonant with Daniel-Hughes's description of Tertullian's attitude to women's bodies: "It is not enough that Christian modesty seems to be true; it must be seen to be true." Daniel-Hughes, *Salvation of the Flesh*, 99.
6. Foucault, *Power/ Knowledge*. See also Jean-Michel Landry, "Généalogie politique de la psychologie: Une lecture du cours de Michel Foucault du gouvernement de vivants (Paris: Collège De France, 1980)," *Raisons politiques* 1, no. 25 (2007): 31–45.
7. Cf. Jordan, *Convulsing Bodies*.
8. Michel Foucault, *Abnormal: Lectures at the Collège De France 1974–1975* (New York: Picador, 2003), 179.
9. Foucault, *Abnormal*, 187.
10. Foucault, *Abnormal*, 186.
11. Foucault, *Abnormal*, 187.
12. Foucault, *Abnormal*, 188. When he describes this development as one that would "lay bare," "beneath the surface of the sins . . . the unbroken nervure of the flesh," Foucault is portraying a view and speaking a language that his analysis deconstructs. *The History of Sexuality: An Introduction*, trans. Robert Hurley (New York: Pantheon, 1978), 1:20.
13. Foucault, *History of Sexuality*, 1:19.
14. Rom 7:23.
15. Foucault, *Abnormal*, 189.
16. The representation of flesh as pinned to the body is a significant departure from medieval theologies in which "corporeal materiality" is "merely identified as the origin of sin," Foucault observes. Foucault, *Abnormal*, 201.
17. Foucault, *Abnormal*, 202.
18. Foucault, *Abnormal*, 201.
19. He states, similarly, "flesh *appears* as the correlate of a system or mechanism of power." Foucault, *Abnormal*, 203. My italics.
20. Jordan, *Convulsing Bodies*.
21. Rom 7:5.
22. Foucault, *Abnormal*, 192.
23. "The convulsive flesh is the body penetrated by the right of examination and subject to the obligation of exhaustive confession and the body that bristles against this right and this obligation. It is the body that opposes silence or the scream to the rule of obedient direction with intense shocks of involuntary revolt or little betrayals of secret connivance." Foucault, *Abnormal*, 213.
24. Foucault, *History of Sexuality*, 1:143.
25. Foucault, *Abnormal*, 223. "Since the eighteenth century, the nervous type is the rational and scientific body of this same flesh. The nervous system takes the place of concupiscence by right. It is the material and anatomical version of the old concupiscence." Foucault, *Abnormal*, 223.
26. On the impact of colonial racialization of normalizing discourses suggested by but underdeveloped in Foucault's work, see Ann Laura Stoler, *Race and the Education of Desire: Foucault's History of Sexuality and the Colonial Order of Things* (Durham, NC: Duke University Press, 1995).

27. I am here drawing on Mark Jordan's observation that while Foucault alludes to the "religious images or concepts that might survive into secular speech about sex," he is much more interested "in the continuity of the energies of religious rhetoric." Cf. "Sexuality and the After-Life of Christianity," in Jordan, *Convulsing Bodies*, 104.
28. Michel Foucault, "Le combat de la chasteté," *Comunications* 35, no. 35 (1982), 17. "Mortification radicale par conséquent qui nous laisse vivre dans notre corps en nous affranchissant de la chair. 'Sortir de la chair tout en demeurant dans le corps.'"
29. Jean-Luc Nancy, *Noli Me Tangere: On the Raising of the Body*, trans. Sarah Clift, Pascale-Anne Brault, and Michael Naas (New York: Fordham University Press, 2008), 27.
30. Jean-Luc Nancy, *Corpus*, trans. Richard A. Rand (New York: Fordham University Press, 2008). The essays included in *Corpus* were originally published in French between 2000 and 2006. Throughout the chapter I have modified Rand's translation, using "is" rather than the contraction with apostrophe *s* that he prefers.
31. Nancy, *Corpus*, 61.
32. Nancy, *Corpus*, 61. Italics in the original. Translation modified: "broyat, lysat de corps dans le suave ineffable grouillant de *cette chose qui n'a de nom dans aucune langue*."
33. Merleau-Ponty, *Visible and the Invisible*, 139.
34. Nancy, *Corpus*, 47.
35. The darkness of the womb—cited by Tertullian as well as Merleau-Ponty—is an image of intimate differentiation.
36. Nancy, *Corpus*, 132.
37. Nancy, *Corpus*, 132.
38. Nancy, *Corpus*, 132.
39. Nancy, *Corpus*, 77.
40. As we saw, Merleau-Ponty addressed this problem by insisting that the sensing and the sensed are one and the same body, enfolded.
41. Nancy, *Corpus*, 69. For Merleau-Ponty, "the spirit is not what descends into the body in order to organize it, but is what emerges from it." Cited in Coole and Frost, *New Materialisms*, 103.
42. Nancy, *Corpus*, 87.
43. Nancy, *Corpus*, 65.
44. Nancy, *Corpus*, 65.
45. Jean-Luc Nancy, *Dis-Enclosure: The Deconstruction of Christianity*, trans. Bettina Bergo, Gabriel Malefant, and Michael B. Smith (New York: Fordham University Press, 2008), 81–84.
46. Nancy, *Dis-Enclosure*, 82.
47. Nancy, *Dis-Enclosure*, 82.
48. Nancy, *Dis-Enclosure*, 82.
49. Merleau-Ponty did not question that chronological reading in his early discussion of its implications for Christian ethics.

50. Virginia Burrus, "Creatio Ex Libidine: Reading Ancient Logos *Differantly*," in *Derrida and Religion: Other Testaments*, ed. Yvonne Sherwood and Kevin Hart (New York: Routledge, 2004).
51. Studies suggest that verbal abuse can create risks of posttraumatic stress disorder. "Verbal Beatings Hurt as Much as Sexual Abuse," *Harvard Gazette*, April 26, 2007. In contrast, self-disclosure can be inherently rewarding—even as pleasurable as sex. Diana I. Tamir and Jason P. Mitchell, "Disclosing Information about the Self Is Intrinsically Rewarding," *PNAS* 109, no. 21 (2012): 8038–43.
52. For analyses of the misleading popularizations of genetic science, see Judith Roof, *The Poetics of DNA* (Minneapolis: University of Minnesota Press, 2007); and Rose, *Politics of Life Itself*.
53. About 4–8 percent of the human genome is composed of DNA sequences from exogenous retroviral infections that took place millions of years ago and since then have become part of our genetic makeup. Strong evidence suggests that these "fossil viruses" conferred to us changes in genetic expression that provided advantages in our evolutionary journey. The continuity between species makes possible experiments in which genetic material from one species is transplanted into another. See, for example, Lawrence K. Altman, "First Human to Get Baboon Liver Is Said to Be Alert and Doing Well; Surgeon Is Optimistic about Interspecies Transplant," *New York Times*, June 30, 1992; and Marla Paul, "Interspecies Transplant Works in First Step for New Diabetes Therapy," *Life Science Weekly*, June 30, 2013.
54. Critical organelles within our cells called mitochondria arose from an ancient cell literally engulfing, or enfolding, its membrane around another bacterial cell and using its machinery for its purposes. Over time mitochondria became part of our contemporary cells but to this day they replicate independently from the cell and contain a distinct form of DNA.
55. Michael Pollan, "Some of My Best Friends Are Germs," *New York Times*, May 15, 2013.
56. Specifically whether the "information" of a gene will be effectively "expressed" in the production of a cell. Scientists call these processes "epigenetic," because they work around (*epi*) genetics. Epigenetic changes are changes that affect gene expression and phenotype in a way that does not affect what is traditionally considered the "genetic code" or the sequence of base pairs in DNA. These changes are stable and/or heritable.
57. Manufacturing chemicals such as bisphenol A (BPA), used to make plastics for the linings of cans, food packaging, and some water bottles, are found in astounding quantities in human bodies. They have been found to cause dramatic developmental changes and produce epigenetic effects. One study found that male rats exposed to BPA early in life showed modification in their epigenetic patterns that resulted in changes to hormone-related genes and altered testicular functioning during sexual maturity after BPA was no longer in their bodies. These kinds of changes have been found in the uterus and brain as well.

An alarming amount of evidence has shown that BPA exposure has significant effects on sexual differentiation and behavior. Brandon Moore and Wendy Hessler, "Genes Change Message after Newborn Rats Given Bpa," *Environmental Health News*, October 5, 2011.

58. Diana Coole, "The Inertia of Matter and the Generativity of Flesh," in *New Materialisms: Ontology, Agency, and Politics*, ed. Diana Coole and Samantha Frost (Durham, NC: Duke University Press, 2010), 94, 93.
59. Coole, "The Inertia of Matter and the Generativity of Flesh," 97.
60. Barad, "On Touching," 213.
61. Barad, "On Touching," 214.
62. Merleau-Ponty, "In Praise of Philosophy," 46.
63. Barad, "On Touching," 216.
64. Barad, "On Touching," 216.
65. Luce Irigaray, *An Ethics of Sexual Difference* (Ithaca, NY: Cornell University Press, 1993), 151.
66. Irigaray, *Ethics of Sexual Difference*, 152.
67. Irigaray, *Ethics of Sexual Difference*, 10.
68. Irigaray, *Ethics of Sexual Difference*, 11.
69. Irigaray, *Ethics of Sexual Difference*, 18.
70. Irigaray, *Ethics of Sexual Difference*, 5.
71. Irigaray, *Ethics of Sexual Difference*, 154.
72. On the parallels between Merleau-Ponty's and more recent theories of the senses, see Willian E. Connolly, "Materialities of Experience," in *New Materialisms: Ontology, Agency, and Politics*, ed. Diana Coole and Samantha Frost (Durham, NC: Duke University Press, 2010).
73. Merleau-Ponty, *Visible and the Invisible*, 131.
74. Irigaray, *Ethics of Sexual Difference*, 165.
75. The possibilities for differential conditions for visibility multiply if we consider the role of technology, in which a body is able to inhabit drastically different environmental conditions from what is seen. And this is just one of the many ways in which social conditions affect visibility, as we will see in part III.
76. Cathryn Vasseleu, *Textures of Light: Vision and Touch in Irigaray, Levinas and Merleau-Ponty*, ed. Andrew Benjamin, Warwick Studies in European Philosophy (London: Routledge, 1998).
77. Irigaray, *Ethics of Sexual Difference*, 165.
78. Irigaray, *Ethics of Sexual Difference*.
79. Irigaray, *Ethics of Sexual Difference*, 154.
80. Irigaray, *Ethics of Sexual Difference*, 156.
81. Irigaray, *Ethics of Sexual Difference*, 162.
82. Judith Butler, "Sexual Difference as a Question of Ethics: Alterities of the Flesh in Irigaray and Merleau-Ponty," *Chiasmi International* 10 (2008), 344.
83. Gn 2:23.
84. Gn 2:24.

85. Johnson, "Desire and Invisibility in 'Eye and Mind.'" Beata Stawarska, "Psychoanalysis," in *Merlau-Ponty: Key Concepts*, ed. Rosalyn Diprose and Jack Reynolds (Stocksfield, UK: Acumen, 2008).
86. Unless one thinks of sensibility at a molecular or atomic level, perhaps, but that would need to be defined as both human and not.
87. Glissant, *Poetics of Relation*, 154.

Chapter 6. Inescapable Bodies

1. J. Michael Dash, "Writing the Body: Edouard Glissant's Poetics and Re-Membering," *World Literature Today* 63, no. 4 (1989): 610.
2. The title "L'expérience vécue du noir" was intriguingly translated as "The Fact of Blackness" in the English edition. Frantz Fanon, *Black Skin, White Masks* (New York: Grove Press, 1967).
3. Fanon, *Black Skin, White Masks*, 13.
4. Alejandro J. de Oto, *Frantz Fanon: Política y poética del sujeto poscolonial* (Mexico D. F.: El Colegio de Mexico, 2003), 47. As I said in chapter 4, Merleau-Ponty considers parables the paradigmatic genre of the gospels. A parable conveys the qualities of embodied knowledge. It draws attention to the emergence of knowledge through engagements with the sensible world, engagements that are necessarily situated and constitutive of the knower.
5. Maurice Merleau-Ponty, *The Visible and the Invisible*, trans. Alphonso Lingis (Evanston, IL: Northwestern University Press, 1968), 127. See chapter 4.
6. Gloria Anzaldúa, "*Cihuatlyotl*, Woman Alone," in Gloria Anzaldúa, *Borderlands/La Frontera: The New Mestiza* (San Francisco: Aunt Lute Books, 1999), 195.
7. Fanon, *Black Skin, White Masks*, 110.
8. Merleau-Ponty's example is of a person locating an ashtray on his desk and grabbing his pipe. Merleau-Ponty, *Phenomenology of Perception*, 115.
9. Fanon, *Black Skin, White Masks*, 111.
10. Merleau-Ponty, *Phenomenology of Perception*, 165, 67.
11. Merleau-Ponty, *Phenomenology of Perception*, 165, 67, my italics.
12. Fanon, *Black Skin, White Masks*, 111. My italics. Merleau-Ponty observes that "our body does not impose definite instincts upon us from birth, as it does upon animals." Merleau-Ponty, *Phenomenology of Perception*, 169.
13. Both Merleau-Ponty and Fanon cite neurologist Jean Lhermitte's *L'image de notre corps*. Lhermitte also wrote on spirit possession. This datum is significant, given Foucault's argument that the antecedents for discourses about instincts are the studies of possessions.
14. Fanon, *Black Skin, White Masks*, 111.
15. Fanon, *Black Skin, White Masks*, 112.
16. Fanon, *Black Skin, White Masks*, 112.
17. Fanon, *Black Skin, White Masks*, 113.
18. Fanon, *Black Skin, White Masks*, 112.
19. Jeremy Weate argues that epidermal schema represents a later stage in a person's psychosomatic disintegration and alienation. "The epidermal masks the stage

where historical construction and contingency is effaced and replaced with the facticity of flesh." Jeremy Weate, "Fanon, Merleau-Ponty and the Difference of Phenomenology," in *Race*, ed. Robert Bernasconi (Oxford: Blackwell, 2001), 174. But Fanon's narrative moves between the two notions, making it difficult to conclude whether he would temporally substitute one for the other.

20. Fanon, *Black Skin, White Masks*, 116.
21. Fanon, *Black Skin, White Masks*, 120.
22. This is followed by a quotation from Merleau-Ponty's *Phenomenology of Perception*: "For a being who has acquired consciousness of himself and of his body, who has attained to the dialectic of subject and object, the body is no longer a cause of the structure of consciousness, it has become an object of consciousness" (Fanon, *Black Skin, White Masks*, 225). Fanon leaves the citation without comments.
23. Aimé Césaire, *Notebook of a Return to the Native Land*, trans. A. James Arnold and Clayton Eshleman (Middletown, CT: Wesleyan University Press, 2013).
24. Commentators link Césaire's use of "O" and "Eia" in that section to Greek tragedy but also to the Latin mass. Césaire's translators, A. James Arnold and Clayton Eshleman, note, for example, the use of "Eia Mater" in "Stabat Mater." Translators' note in the appendix of Césaire, *Notebook of a Return to the Native Land*, 64.
25. Césaire, *Notebook of a Return to the Native Land*, 37.
26. Césaire, *Notebook of a Return to the Native Land*, 37.
27. Césaire, *Notebook of a Return to the Native Land*, 37. Translation modified.
28. Césaire, *Notebook of a Return to the Native Land*, 57.
29. "enroule-toi, vent, autour de ma nouvelle croissance . . . je te livre ma conscience et son rythme de chair . . . lie ma noire vibration au nombril même du monde (64–64). See also Aimé Césaire, *Cahier d'un retour au pays natal* (Paris: Présence Africane, 1983), 47.
30. Césaire, *Notebook of a Return to the Native Land*, 16: "ce pays dont le limon entre dans la composition de ma chair."
31. Fanon, *Black Skin, White Masks*, 125.
32. "I revive Onan who entrusted his sperm to the fecund earth and the water of life circumvents the papilla of the morne" (Césaire, *Notebook of a Return to the Native Land*, 47). Onan refers to Genesis. See translators' commentary in the appendix of *Notebook of a Return to the Native Land*, 65.
33. Fanon, *Black Skin, White Masks*, 126.
34. Fanon cites, for instance, Senghor's statement that "emotion is completely Negro as reason is Greek." *Black Skin, White Masks*, 127.
35. Fanon, *Black Skins, White Masks*, 127.
36. Fanon, *Black Skins, White Masks*, 132.
37. Fanon, *Black Skins, White Masks*, 221.
38. Fanon, *Black Skins, White Masks*, 122. My emphasis.
39. Fanon, *Black Skins, White Masks*, 122.
40. Fanon, *Black Skins, White Masks*, 109.

41. I agree with Jeremy Weate's argument that an ontology is implicit in the thought of difference. "The phenomenon of difference must be understood as that which defers (and deters) being" (13). But I wonder if the rethinking of ontology would require more than "an assertion of the difference of black lived experience," an account of ontologies as historical constructs with productive power. Weate, "Fanon, Merleau-Ponty and the Difference of Phenomenology," 13.
42. Notes for a lecture on Descartes, cited in de Saint Aubert, *Dulien des êtres aux éléments de l'être*, 259, my translation.
43. Aimé Césaire and Pablo Picasso, *Lost Body*, trans. Clayton Eshleman and Annette Smith (New York: George Braziller, 1986), 7.
44. Translators' introduction to Césaire, *Notebook of a Return to the Native Land*, xiv.
45. As Jean Khalfa explains, in his correspondence with Francis Jeanson, "Fanon stressed that some of his sentences aimed at the affectivity of the reader, at transmitting an experience, rather than an explanation or a system of concepts." Jean Khalfa, "My Body, This Skin, This Fire: Fanon on Flesh," *Wasafiri* 20, no. 44 (2005): 42.
46. Glissant, *Poetics of Relation*, 148.
47. Fanon, *Black Skin, White Masks*, 140.
48. Fanon, *Black Skin, White Masks*, 140.
49. Fanon, *Black Skin, White Masks*, 140.
50. Fanon, *Black Skin, White Masks*, 231.
51. Fanon's misogynist arguments, most prominent in his chapter on psychoanalysis, are well known. For this writer, engaging the violence of his words seemed more destructive than confining them to this indirect footnote. On the function of the "crip" as a figure of abject vulnerability, see Sharon V. Betcher, *Spirit and the Politics of Disablement* (Minneapolis: Fortress Press, 2007).
52. Fanon, *Black Skin, White Masks*, 23.
53. Fanon, *Black Skin, White Masks*, 231.
54. Fanon, *Black Skin, White Masks*, 231. The prayer is reminiscent of Césaire's, which Fanon cites earlier in the book. "And more than anything, *my body*, as well as my soul, do not allow yourself to cross your arms like a sterile spectator." Césaire, *Notebook of a Return to the Native Land*, cited in Fanon, *Black Skin, White Masks*, 187. My italics.

Chapter 7. Carnal Relations

1. Adrienne Rich, "Waking in the Dark," in *Poems, Selected and New, 1950–1974* (New York: W. W. Norton, 1975), 18.
2. Michael Ondaatje, *The English Patient* (New York: Vintage Books, 1992), 261.
3. Linda Martín Alcoff, *Visible Identities: Race, Gender, and the Self* (Oxford: Oxford University Press, 2006), 102.
4. Simone de Beauvoir, *The Second Sex*, trans. Constance Borde and Shiela Malovany Chevallier (New York: Vintage Books, 2011), 283.
5. Butler, "Sex and Gender in Simone de Beauvoir's *Second Sex*," 36.
6. Judith Butler, *Gender Trouble: Feminism and the Subversion of Identity* (New York: Routledge, 1999), 11. Italics mine.

7. Conceiving gender as "a cultural inscription of meaning on a pregiven sex," Butler argued, loses sight of the cultural history of sex. Butler, *Gender Trouble*, 10.
8. Butler, *Gender Trouble*, 10. As Butler describes the relationship, she seeks to understand how race and sex condition one another, "how one becomes the unmarked background for the action of the other" (Vikki Bell, "On Speech, Race, and Melancholia: An Interview with Judith Butler," *Theory, Culture and Society* 16 no. 2 [1999], 168). Her approach for an analysis of sex and race is neither an absolute synthesis nor an analogy, but a shift between perspectives to allow for some "interarticulation" between the different narratives.
9. As I write this, news about the shooting by the police of an unarmed young African American, Michael Brown, has moved communities all over the United States to protest. The proliferation of incidents in which the police kills unarmed black and brown men and women is a poignant example of more widespread phenomena in which visible identities lead to bodily harm.
10. Martín Alcoff, *Visible Identities*, 183; cf. Khalfa, "My Body, This Skin, This Fire."
11. Based on Gramsci's statement, "Despite its felt naturalness . . . common sense is 'culturally constituted—not as false consciousness is, by imposition from above, but by the sediment' of past historical beliefs and practices of a given society and culture." Martín Alcoff, *Visible Identities*, 185.
12. Martín Alcoff, *Visible Identities*, 126.
13. Merleau-Ponty, *Phenomenology of Perception*, 512–13.
14. Martín Alcoff, *Visible Identities*, 185.
15. Merleau-Ponty, *Phenomenology of Perception*, cited in Martín Alcoff, *Visible Identities*, 188.
16. Martín Alcoff, *Visible Identities*, 188.
17. Butler analyzes, for example, the practice of viewing videos during the trial of police officers for beating an African American man, Rodney King. Gazing at the beating conjures other images of race and constructs race. The "performativity" of this "kind of visual reading practice" is part of "racialization"—the practices by which bodies are raced. Vikki Bell, "On Speech, Race and Melancholia: An Interview with Judith Butler," *Theory, Culture and Society* 16, no. 2 (1999): 169.
18. Martín Alcoff, *Visible Identities*, 194.
19. Martín Alcoff, *Visible Identities*, 111.
20. Merleau-Ponty, *Visible and the Invisible*, 135.
21. Merleau-Ponty, *Visible and the Invisible*, 135.
22. Homi K. Bhabha, *The Location of Culture* (London: Routledge, 1994).
23. The following is just a sample of the types of works to which I am referring: Nao Hagiwara et al., "Racial Attitudes, Physician-Patient Talk Time Ratio, and Adherence in Racially Discordant Medical Interactions," *Social Science and Medicine* 87 (2013): 123–31; May Lau, Hua Lin, and Glenn Flores, "Racial/Ethnic Disparities in Health and Health Care among U.S. Adolescents," *Health Services Research* 47, no. 5 (2012): 2031–59; Alan Nelson, "Unequal Treatment: Confronting Racial and Ethnic Disparities in Health Care," *Journal of the National Medical Association*

94, no. 8 (2003): 666–68; and Janice Sabin, Frederick Rivara, and Anthony Greenwald, "Physician Implicit Attitudes and Stereotypes about Race and Quality of Medical Care," *Medical Care* 46, no. 7 (2008): 678–85. On the effects of racism in the terms of loans, see Alan M. White, "Borrowing While Black: Applying Fair Lending Laws to Risk-Based Mortgage Pricing," *South Carolina Law Review* 60 no. 3 (2009); and Christine Van Dusen, "Racial Disparity in Loans Studied: Advocacy Group Finds Widening Gap between Black/Latino Mortgage Rejection Rates and Those of Whites in Metro Area," *Atlanta Journal-Constitution*, October 2, 2002. On environmental racism see, Ryan Holifield, "Defining Environmental Justice and Environmental Racism," *Urban Geography* 22, no. 1 (2001): 78–90; William T. Markham and Eric Rufa, "Class, Race, and the Disposal of Urban Waste: Locations of Landfills, Incinerators, and Sewage Treatment Plants," *Sociological Spectrum* 17, no. 2 (1997): 235–48; Jim Motavelli, "Toxic Targets: Polluters That Dump on Communities of Color Finally Being Brought to Justice," *E Magazine*, July–August 1998; and "In Whose Backyard? Pollution and Race," *Economist*, December 4, 2010.

24. Briana Mezuk et al., "Reconsidering the Role of Social Disadvantage in Physical and Mental Health: Stressful Life Events, Health Behaviors, Race, and Depression," *American Journal of Epidemiology* 172, nos. 1238–1249 (2010): 1238–49; R. A. Miech and M. J. Shanahan, "Socioeconomic Status and Depression over the Life Course," *Journal of Health and Social Behavior* 41, no. 2 (2000): 162–76; Tony Morris, Melissa Moore, and Felicity Morris, "Stress and Chronic Illness: The Case of Diabetes," *Journal of Adult Development* 18, no. 2 (2011): 70–80; Sarah Rosenfield, "Triple Jeapordy? Mental Health at the Intersection of Gender, Race, and Class," *Social Science and Medicine* 74, no. 11 (2012): 1791–801.
25. Merleau-Ponty, *Phenomenology of Perception*, 92.
26. Merleau-Ponty, *Phenomenology of Perception*, 92–93.
27. See Martín Alcoff's discussion of relevant works by Iris Marion Young and George Lakoff in Martín Alcoff, *Visible Identities*.
28. Butler, "Sex and Gender in Simone de Beauvoir's *Second Sex*," 35.
29. Butler, "Sex and Gender in Simone de Beauvoir's *Second Sex*," 35.
30. Butler, *Bodies That Matter*, 94.
31. Butler, *Gender Trouble*, 164. There is, to be sure, enticement from the world; but, as Beauvoir suggested, one can be enticed into one's own alienation. Butler, "Sex and Gender in Simone de Beauvoir's *Second Sex*," 42.
32. Butler, *Bodies That Matter*, 9.
33. Butler, "Merleau-Ponty and the Touch of Malebranche," 181.
34. Butler, "Merleau-Ponty and the Touch of Malebranche," 203. Italics mine. *Giving an Account of Oneself* (New York: Fordham University Press, 2005), 203. In that book, Butler relies on Levinas, not Merleau-Ponty. In the epigraph to chapter 3, Levinas describes body in terms similar to Merleau-Ponty's, as a "knot or denoument of being" (83).
35. Butler, "Merleau-Ponty and the Touch of Malebranche," 203.

36. Amy Hollywood, "Performativity, Citationality, Ritualization," in *Bodily Citations: Religion and Judith Butler*, ed. Ellen T. Armour and Susan M. St. Ville (New York: Columbia University Press, 2006).
37. Hollywood, "Performativity, Citationality, Ritualization," 253.
38. See the discussion of Jean-Luc Nancy's neologism in chapter 5.
39. Dan Hurley, "Grandma's Experiences Leave a Mark on Your Genes," *Discovery*, May 2013, accessed June 11, 2013, http://discovermagazine.com/2013/may/13-grandmas-experiences-leave-epigenetic-mark-on-your-genes. Research suggests that PTSD markers may be passed on to offspring. See also Nathan Seppa, "Epigenetic Shifts Linked to PTSD," *Science News* 177 no. 12 (June 5, 2010): 9.
40. In a small study published in *PLOS ONE* in January, researchers found that childhood adversity in the form of maltreatment, parental loss, or abandonment altered a control mechanism for a key gene that regulates the brain's ability to handle stress hormones. The subjects weren't aware of the change; it happened silently as their environment influenced their genes. The effects of early life stress and hormone disruption, said the researchers, are a risk factor for major depression and posttraumatic stress disorder.
41. Rosalyn Diprose, *Corporeal Generosity: On Giving with Nietzsche, Merleau-Ponty, and Levinas* (Albany: State University Press of New York, 2002), 55.
42. Diprose, *Corporeal Generosity*, 55.
43. Butler, *Bodies That Matter*, 4. The text continues, "Although political discourses that mobilize identity categories tend to cultivate identifications in the service of a political goal, it may be that the persistence of *dis*identification is equally crucial to the rearticulation of democratic contestation. . . . Such collective disidentification can facilitate a reconceptualization of which bodies matter and which bodies are yet to emerge as critical matters of concern" (4).
44. Judith Butler, *Undoing Gender* (New York: Routledge, 2004), 195.
45. Butler, *Undoing Gender*, 195. My italics.
46. Martín Alcoff, *Visible Identities*, 93. Martín Alcoff argues that "by offering a psychoanalytic rather than historical account of subject formation [Butler] renders inevitable and ahistorical the link between subjection and subjectification" (76).
47. Bell, "On Speech, Race and Melancholia," 164.
48. Martín Alcoff does not discount biological elements in gender; even if they are not enough to cause gender difference, she argues for a "metaphysics of gender" focusing on the possibility of reproduction. She rejects a parallel structure for race. Martín Alcoff's idea of a metaphysics of gender suggests her interest in retrieving elements of a corporeal self that cannot be fully accounted for by an appeal to social processes.
49. Catherine Keller traces the movement toward a more explicit social ontology in Butler's work. In the early works, the ones I have been discussing, what is brought to the fore is the "regulatory force of sociality," following Foucault. Even if psychoanalysis gives the account relational elements, particularly as it relates to the family, Keller observes, "the dissolution of the substance essentialism into a stylized repetition . . . does not, in itself, entail an affirmative relational-

ism." The second phase of Butler's work, which was in response to the events following the attacks on the United States on September 11, 2001, offers a more explicit social ontology. As Keller observes, Butler's work on collective trauma shows an "ethical widening of our constituent relationality through and beyond the intimate circles of the formative family" (Catherine Keller, "Undoing and Unknowing: Judith Butler in Process," in *Butler on Whitehead: On the Occasion*, edited by Roland Faber, Michael Halewood, and Deena Lin, 47–48 (Lanham, MD: Lexington Books, 2012).

50. Butler admits, "I failed to know and consider those interactive models that seek to establish that biology is responding to culture, and culture to biology." Butler, "On This Occasion," 11.
51. She also notes the need to rethink notions of "causality": "What is it about the materiality of bodies that makes it susceptible to the enactment of the intertwined forces of biology and history?" Drawing from scientific insights about the relationship between the seer and the seen—and thus between subject and object—Barad proposes a relational ontology. It explains discursive practices as implicated in the activities of materialization. Barad, *Meeting the Universe Halfway*, 65.
52. Barad, *Meeting the Universe Halfway*, 133.
53. Karen Barad, "Posthumanist Performativity: Toward an Understanding of How Matter Comes to Matter," *Signs* 28, no. 3 (2003): 809.
54. In August 2011, the *New York Times* published an article that begins with this sentence: "Gruesome details of American-run venereal disease experiments on Guatemalan prisoners, soldiers and mental patients in the years after World War II were revealed this week during hearings before a White House bioethics panel investigating the study's sordid history." Sadly, the story has repeated itself in many places. Donald G. McNeil Jr., "Panel Hears Grim Details of Venereal Disease Tests," *New York Times*, August 30, 2011.
55. Terry Tempest Williams, "The Clan of One-Breasted Women," in *Refuge: An Unnatural History of Family and Place* (New York: Random House Vintage, 1991), 281.
56. Anzaldúa, *Borderlands/ La Frontera*, 2.
57. Joanna Blythman, "Can Vegans Stomach the Unpalatable Truth about Quinoa?" *Guardian*, January 16, 2013.

Conclusion

1. Merleau-Ponty, "Faith and Good Faith," 179.

BIBLIOGRAPHY

Alaimo, Stacy, and Susan Hekman. *Material Feminisms*. Bloomington: Indiana University Press, 2008.

Alexandre, Jérôme. *Une chair pour la gloire: L'anthropologie réaliste et mystique de Tertullien*. Paris: Beauchesne Éditeur, 2001.

Althaus-Reid, Marcella, ed. *Liberation Theology and Sexuality*. Burlington, VT: Ashgate, 2006.

Altizer, Thomas J. J. "Paul and the Birth of Self-Consciousness." *Journal of the American Academy of Religion* 51, no. 3 (1983): 359–70.

Altman, Lawrence K. "First Human to Get Baboon Liver Is Said to Be Alert and Doing Well; Surgeon Is Optimistic about Interspecies Transplant." *New York Times*, June 30, 1992.

Alves, Rubem. *I Believe in the Resurrection of the Body*. Eugene, OR: Wipf and Stock, 1986.

Anselm. "Monologium." In *Proslogium; Monologium; An Appendix in Behalf of the Fool by Gaunilon; and Cur Deus Homo*, translated by Sidney Norton Deane. La Salle, IL: Open Court, 1951.

Anzaldúa, Gloria. *Borderlands/ La Frontera: The New Mestiza*. San Francisco: Aunt Lute Books, 1999.

Aristotle. *De Anima*. Translated by D. W. Hamlyn. Claredon Aristotle Series. Oxford: Oxford University Press, 1993.

Asher, Jeffrey R. *Polarity and Change in 1 Corinthians 15*. Tübingen: Mihn Siebeck, 2000.

Ashton, John. *Understanding the Fourth Gospel*. 2nd ed. New York: Oxford University Press, 2009.

Athanasius. *De Incarnatione*. Edited by Frank L. Cross. Eugene, OR: Wipf and Stock, 2010.

Augustine. *The Confessions*. Translated by Philip Burton. New York: Alfred A. Knopf, 2001.

Ayres, Jennifer R. *Good Food: Grounded Practical Theology*. Waco, TX: Baylor University Press, 2013.

Bachelard, Gaston. *Earth and the Reveries of Will: An Essay on the Imagination of Matter*. Translated by Kenneth Haltman. Dallas: Dallas Institute of Publications, 2002.

Badiou, Alain. *Saint Paul: The Foundation of Universalism*. Translated by Ray Brassier. Cultural Memory in the Present. Stanford, CA: Stanford University Press, 2003.

Barad, Karen. *Meeting the Universe Halfway: Quantum Physics and the Entanglement of Matter and Meaning*. Durham, NC: Duke University Press, 2007.

———. "On Touching: The Inhuman That Therefore I Am." *Differences* 25, no. 3 (2012): 206–23.

———. "Posthumanist Performativity: Toward an Understanding of How Matter Comes to Matter." *Signs* 28, no. 3 (2003): 801–31.

———. "Posthuman Performativity: Toward an Understanding of How Matter Comes to Matter." In *Material Feminisms*, edited by Stacy Alaimo and Susan Hekman, 120–54. Indianapolis: Indiana University Press, 2008.

Bell, Vikki. "On Speech, Race and Melancholia: An Interview with Judith Butler." *Theory, Culture and Society* 16, no. 2 (1999): 163–74.

Belluck, Pam. "In Study, Fatherhood Leads to Drop in Testosterone." *New York Times*, September 12, 2011.

Betcher, Sharon V. "Becoming Flesh of My Flesh: Feminist and Disability Theologies on the Edge of Posthumanist Discourse." *Journal of Feminist Studies in Religion* 26, no. 2 (2010): 107–39.

———. *Spirit and the Obligation of Social Flesh: A Secular Theology for the Global City*. New York: Fordham University Press, 2013.

———. *Spirit and the Politics of Disablement*. Minneapolis: Fortress Press, 2007.

Bhabha, Homi K. *The Location of Culture*. London: Routledge, 1994.

Boyarin, Daniel. *Carnal Israel: Reading Sex in Talmudic Culture*. Berkeley: University of California Press, 1995.

———. "The Gospel of the Memra: Jewish Binitarianism and the Prologue to John." *Harvard Theological Review* 94, no. 3 (2001): 243–84.

———. *A Radical Jew: Paul and the Politics of Identity*. Berkeley: University of California Press, 1994.

———. *Unheroic Conduct: The Rise of Heterosexuality and the Invention of the Jewish Man*. Berkeley: University of California Press, 1997.

Braun, René. "Sacralité et sainteté chez Tertullien." *Bulletin de l'Association Guillame Budé: Lettres d'humanité* 48 no. 4 (1989): 339–44.

Brown, Raymond E. *The Gospel according to John*. The Anchor Bible. Vol. 29. New York: Doubleday, 1966.

Buell, Denise Kimber. "Hauntology Meets Posthumanism: Some Payoffs for Biblical Studies." In *The Bible and Posthumanism*, edited by Jennifer L. Koosed, 27–56. Atlanta: Society of Biblical Literature, 2014.

———. "Imagining Human Transformation in the Context of Invisible Powers: Instrumental Agency in Second-Century Treatments of Conversion." In *Metamorphoses:*

Resurrection, Body and Transformative Practices in Early Christianity, edited by Turid Karlsen Seim and Jorunn Økland, 249–70. Berlin: Walter de Gruyter, 2009.

Burrus, Virginia. "Creatio Ex Libidine: Reading Ancient Logos Differantly." In Derrida and Religion: Other Testaments, edited by Yvonne Sherwood and Kevin Hart, 141–56. New York: Routledge, 2004.

———. "An Embarrassment of the Flesh." In Saving Shame: Martyrs, Saints, and Other Abject Subjects, 44–80. Philadelphia: University of Pennsylvania Press, 2008.

———. "Seducing Theology." Theology and Sexuality 18, no. 2 (2013): 1–4.

———. "Carnal Excess: Flesh at the Limits of Imagination." Journal of Early Christian Studies. 17, no. 2 (Summer 2009): 247–65.

Burrus, Virginia, Mark D. Jordan, and Karmen MacKendrick. Seducing Augustine: Bodies, Desires, Confessions. New York: Fordham University Press, 2010.

Butler, Judith. Bodies That Matter: On the Discursive Limits of "Sex." New York: Routledge, 1993.

———. Gender Trouble: Feminism and the Subversion of Identity. 1990. Reprint, New York: Routledge, 1999.

———. Giving an Account of Oneself. New York: Fordham University Press, 2005.

———. "Merleau-Ponty and the Touch of Malebranche." In The Cambridge Companion to Merleau-Ponty, edited by Taylor Carman and Mark B. N. Hansen, 181–205. Cambridge: Cambridge University Press, 2005.

———. "On This Occasion . . ." In Butler on Whitehead: On the Occasion, edited by Roland Faber, Michael Halewood, and Deena Lin, 3–18: Lanham, MD: Lexington, 2012.

———. "Sex and Gender in Simone De Beauvoir's Second Sex." Yale French Studies 72 (1986): 35–49.

———. "Sexual Difference as a Question of Ethics: Alterities of the Flesh in Irigaray and Merleau-Ponty." Chiasmi International 10 (2008): 333–47.

———. Undoing Gender. New York: Routledge, 2004.

Carney, Dana R., Amy J. C. Cuddy, and Andy J. Yap. "Power Posing: Brief Nonverbal Displays Affect Neuroendocrine Levels and Risk Tolerance." Psychological Science 20, no. 10 (2010): 1–6.

Cary, Phillip. Augustine's Invention of the Inner Self: The Legacy of a Christian Platonist. Oxford: Oxford University Press, 2000.

Castelli, Elizabeth. Martyrdom and Memory: Early Christian Culture Making. New York: Columbia University Press, 2004.

Césaire, Aimé. Cahier d'un retour au pays natal. 1939. Paris: Présence Africane, 1983.

———. Notebook of a Return to the Native Land. 1939. Translated by A. James Arnold and Clayton Eshleman. Middletown, CT: Wesleyan University Press, 2013.

Césaire, Aimé, and Pablo Picasso. Lost Body. 1950. Translated by Clayton Eshleman and Annette Smith. New York: George Braziller, 1986.

Cixous, Hélène. "The Laugh of the Medusa." Signs 1, no. 4 (1976): 875–93.

Connolly, Willian E. "Materialities of Experience." In New Materialisms: Ontology, Agency, and Politics, edited by Diana Coole and Samantha Frost, 178–200. Durham, NC: Duke University Press, 2010.

Coole, Diana. "The Inertia of Matter and the Generativity of Flesh." In *New Materialisms: Ontology, Agency, and Politics*, ed. Diana Coole and Samantha Frost, 92–115. Durham, NC: Duke University Press, 2010.
Coole, Diana, and Samantha Frost, eds. *New Materialisms: Ontology, Agency, and Politics*. Durham, NC: Duke University Press, 2010.
Cross, Bryan. "Horton on Being Made One Flesh with Christ." *Called to Communion*, September 27, 2009, http://www.calledtocommunion.com/2009/09/horton-on-being-made-one-flesh-with-christ/.
Daniel-Hughes, Carly. *The Salvation of the Flesh in Tertullian of Cathage: Dressing for Resurrection*. New York: Palgrave Macmillan, 2011.
Dash, J. Michael. "Writing the Body: Edouard Glissant's Poetics and Re-Membering." *World Literature Today* 63, no. 4 (1989): 690–712.
de Beauvoir, Simone. *The Second Sex*. Translated by Constance Borde and Shiela Malovany Chevallier. New York: Vintage Books, 2011.
de Oto, Alejandro J. *Frantz Fanon: Política y poética del sujeto poscolonial*. Mexico D.F.: El Colegio de México, 2003.
de Saint Aubert, Emmanuel. *Du lien des êtres aux éléments de l'être: Merleau-Ponty au tournant des années 1945–1951*. Paris: Vrin, 2004.
———. "'L'incarnation change tout' Merleau-Ponty Critique De La 'Théologie Explicative.'" *Archives de Philosophie* 71, no. 3 (2008): 371–405.
Derrida, Jacques. *On Touching—Jean-Luc Nancy*. Translated by Christine Irizarry. Stanford, CA: Stanford University Press, 2005.
Dickinson, Emily. *Poems*. Vol. 1. Raleigh, NC: Hayes Barton, 1955.
Diprose, Rosalyn. *Corporeal Generosity: On Giving with Nietzsche, Merleau-Ponty, and Levinas*. Albany: State University Press of New York, 2002.
Dunning, Benjamin H. *Specters of Paul: Sexual Difference in Early Christian Thought*. Philadelphia: University of Pennsylvania Press, 2011.
Dussel, Enrique. *Beyond Philosophy: Ethics, History, Marxism, and Liberation Theology*. Lantham, MA: Rowman and Littlefield, 2003.
———. *El humanismo Helénico*. Buenos Aires: Editorial Universitaria de Buenos Aires, 1975.
———. *El humanismo Semita: Estructuras intencionales radicales del pueblo de Israel y otros Semitas*. Buenos Aires: Editorial Universitaria de Buenos Aires, 1969.
Engberg-Pedersen, Troels. *Cosmology and the Self in the Apostle Paul: The Material Spirit*. Oxford: Oxford University Press, 2010.
Fanon, Frantz. *Black Skin, White Masks*. 1952. New York: Grove Press, 1967.
Foucault, Michel. *Abnormal: Lectures at the Collège De France 1974–1975*. New York: Picador, 2003.
———. "Le combat de la chastité." *Comunications* 35 (1982): 15–25.
———. *The History of Sexuality: An Introduction*. Translated by Robert Hurley. 3 vols. New York: Pantheon, 1978.
———. *Power/ Knowledge: Selected Interviews and Other Writings 1972–1977*. New York: Pantheon Books, 1980.

Fredouille, Jean-Claude. "Observations sur la terminologie anthropologique de Tertullien: Constantes et variations." In *Les pères de l'église face à la science médicale de leur temps*, edited by Véronique Boudon-Millot and Bernard Pouderon, 321–44. Paris: Beauchesne Éditeur, 2005.

Fulton, Alice. "After the Angelectomy." *Chronicle of Higher Education*. May 12, 2012. chronicle.com/blogs/brainstorm/mondays-poem-after-the-angelectomy-by-alice-fulton/46716.

Gibran, Kahlil. *Jesus, the Son of Man*. Kahlil Gibran Pocket Library. New York: Alfred A. Knopf, 1995.

Glancy, Jennifer A. *Corporeal Knowledge: Early Christian Bodies*. Oxford: Oxford University Press, 2010.

———. *Slavery in Early Christianity*. Minneapolis: Fortress Press, 2006.

Glissant, Édouard. *Poetics of Relation*. Translated by Betsy Wing. Ann Arbor: University of Michigan Press, 1997.

Grosz, Elizabeth. "Irigaray and the Divine." In *Transfigurations: Theology and French Feminism*, edited by C. W. Maggie Kim, Susan M. St. Ville, and Susan M. Simonatis, 199–214. Eugene, OR: Wipf and Stock, 2002.

Hagiwara, Nao, Louis A. Penner, Richard Gonzalez, Susan Eggly, John F. Dovidio, Samuel L. Gaertner, Tessa West, and Terrance L. Albrecht. "Racial Attitudes, Physician-Patient Talk Time Ratio, and Adherence in Racially Discordant Medical Interactions." *Social Science and Medicine* 87 (June 2013): 123–31.

Heyward, Carter. *Touching Our Strength: The Erotic as Power and the Love of God*. San Francisco: Harper San Francisco, 1989.

Hodge, Caroline E. Johnson. *If Sons, Then Heirs: A Study of Kinship and Ethnicity in the Letters of Paul*. Oxford: Oxford University Press, 2007.

Holifield, Ryan. "Defining Environmental Justice and Environmental Racism." *Urban Geography* 22, no. 1 (2001): 78–90.

Hollywood, Amy. "Performativity, Citationality, Ritualization." In *Bodily Citations: Religion and Judith Butler*, edited by Ellen T. Armour and Susan M. St. Ville, 252–75. New York: Columbia University Press, 2006.

Howe, Marie. *The Kingdom of Ordinary Time: Poems*. New York: W. W. Norton, 2008.

Hurley, Dan. "Grandma's Experiences Leave a Mark on Your Genes." *Discovery*, May 2013.

"In Whose Backyard? Pollution and Race." *Economist*, December 4, 2010.

Iranaeus. "Against Heresies." In *Ante-Nicene Fathers Volume I*. Edited by Alexander Roberts and James Donaldson. Peabody, MA: Hendrickson Publishers, 1994.

Irigaray, Luce. *An Ethics of Sexual Difference*. Ithaca, NY: Cornell University Press, 1993.

Jantzen, Grace M. *Becoming Divine: Towards a Feminist Philosophy of Religion*. Bloomington: Indiana University Press, 1999.

Johnson, Gale A. "Desire and Invisibility in 'Eye and Mind': Some Remarks on Merleau-Ponty's Spirituality." In *Merleau-Ponty in Contemporary Perspectives*, edited by Patrick Burke and Jan Van der Veken, 85–98. Dordrecht, the Netherlands: Kluwer Academic Publishers, 1993.

Jordan, Mark. *Convulsing Bodies: Religion and Resistance in Foucault.* Stanford, CA: Stanford University Press, 2014.

Kearney, Richard. "Ecrire la chair: L'expression diacritique chez Merleau-Ponty." *Chiasmi International* (Fall 2013): 183–96.

Keller, Catherine. *Cloud of the Impossible: Negative Theology and Planetary Entanglement.* New York: Columbia University Press, 2014.

———. "Undoing and Unknowing: Judith Butler in Process." In *Butler on Whitehead: On the Occasion*, edited by Roland Faber, Michael Halewood, and Deena Lin, 43–60. Lanham, MD: Lexington, 2012.

Kelly, Sean Dorrance. "Merleau-Ponty on the Body." *Ratio* 15 (2002): 376–91.

Khalfa, Jean. "My Body, This Skin, This Fire: Fanon on Flesh." *Wasafiri* 20, no. 44 (2005): 42–50.

King, Karen. *The Gospel of Mary of Magdala: Jesus and the First Woman Apostle.* Santa Rosa, CA: Polebridge Press, 2003.

———. "Response." In *Galatians and Gender Trouble: Primal Androgyny and the First-Century Origins of a Feminist Dilemma*, edited by Christopher Ocker. Berkeley: Center for Hermeneutical Studies, 1992.

Kirby, Vicki. "Corporeal Habits: Addressing Essentialism Differently." *Hypatia* 6, no. 3 (1991): 4–24.

———. "Natural Convers(at)ions: Or, What If Culture Was Really Nature All Along." In *Material Feminisms*, edited by Stacy Alaimo and Susan Hekman, 214–36. Indianapolis: Indiana University Press, 2008.

———. "Postructural Feminisms, Part 2: Substance Abuse: Judith Butler." In *Telling Flesh: The Substance of the Corporeal.* New York: Routledge, 1997.

———. *Quantum Anthropologies: Life at Large.* Durham, NC: Duke University Press, 2011.

Labelle, Gilles. "Merleau-Ponty et le Christianisme." *Laval théologique et philosophique* 58, no. 2 (2002): 317–40.

Landry, Jean-Michel. "Généalogie politique de la psychologie: Une lecture du cours de Michel Foucault du gouverment de vivants (Collège De France, 1980)." *Raisons politiques* 1, no. 25 (2007): 31–45.

Lau, May, Hua Lin, and Glenn Flores. "Racial/Ethnic Disparities in Health and Health Care among U.S. Adolescents." *Health Services Research* 47, no. 5 (2012): 2031–59.

Loughlin, Gerard, ed. *Queer Theology: Rethinking the Western Body.* Malden, MA: Blackwell, 2007.

Luther, Martin. "An Argument in the Defense of All the Articles of Dr. Martin Luther Wrongly Condemned in the Roman Bull." Translated by C. M. Jacobs. In *Works of Martin Luther*, 5–116. Grand Rapids, MI: Baker Book House, 1982.

———. "The Estate of Marriage." In *Luther's Works: The Christian in Society*, edited by Walter I. Brandt. Philadelphia: Muhlenberg Press, 1962.

MacKendrick, Karmen. *Word Made Skin: Figuring Language at the Surface of Flesh.* New York: Fordham University Press, 2004.

Markham, William T., and Eric Rufa. "Class, Race, and the Disposal of Urban Waste: Locations of Landfills, Incinerators, and Sewage Treatment Plants." *Sociological Spectrum* 17, no. 2 (1997): 235–48.

Martín Alcoff, Linda. *Visible Identities: Race, Gender, and the Self.* Oxford: Oxford University Press, 2006.

Martin, Dale B. *The Corinthian Body.* New Haven, CT: Yale University Press, 1995.

———. *Slavery as Salvation: The Metaphor of Slavery in Pauline Christianity.* New Haven, CT: Yale University Press, 1990.

McFague, Sallie. *The Body of God.* Minneapolis: Fortress Press, 1993.

McVay, John K. "The Human Body as Social and Political Metaphor in Stoic Literature and Early Christian Writers." *Bulletin of the American Society of Papyrologists* 37, no. 1–4 (2000): 135–47.

Méndez-Montoya, Angel F. *The Theology of Food: Eating and the Eucharist.* Malden, MA: Wiley-Blackwell, 2009.

Menn, Stephen Philip. *Descartes and Augustine.* Cambridge: Cambridge University Press, 1998.

Merleau-Ponty, Maurice. "The Battle over Existentialism." In *Sense and Non-Sense*, translated by Patricia Allen Dreyfus, 71–82. Evanston, IL: Northwestern University Press, 1964.

———. "Bergson in the Making." Translated by Richard C. McCleary. In *Signs*, translated by Richard M. McCleary, 182–91. Evanston, IL: Northwestern University Press, 1964.

———. "The Child's Relations with Others." In *The Primacy of Perception: And Other Essays on Phenomenological Psychology, the Philosophy of Art, History and Politics*, edited by James M. Edie, 95–158. Evanston, IL: Northwestern University Press, 1964.

———. "Christianity and *Ressentiment*." In *Texts and Dialogues: On Philosophy, Politics, and Culture*, edited by Hugh J. Silverman and James Barry, 85–100. Amherst, NY: Humanity Books, 1992.

———. "Everywhere and Nowhere." Translated by Richard C. McCleary. In *Signs*, 126–58. Evanston, IL: Northwestern University Press, 1964.

———. "Faith and Good Faith." In *Sense and Non-Sense*, 172–81. Evanston, IL: Northwestern University Press, 1964.

———. "Indirect Language and the Voices of Silence." Translated by Richard C. McCleary. In *Signs*, 39–83. Evanston, IL: Northwestern University Press, 1964.

———. "In Praise of Philosophy." Translated by John Wild and James M. Edie. In *In Praise of Philosophy*, 3–67. Evanston, IL: Northwestern University Press, 1963.

———. "La philosophie de l'existence." *Dialogue* 5, no. 3 (1966): 307–22.

———. *Nature: Course Notes from the Collège de France.* 1995. Evanston, IL: Northwestern University Press, 2003.

———. *Phenomenology of Perception.* 1945. New York: Routledge, 1962.

———. "The Philosopher and His Shadow." Translated by Richard C. McCleary. In *Signs*, 159–81. Evanston, IL: Northwestern University Press, 1964.

———. "The Philosophy of Existence." Translated by Allen S. Weiss. In *Texts and Dialogues: On Philosophy, Politics, and Culture*, edited by Hugh J. Silverman and James Barry, 129–39. Amherst, NY: Humanity Books, 1992.

———. *Signs.* Translated by Richard C. McCleary. Evanston, IL: Northwestern University Press, 1964.

———. *The Visible and the Invisible*. Translated by Alphonso Lingis. Evanston, IL: Northwestern University Press, 1968.

Mezuk, Briana, Jane A. Rafferty, Kiarri N. Kershaw, Darrell Hudson, Cleopatra M. Abdou, Hedwig Lee, William W. Eaton, and James S. Jackson. "Reconsidering the Role of Social Disadvantage in Physical and Mental Health: Stressful Life Events, Health Behaviors, Race, and Depression." *American Journal of Epidemiology* 172, no. 11 (2010): 1238–49.

Miech, R. A., and M. J. Shanahan. "Socioeconomic Status and Depression over the Life Course." *Journal of Health and Social Behavior* 41, no. 2 (2000): 162–76.

Moore, Brandon, and Wendy Hessler. "Genes Change Message after Newborn Rats Given Bpa." *Environmental Health News*, October 5, 2011.

Moore, Stephen D. *Poststructuralism and the New Testament: Derrida and Foucault at the Foot of the Cross*. Minneapolis: Fortress Press, 1994.

Morris, Tony, Melissa Moore, and Felicity Morris. "Stress and Chronic Illness: The Case of Diabetes." *Journal of Adult Development* 18, no. 2 (2011): 70–80.

Motavelli, Jim. "Toxic Targets: Polluters That Dump on Communities of Color Finally Being Brought to Justice." *E Magazine*, July–August 1998.

Nancy, Jean-Luc. *Corpus*. Translated by Richard A. Rand. New York: Fordham University Press, 2008.

———. *Dis-Enclosure: The Deconstruction of Christianity*. Translated by Bettina Bergo, Gabriel Malefant, and Michael B. Smith. New York: Fordham University Press, 2008.

———. *Noli Me Tangere: On the Raising of the Body*. 2003. Translated by Sarah Clift, Pascale-Anne Brault, and Michael Naas. New York: Fordham University Press, 2008.

———. *The Sense of the World*. Minneapolis: University of Minnesota Press, 1997.

Nasrallah, Laura. *An Ecstasy of Folly: Prophecy and Authority in Early Christianity*. Cambridge, MA: Harvard Theological Studies, 2003.

Nelson, Alan. "Unequal Treatment: Confronting Racial and Ethnic Disparities in Health Care." *Journal of the National Medical Association* 94, no. 8 (2003): 666–68.

Nelson, James B. *Body Theology*. Louisville, KY: Westminster/John Knox Press, 1992.

Nightingale, Andrea. *Once out of Nature: Augustine on Time and the Body*. Chicago: University of Chicago Press, 2011.

Ondaatje, Michael. *The English Patient*. New York: Vintage, 1992.

Origen. "De Principis (On First Principles)." In *The Ante-Nicene Fathers, Volume IV*. Grand Rapids, MI: Wm. B. Eerdmans, 1951.

Paul, Marla. "Interspecies Transplant Works in First Step for New Diabetes Therapy." *Life Science Weekly*, June 30, 2013.

Perkins, Judith. "The Rhetoric of the Maternal Body in the Passion of Perpetua." In *Mapping Gender in Ancient Religious Discourses*, edited by Todd C. Penner and Caroline Vander Stichele, 313–32. Leiden: Brill, 2007.

Pollan, Michael. "Some of My Best Friends Are Germs." *New York Times*, May 15, 2013.

Reinhartz, Adele. *Befriending the Beloved Disciple: A Jewish Reading of the Gospel of John*. London: Bloomsbury Academic, 2002.

Rich, Adrienne. "Waking in the Dark." In *Poems, Selected and New, 1950–1974*, 18. New York: W. W. Norton, 1975.

Rivera, Mayra. "Flesh of the World: Corporeality in Relation." *Concilium*, no. 2 (2013): 83–96.

Roof, Judith. *The Poetics of DNA*. Minneapolis: University of Minnesota Press, 2007.

Rose, Nikolas. *The Politics of Life Itself: Biomedicine, Power, and Subjectivity in the Twenty-First Century*. Princeton, NJ: Princeton University Press, 2007.

Rosenfield, Sarah. "Triple Jeapordy? Mental Health at the Intersection of Gender, Race, and Class." *Social Science & Medicine* 74, no. 11 (2012): 1791–801.

Sabin, Janice, Frederick Rivara, and Anthony Greenwald. "Physician Implicit Attitudes and Stereotypes about Race and Quality of Medical Care." *Medical Care* 46, no. 7 (2008): 678–85.

Said, Edward W. "Labyrinth of Incarnations: The Essays of Maurice Merleau-Ponty." *Kenyon Review* 29, no. 1 (1967): 54–68.

Schneider, Laurel. *Beyond Monotheism: A Theology of Multiplicity*. London: Routledge, 2008.

Schüssler Fiorenza, Elisabeth. *In Memory of Her: A Feminist Theological Reconstruction of Christian Origins*. New York: Crossroad, 1994.

———. *Jesus: Miriam's Child, Sophia's Prophet*. New York: Bloomsbury Academic, 1994.

———. "Slave Wo/Men and Freedom: Some Methodological Reflections." In *Postcolonial Interventions*, edited by Tat-siong Benny Liew, 123–46. Sheffield, UK: Sheffield Phoenix Press, 2009.

Seppa, Nathan. "Epigenetic Shifts Linked to PTSD." *Science News* 177 no. 12 (June 5, 2010): 9.

Songe-Møller, Vigdis. "With What Kind of Body Will They Come? Metamorphosis and the Concept of Change: From Platonic Thinking to Paul's Notion of the Resurrection of the Dead." In *Metamorphoses: Resurrection, Body, and Transformative Practices in Early Christianity*, edited by Turid K. Seim and Jorunn Økland, 109–22. Berlin: Walter de Gruyter, 2009.

Spivak, Gayatri Chakravorty. "Response to Jean-Luc Nancy." In *Thinking Bodies*, edited by Juliet Flower MacCannell and Laura Zakarin. Stanford, CA: Stanford University Press, 1994.

Staten, Henry. "How the Spirit (Almost) Became Flesh: Gospel of John." *Representations* 41 (Winter 1993): 34–57.

Stawarska, Beata. "Psychoanalysis." In *Merleau-Ponty: Key Concepts*, edited by Rosalyn Diprose and Jack Reynolds, 57–69. Stocksfield, UK: Acumen, 2008.

Stoler, Ann Laura. *Race and the Education of Desire: Foucault's History of Sexuality and the Colonial Order of Things*. Durham, NC: Duke University Press, 1995.

Stowers, Stanley K. *A Reading of Romans: Justice, Jews, and Gentiles*. New Haven, CT: Yale University Press, 1994.

Tamir, Diana I., and Jason P. Mitchell. "Disclosing Information about the Self Is Intrinsically Rewarding." *PNAS* 109, no. 21 (2012): 8038–43.

Tat-siong, Benny Liew. *What Is Asian American Biblical Hermeneutics? Reading the New Testament*. Honolulu: University of Hawai'i Press, 2008.

———. "When Margins Become Common Ground: Questions of and for Biblical Studies." In *Still at the Margins: Biblical Scholarship Fifteen Years after Voices from the Margin*, edited by R. S. Sugirtharajah, 40–55. London: T and T Clark, 2008.

———. "The Word of Bare Life: Workings of Death and Dream in the Fourth Gospel." In *Anatomies of the Fourth Gospel: The Past, Present, and Futures of Narrative Criticism*, edited by Tom Thatcher and Stephen Moore, 167–93. Atlanta: SBL, 2008.

Tertullian. *Adversus Marcion (Against Marcion)*. Translated by Ernest Evans. Oxford: Clarendon Press, 1972.

———. *De Carne Christi Liber (On the Flesh of Christ)*. Edited by Ernest Evans. London: SPCK, 1956.

———. *On the Resurrection*. Translated by Ernest Evans. London: SPCK, 1960.

Tiemersma, Douwe. *Body Schema and Body Image: An Interdisciplinary and Philosophical Study*. Amsterdam: Swets and Zeitlinger, 1989.

Van Dusen, Christine. "Racial Disparity in Loans Studied: Advocacy Group Finds Widening Gap between Black/Latino Mortgage Rejection Rates and Those of Whites in Metro Area." *Atlanta Journal-Constitution*, October 2, 2002.

Vasseleu, Cathryn. *Textures of Light: Vision and Touch in Irigaray, Levinas and Merleau-Ponty*. Edited by Andrew Benjamin. Warwick Studies in European Philosophy. London: Routledge, 1998.

"Verbal Beatings Hurt as Much as Sexual Abuse." *Harvard Gazette*, April 26, 2007.

Walcott, Derek. "The Antilles: Fragments of Epic Memory, Nobel Lecture." In Derek Walcott, *What the Twilight Says: Essays*, 3–35. New York: Farrar, Straus, and Giroux. 1992.

Wallace, David Foster. *Both Flesh and Not*. New York: Little, Brown, 2012.

Wasserman, Emma. *The Death of the Soul in Romans 7: Sin, Death, and the Law in Light of Hellenistic Moral Psychology*. Tübingen: Mohr Siebeck, 2008.

Weate, Jeremy. "Fanon, Merleau-Ponty and the Difference of Phenomenology." In *Race*, edited by Robert Bernasconi, 169–83. Oxford: Blackwell, 2001.

Weinandy, Thomas. *In the Likeness of Sinful Flesh: An Essay on the Humanity of Christ*. Edinburgh: T and T Clark, 1993.

Weheliye, Alexander G. *Habeas Viscus: Racializing Assemblages, Biopolitics, and Black Theories of the Human*. Durham, NC: Duke University Press, 2014.

Westhelle, Vitor. *The Scandalous God: The Use and Abuse of the Cross*. Minneapolis: Fortress Press, 2007.

White, Alan M. "Borrowing While Black: Applying Fair Lending Laws to Risk-Based Mortgage Pricing." *South Carolina Law Review* 60 no. 3 (2009): 677–706.

Williams, Terry Tempest. "The Clan of One-Breasted Women." In *Refuge: An Unnatural History of Family and Place*. New York: Random House Vintage, 1991.

Wright, M. R. *Cosmology in Antiquity*. London: Routledge, 1995.

Žižek, Slavoj. *The Ticklish Subject: The Absent Centre of Political Ontology*. London: Verso, 1999.

INDEX

"according to the flesh," 40, 159n1
action: beyond the subject, 133–34, 144, 148, 150–52; constraint of, 143, 147, 156; God's, 64–65; mystery of, 36; rational, 37; shaping flesh, 134, 146, 157
affect, 69–70, 76–77, 94, 119, 128–29
affirmation, 124, 128, 147–49, 158
Agamben, Giorgio, 24
agency, 149–50, 167n39
Altizer, Thomas, 34
Alves, Rubem, 59
animals, 10, 41, 125, 171n11
animation, 79, 82, 101, 104, 144, 155; animate and inanimate, 102
anti-Semitism, 2, 19–20, 22, 40, 147, 154, 159n1, 163n6
Anzaldúa, Gloria, 119, 151
apophasis/apophatic, 73–74, 78. *See also* negative theology
Aristotle, 78, 99
Arnold, A. James, 128
art, 3, 83–84, 105
Augustine, 18, 36–37, 40, 62, 65, 167n42, 168n45
autonomy, 136, 153, 167n39

Bachelard, Gaston, 78–79, 105
Barad, Karen, 104, 149–50, 177n58, 191n51
"bare life," 24

becoming: divine, 44, 155; flesh's eternal, 49; God becoming flesh, 63, 100, 154–55; human, 130; process of, 13; a woman, 143
Benny Liew, Tat-siong, 18, 24
Bergson, Henri, 78–79
Betcher, Sharon, 7
biological, 6, 136–39
birth, 44–45, 48–49, 52, 105, 154, 171n9, 171n12
blood, 23, 25, 45, 48, 121, 155
body: in advertising, 95; body-in-the-world, 60, 65–67, 70–71, 100; "body of sense," 102; body/spirit dualism, 6; of Christ, 23, 38–41, 45, 49–50, 99; disabled, 7, 129; glorified, 81, 85; imaginary, 60, 69–70, 82, 125, 141; in childhood development, 67–69, 102; in feminist thought, 6–7, 136; of God, 6, 161n15; in liberation theology, 5–6, 59; race and, 8, 118–22, 128–31, 141; resurrected, 30, 33–36, 48–51; of sin, 35–38; sinful, 12, 35, 37–39, 91–93, 154; subject, 145; tangible, 74–76, 101, 106–7, 109; visible, 9, 60, 70, 76, 101, 114, 126, 156. *See also* carnality
Boyarin, Daniel, 35, 40
bread, 21–26, 30, 54, 83, 155, 163n16, 164n20

breath, 31, 47, 118, 123
Burrus, Virginia, 4, 44, 49
Butler, Judith, 8–9, 13, 108, 114, 135–37, 143–49, 179n93, 188n17, 190n49

carnality, 11, 38–41, 43–45, 54, 82, 88, 109–10, 118, 153–56; "carnal adherence," 77; carnal God, 64; carnal ontology, 97; carnal poetics, 23, 87, 101; and knowledge, 80, 158; and language, 83, 94; and perception, 61, 80, 83; and sin, 91; social-material world and human, 134
Cassian, John, 94
Césaire, Aimé, 12, 118–19, 122–30, 158
Christ, 30, 32–35, 37, 40, 48–52; body of, 23, 38–41, 49–50, 99; flesh of, 44–47
Christian body, 5–7, 11, 17, 21, 34, 36–37, 59, 95, 100
Cixous, Helene, 2, 159
Claudel, Paul, 81–82
colonial discourses, 57–58, 93, 117–20, 122–28, 141, 157, 181n26
confession, 90–93, 102, 181n23. *See also* Foucault, Michel
consciousness, 67, 72, 75, 138–39, 186n22; self-consciousness, 65
Coole, Diana, 104
corporeal schema, 66–70, 84, 119, 121, 126, 142–43
corpus, 10, 50–52
Cox Miller, Patricia, 43
creation, 31–32, 46–49, 72, 105, 128, 154, 168n45, 172n26, 172n37

Dash, Michael, 118
De Oto, Alejandro, 118
De Saint Aubert, Emmanuel, 64
death, 23–24, 30–37, 44, 95, 128, 166n10; of God, 97; of Jesus, 21, 24–26, 48–49, 51, 99
Deleuze, Gilles, 11
Derrida, Jacques, 11, 174n4
Descartes, Rene, 62, 65, 104, 175n13; Cartesian, 98
desire, 77, 95, 109, 119–20, 143; Christianity and, 5, 57, 91–92; the desire to philosophize, 88–89, 143; God's, 59; Pauline, 9, 36–37
Diprose, Rosalyn, 146
disability, 7–8, 119, 129, 154
discipline, 39, 53, 90, 95
discourse: critiques of discourse theories, 8–9, 149–50; gender as set of, 114; modern, 91; production of biological effects, 137; scientific, 93, 117. *See also* colonial discourse; gendering; racialization
Dunning, Benjamin, 44, 166n11, 173n54
Dussel, Enrique, 6, 23

earth, 47–49, 79, 123–24, 155, 157; earthy bodies, 30–36, 50; "earthy man," 32–33, 50–51; humanity and, 46, 54; love of, 128, 154; virgin, 46. *See also* nature
elements, 20–26, 45–46, 78–79, 82–84, 95–96, 123–24, 152, 168n45; elemental flesh, 109; social norms materializing in, 13, 135, 152
Engberg-Pederson, 34, 165n7
entanglement, 160n8; bodily, 72, 92, 126; of knowledge with the world, 63; relational, 4, 110, 158
epidermal schema, 119–22, 138, 185n19
essentialism, 102, 128, 190n49
existentialism, 61, 174n3
"ex-peau-sure," 101, 146, 152
exposure, 7, 97, 100–103, 133. *See also* "ex-peau-sure"

faith, 61–64, 76, 155
feminism, 6–7, 57, 136, 160n14
feminist theology, 6, 161n15
"flesh of my flesh," 77, 108
folded flesh, 104, 152
Foucault, Michel, 12, 53, 87, 137, 158; Christianity and, 89–90, 93, 94, 122; flesh and, 90–91, 122; power and, 92, 94; sexuality and, 91, 117
fragmentation, 3, 17, 78, 121

gaze, 70, 76, 101, 106, 120, 124–26, 129, 139–41; sovereign, 74

gender, 40, 46, 53–54, 88, 108–9; denaturalizing, 6, 9, 136–37; difference, 32, 52, 169n70
gendering, 72, 114, 135, 139, 143; norms, 2, 114, 135, 141–43; performativity of, 143, 147
genetics, 8–9, 102–3, 122, 125, 136–37, 150, 161n22, 183n53; epigenetics, 183n56, 183n57, 190n39
Gibran, Khalil, 25
Glissant, Édouard, 2–4, 110, 128–29, 153
glory, 20–21, 25–26, 29, 31, 33–34, 51, 100, 153
God, 34–38, 43, 154; becoming human, 21; body of, 6, 161n15; carnal God, 64; creation and, 20, 31, 46–47, 52, 54; emptying, 59, 62, 64, 100; essence of, 34; as father, 53; image of, 32; immateriality of, 6, 98; kingdom of, 30, 51; philosophy and, 58, 61–64, 72, 78, 87, 97–100, 104; power of, 49; touching, 96

habit, 66–67, 70, 120, 126, 135, 139–40, 142–43, 146
health, 141, 146, 150–51
historico-racial schema, 121, 140–41
history, 56, 61, 128, 136, 148; entanglement of biology and, 150, 191n51; evolutionary, 103, 134; Foucault's hyperbolic, 89–90; historical myth, 122, 156; material, 98, 100, 114, 134; social, 139
Hodge, Caroline Johnson, 40
Hollywood, Amy, 145
Howe, Marie, 19
human, 24, 32–34; creativity, 85; development, 70, 125; inter-human exchanges, 70–72, 144, 146; mastery and, 129–30; 6; nonhuman and, 10, 41, 44, 47, 49, 95, 109, 135, 149–52; nonhuman in the, 2, 103, 110, 157; permeability of, 39; reproduction, 136–37

ideality, 80–82
identity, 1, 40, 77, 90–91, 143, 147, 162n29
ideology, 138–9
imago dei, 62
imaginary: affirmative imaginary, 123; bodies, 60, 82, 114, 125, 141; carnal, 118; as an element, 79; poetics and, 2; self, 69, 70, 126
incarnation, 2, 88, 144–45, 154–71; in Christian sources, 18–19, 21, 29, 44–46, 50–53; Foucault and 92–93, 113; incarnations of the social, 125, 134, 145–46; Merleau-Ponty and, 56, 60–65, 71–72, 84, 175n18; Nancy's critique of the, 96–101. *See also* intercarnations
"inner man," 175n13; Pauline, 36–37; performativity as challenge to, 148; in philosophy, 61–62, 65, 75, 96
instinct, 2, 10, 89, 93, 109, 117, 122, 155, 185n12
inter-corporeality, 65, 67–71, 125
intercarnations, 145–46
interdependence, 7, 103, 144
Irenaeus, 43, 46
Irigaray, Luce, 12, 88, 105–8

Jantzen, Grace, 6
Jews, 2, 20, 22–23, 35, 40, 147, 154, 163n6
Jordan, Mark, 89–90, 182n27
justice, 59–61, 129–30, 157

Kearney, Richard, 83
Keller, Catherine, 160n8, 190n49
Kelly, Sean, 176n32
King, Karen, 40, 169n70, 171n6
Kirby, Vicki, 8–9, 162n27
kosmotheoros, 74

language, 63, 73–74, 83–84; bodies in relation to, 9, 82–83, 94; literary, 141; poetics and, 105, 158; transformation and, 115
law, 34–40, 61, 90–93, 109, 114, 138, 145–47, 167n32, 167n36
Levinas, 160n12
liberation theology, 5–6, 23, 60
Liew, Tat-siong Benny, 18, 24

Index   205

life, 6, 20–27, 37–40, 46, 48, 62, 73, 93–94, 99–100; prenatal life, 107
light, 20–21, 27, 49, 62, 73–74, 81, 83, 99, 105–57, 158
literature, 4, 80–81, 85, 121, 148; Caribbean, 118; colonial, 125

MacKendrick, Karmen, 20
Marcel, Gabriel, 59–61
Martin, Dale, 31
Martín Alcoff, Linda, 13, 135, 136, 138–40, 148
materialism, 9–10, 104, 101n25
materiality, 2, 149–50, 157–58, 162n27
materialization, 9, 13, 137, 144–50, 155, 191n51
matter, 9–10, 33, 74, 78–79, 98, 100, 103–34, 144, 149; mystery and, 61; spirit/matter dualism, 6, 33, 53
Merleau-Ponty, Maurice: childhood development in the work of, 67–69; experience of my body in, 70–71; expression and perception, 83; *Everywhere and Nowhere*, 56; faith in, 63–64; "Faith and Good Faith," 61; flesh, 73, 76–82; God and, 58–63; imagination in, 78–79; incarnation and, 60–66, 72, 84–85; "Indirect Language and the Voices of Silence, 83–84; inner man and, 61–62; language and, 80–84; *L'entrelacs*, 73–83; light in, 79–80; objective body versus corporeal schema, 65–67; painting in, 83; perception, 63–65, 68–70, 72, 74–76, 84; *Phenomenology of Perception*, 65–72; philosophy of language and, 63; poetics and, 83–84; task of philosophy and, 58. *See also* body-in-the-world; corporeal schema; tangibility; visibility
metamorphosis, 30, 54, 81–82
metaphysics, 27, 88, 96–97, 102, 104, 109, 157
mirror stage, 68–70, 82
Moore, Stephen, 26
mystery, 61, 79, 96–97, 105; divine, 62–63; of materiality, 61

Nancy, Jean-Luc, 96–101; critique of flesh as metaphysical concept, 88, 96–97; critique of incarnation, 98–101; deconstruction of ontotheology, 12; impenetrable bodies, 97–98; "sense of the body," 98. *See also* "ex-peau-sure"
Nasrallah, Laura, 39, 169n60
natural body, 31, 33–34, 50, 52–53, 136
nature, 6–7, 49, 130, 137, 159n1, 162n27
negative philosophy, 74
negative theology, 74. *See also* apophasis
Négritude, 123–24
new materialisms, 9, 104, 178n84
nonhuman, 10, 44, 49, 95, 134–35, 156; performativity of, 150

objects, 63; bodies and, 65–66, 84, 102, 141; constructions of objects of knowledge, 61–62, 93, 96; perception of, 63, 65–67
ontology, 60, 64, 85, 107, 118, 127; bodily, 8, 57, 97; materialist, 104. *See also* carnal ontology
ontotheology, 12, 88
opacity, 144, 158; of the body, 4, 80, 103; of flesh, 54, 80, 88; rejection of, 98; of relation, 3–4, 144
otherness, 26, 80, 98, 105, 129, 144, 157–58; constitution by, 144

passivity, 79, 104
perception, 32, 61; impact of social relations on, 126–30, 138–42, 156; "incarnation of perception," 71; Merleau-Ponty and, 63–65, 68–70, 72, 74–76, 84. *See also* senses
performativity, 135, 143–50, 188n17
Philo, 32, 37
philosophy, 58, 61, 63, 78–79, 83–84, 106
pneuma, 34
poetics, 2–5, 18, 20, 58–59, 79, 83–84, 105, 110, 154–55, 158
poiesis, 3. *See also* theopoiesis
porneia, 38, 108
postmodern: body, 5; critiques of the flesh, 57–58; philosophy and theory, 1, 9, 36, 160n27; science, 160n8

power, 7, 9, 39, 67, 70, 95, 136–37, 147, 150; colonial, 93, 120–21, 130; in Foucault, 89–94; God's, 49, 78, 165n9; social, 147–50, 157
Prado, Adélia, 16

race, 5–6, 117–18, 121–22, 125, 128–30, 157; denaturalization of, 9, 136–39, 143, 188n8, 188n17
racialization, 12, 57, 72, 114, 125, 145, 181n26
rationality, 37, 75
relation: collective body and, 39; constitution of bodies by, 11–12, 65–66, 70–72; to earth, 124; flesh as a site of, 44, 58, 73, 77, 94–95, 102, 109, 154, 158; Glissant on, 3–4, 110, 160n8; matter and, 10, 104, 142, 155; social relations, 13, 113, 134–37, 146, 149–52, 156
reproduction, 88, 105, 136–37, 190n48
reproductive technology, 10, 137
resistance, 147
resurrection, 30, 33–36, 41, 46–51, 59, 82, 98, 164n24

Sartre, Jean Paul, 61, 71, 80, 118
Schneider, Laurel, 161n15, 170n5
Schüssler Fiorenza, Elizabeth, 169n63
science: genetics in popularized science, 102, 183n52; racializing, 122; recent developments, 8–9, 137
senses, 107, 125, 175n13; spiritual, 64, 99. *See also* perception
sensing body, 70, 75–77
sexuality, 89–90, 114, 119, 124, 147
shame, 44–46, 171n8

sin, 34–37, 39, 41, 53, 57, 170n73; in Foucault, 89–93
soma, 21, 30–31, 34, 50, 99, 166n25; somatic corporeal imaginary, 11–12, 88, 92–95, 109, 154; somatophobia, 9
spirit, 20, 21, 24–26, 29, 33, 38–57, 62, 98–100, 155, 157
spiritual body, 11, 17, 29, 31–32, 34, 38–39, 40–41, 50, 52–53, 65, 81–82, 95
suffering, 1, 53, 64, 124, 129, 154, 157
Spivak, Gayatri Chakravorty, 88–90

tangibility, 75, 98, 107
technology, 8–9, 137, 184n75
theopoiesis, 21
theosis, 21
touch, 20, 47–49, 54, 62, 67, 73–77, 78–80, 96–77, 104, 106–77, 110, 164n27, 177n58
transcendence, 6
transformation, 11, 24–25, 31, 41, 66–69, 72, 82–83, 103, 113, 123–25, 152, 154

Vasseleu, Cathryn, 107
visibility, 12, 73–74, 76–77, 81–82, 106–7, 126–27, 134–35, 140, 152, 179n87
vitality, 11, 19, 104
vulnerability, 5, 7–8, 12, 24, 44, 48, 53–54, 84, 94, 96, 119, 154, 187n51

Walcott, Derek, 3, 127, 160n5
water, 24–26, 54, 78, 82, 123, 155
Weheliye, Alexander, 161n21
womb, 44–48, 52, 57, 88, 100, 105–9, 171n11, 182n35
wonder, 58, 158

www.ingramcontent.com/pod-product-compliance
Lightning Source LLC
Chambersburg PA
CBHW050243170426
43202CB00015B/2899